# An Introduction to Cybercultures

*An Introduction to Cybercultures* provides an accessible guide to the major forms, practices and meanings of this rapidly-growing field. From the evolution of hardware and software to the emergence of cyberpunk film and fiction, David Bell introduces readers to the key aspects of cyberculture, including email, the Internet, digital imaging technologies, computer games and digital special effects.

Each chapter contains 'hot links' to key articles in *The Cybercultures Reader*, suggestions for further reading, and details of relevant websites.

Individual chapters examine:

- Cybercultures: an introduction
- Storying cyberspace
- Cultural studies in cyberspace
- Community and cyberculture
- Identities in cyberculture
- Bodies in cyberculture
- Cybersubcultures
- Researching cybercultures

**David Bell** is Reader in Cultural Studies at Staffordshire University. He is the co-editor of *The Cybercultures Reader* (Routledge 2000).

# An Introduction to Cybercultures

David Bell

London and New York

First published 2001
by Routledge
11 New Fetter Lane, London EC4P 4EE

Simultaneously published in the USA and Canada
by Routledge
29 West 35th Street, New York, NY 10001

*Routledge is an imprint of the Taylor & Francis Group*

© 2001 David Bell

Typeset in Perpetua by Florence Production Ltd, Stoodleigh, Devon
Printed and bound in Great Britain by TJ International Ltd, Padstow,
Cornwall

*British Library Cataloging in Publication Data*
A catalogue record for this book is available from the British Library

*Library of Congress Cataloguing in Publication Data*
A catalog record for this book has been applied for

ISBN 0–415–24658–X (hbk)
ISBN 0–415–24659–8 (pbk)

# Contents

# Acknowledgements

This is the first book I've written on my own; without the benefit of a co-author or co-editor to bounce ideas around with, I have inevitably had to rely on the generosity of those people around me, and I'd like to thank them for showing interest in what I've been doing, as well as for all the practical help they've given. I couldn't wish to work in a better intellectual environment. Thank you, then, to colleagues and students in Cultural Studies at Staffordshire University, and especially those who've shared the experience of learning about cybercultures on the undergraduate module Technocultures and the postgraduate module Cyberdiscourse. Those with whom I have shared the teaching of these modules deserve special mention: Mark Featherstone, Mark Jayne, Barbara Kennedy and John O'Neill. Extra-special thanks, as always, to Jon Binnie and Ruth Holliday. Rebecca Barden, my 'virtual editor' at Routledge (virtual in the sense that we still haven't managed to meet f2f) has been everything an editor should be: generous, enthusiastic, patient and good-humoured. And good luck with parenthood, Rebecca! Thanks also to Alistair Daniel and Sue Edwards for seeing the book through the production process.

Finally, I'd like to dedicate this book to three people, all of whom 'got me started' in one way or another: to Derek Longhurst, who got me started with Cultural Studies; to Tristan Palmer, who got me started writing books; and in memory of my father, Colin Bell, who got me started with science and technology.

**Note**: In this book, I will be making substantial use of essays published in *The Cybercultures Reader* (edited by Bell and Kennedy 2000). In order to signal the primitive hyperlink between this book and the Reader, when I cite or quote from an essay in the Reader, it's indicated in the text, abbreviated to CR. So, when I cite Andrew Ross' 'Hacking away at the counterculture', I've written (Ross CR), rather than 'Ross (2000)'. Links to the Reader appear at the end of each chapter, not in the bibliography.

# CYBERCULTURES
## An introduction

My personal walkabout in cyberspace has given me glimpses of a truly different world, and I wish to share them.

*David Hakken*

SITTING HERE, AT MY COMPUTER, pondering how to start this book, how to introduce my own 'walkabout' in cyberspace, I find myself struggling. Maybe it's because I've just been reading and writing about hyperlinks and the web as text – as text, moreover, that is open and infinite, that has no beginning or end. But a book is still a linear thing, decidedly non-hypertexty – despite various authors' unsuccessful attempts to simulate on paper the experience of the screen (see, for example, Taylor and Saarinen 1994; Case 1996; Bolter and Grusin 1999). So I have to abide by the logic of the book, even if it seems increasingly contradictory in the digital age to do so. The move from books to bytes, to borrow Anthony Smith's (1993) phrase, is still far from complete – and so here I am, sitting here, the cursor blinking at me, thinking of a way to introduce you to my book.

If I was to try to define in a sentence what this book is about – something I often ask students to do with projects and dissertations – I would have to say that it is about thinking through some of the ways of understanding what the term 'cybercultures' means. It's a series of ideas, issues and questions about what happens when we conjoin the words 'cyber' and 'culture'. Think of it this way, which I borrow from Christine Hine (2000): cyberspace as culture and as cultural artefact. Let's work that formulation through. First, what is cyberspace? It's a slippery term, to be sure; hard to define, multiplicitous. I think of it as combining three things, as the next

1

two chapters of this book show: it has material, symbolic and experiential dimensions. It is machines, wires, electricity, programs, screens, connections, and it is modes of information and communication: email, websites, chat rooms, MUDs. But it is also images and ideas: cyberspace exists on film, in fiction, in our imaginations as much as on our desktops or in the space between our screens. Moreover, and this is the important bit, we experience cyberspace in all its spectacular and mundane manifestations by *mediating* the material and the symbolic. As I attempt to track in Chapters 2 and 3, thinking about what cyberspace 'is' and what it 'means' involves its own hypertextuality, as we mingle and merge the hardware, software and wetware with memories and forecasts, hopes and fears, excitement and disappointment. Cyberspace is, I think, something to be understood as it is lived — while maps and stats give us one kind of insight into it, they are inadequate to the task of capturing the thoughts and feelings that come from, to take a mundane example, sending and receiving email. At one level, thinking of cyberspace as culture emphasizes this point: it is lived culture, made from people, machines and stories in everyday life. That's why I often turn to stories of my own and others' experiences with cyberspace. In Chapter 3 especially, I emphasize my story — not quite a tale of personal transformation from newbie to nerd, but not far off.

Thinking about cyberspace as cultural artefact means considering how we've got cyberspace as it currently exists; it means tracking the stories of its creation and on-going shaping, as well as the stories of on-going meaning-making that make cyberspace over. From the perspective of someone working in cultural studies, it seems relatively straightforward to see cyberspace as cultural, in that any and every thing around us is the product of culture — look at the shape of your computer, for example, and consider why it's turned out that way. The story of how computers ended up on our desktops, and ended up connecting us to each other, is a profoundly cultural tale (Edwards 1996).

The trick is to think about cyberspace as product of and producer of culture simultaneously — another hypertext moment. Keeping both perspectives visible is important, because it avoids the all-too-easy slide into either technophilia or technophobia. And, as Jonathan Sterne (1999) points out, part of the task of cultural studies in cyberspace is to navigate a path between these two extremes, though without necessarily abandoning them totally — especially since they remain important framing discourses circulating in everyday life (from the technophilic hype around 'dot.com' millionaires to the technophobic imagery of *Terminator*).

Chapters 2 and 3 of this book are a joint attempt to work through ways of thinking about cyberspace, therefore. They can't pretend to be comprehensive, authoritarian accounts — they are fragmentary, flickering. I hope that they are read not for grand answers, but for modestly thought-provoking moments. In the chapters that follow, by focusing in on particular aspects of cyberculture, my aim is to get a slightly better understanding of some things that 'cyberculture' means or might mean. To start off, I have tried to think through what cultural studies has to contribute to this, and to suggest some of the theoretical resources we can make use of. This involves establishing a number of different ways of thinking about science, technology, computers and cyberspace, and I hope that by taking a walkabout through some of those ways, I can trace some connections and directions that are productive. That's the agenda for Chapter 4, which 'detours' through theories and theorists that we might make use of in the project understanding cybercultures.

Chapter 5 takes us into one of the most interesting and contested areas of cyberculture. The topic here is community – are new communities forming in cyberspace? Are these replacing or augmenting offline communities? Is this a good thing or a bad thing? The debate about cyber-community crystallizes many of the important issues of cyberculture, therefore. It shows the ways in which cyberspace reworks our understandings of 'community', and the extent to which that reworking is open to contestation. It brings to the surface the troublesome question of marking boundaries between 'virtual life' and 'real life', and asks what meanings and values we attribute to these terms. By approaching cyber-community from a range of perspectives, and letting these rub up against each other, this chapter is my attempt to indicate the implications for how we think about both cyberspace and community.

Chapter 6 shifts our attention to questions of cultural identity in cyberspace, and to do this I focus on race, class, gender and sexuality. Set in the broader context of arguments about identity in contemporary culture – what has been termed the decentring of the self – thinking through the ways in which these aspects of identity are reworked in cyberculture gives us important insights into what goes on when people enter virtual realms, cybercommunities and digital worlds. How much of our 'real life' identity can we jettison – and how much would we want to jettison? Does the possibility of 'playing' with identity in cyberspace mean something productive, or does it merely provide another arena for domination?

Closely but complexly related to questions about cybercultural identity are issues of embodiment, and Chapter 7 takes these up, introducing and exploring narratives about strange new figures on our cultural landscape: posthumans, cyborgs, digital corpses and intelligent machines. From the cyberpunk dream of 'leaving the meat behind' and existing in cyberspace as pure data to the intricate readings of the cyborg provided by Donna Haraway (CR), the shifting shapes and meanings of 'the body' in cyberculture open up a number of important questions and challenges. As we enter into evermore intimate relationships with an ever-increasing diversity of nonhuman others, we have to radically rethink what we mean by 'body', what we mean by 'life' and what we mean by 'human' – and consider the usefulness of

3

retaining categories and boundaries that are becoming increasingly difficult to sustain.

Chapter 8 brings together some of the themes addressed previously, through a focus on what I've termed 'cybersubcultures'. Building on cultural studies of subcultures – groups like punks, eco-warriors and football hooligans – this chapter explores how different subcultural responses to and uses of cyberspace work. In some cases, pre-existing forms of subcultural activity have found a new home in cyberspace, and in this respect I look at fan cultures and 'fringe' political groups (such as conspiracy theorists and neonazis). What we see there is an adaptive relationship to new media technologies that is reshaping the practices and forms that these subcultures take. Moving on from here, I look at subcultures that signal an expressive engagement with cyberspace, focusing on MUDders, cyberpunks, hackers, and neo-Luddites. Each of these groups has its own subcultural take on cyberspace, and each reintroduces debates about identity, embodiment and community in cyberculture.

The final substantive chapter of the book explores the business of research on, in and with cyberspace and cybercultures, and is intended as a partial, critical commentary on the issues that come to the surface when the communities, identities, bodies and subcultures of and in cyberspace are investigated empirically. Two kinds of research are highlighted here: textual approaches to the web and cyberethnography. The methodological challenges and questions that arise when we attempt to do research in and on cyberspace provide us with a different way of thinking through what cyberculture means – indeed, Hine's (2000) neat discussion of cyberspace as culture and as cultural artefact has its origins in her own online fieldwork. How we think about cyberspace shapes how we research it, and how we research cyberspace shapes how we think about it.

All of these chapters share a common architecture, and come with a common set of attachments. At the end of the chapters the following features recur: links to chapters in *The Cybercultures Reader* (Bell and Kennedy 2000), a handful of suggestions for further reading, and some URLs for websites on related topics. The links to the *Reader* are intended to point readers towards essays that illustrate, extend and contest the ideas that I introduce. This book was partly conceived as a companion to the *Reader*, to provide space to work through the issues raised by the essays collected there. So, in a way, that's my own gesture towards hypertexting. While I've tried to make this book make sense in its own right, so these links aren't essential, it's always part of academic writing to stage a primitive hypertextuality by referring across to others' work. When we assembled the *Reader*, our aim was to gather together what we thought to be the most useful and interesting essays on cybercultures – so it's not surprising that I would want to make use of them in this book too.

The further reading and websites at the end of each chapter are a second kind of hypertexting, linking the reader to other places where the themes of the chapter can be explored. The sites were all up and running in January 2001, but given the ephemerality of the web, I can only apologize if any of them have vanished by the time you try to visit them. These sites aren't the result of any kind of exhaustive or systematic survey of available sites, either. Despite Ananda Mitra and Elisia Cohen's (1999) suggestions for ways to evaluate sites, the choice here is more personal than anything: these are sites that I think are useful *ways into* particular topics. Each reader can move from them in their own route, following the links that they find enticing.

At the end of the book, I have added two more resources: a glossary and another guide to further reading. These are my attempt to answer the FAQs that get asked about cybercultures. The glossary is a weird thing – compiling it calls for lots of pondering, decisions about what to include and what can be left out. Terms from cyberspace enter our everyday speech reasonably easily (Shortis 2001), and yet usage in common parlance doesn't always equate with an ability to define any term. All I have done with the glossary is to sift through a few other glossaries provided by authors with a similar assumed audience to mine, and sifted my own text for the appearance of terms that I think could do with defining. The act of definition is itself very tricky, and another partial and contingent thing: while glossaries, like dictionaries and encyclopedias, pretend to be objective texts, we can clearly see that they are the result of *somebody's* thinking. This glossary is no more than the result of mine. If I imagine my audience, I call up my own students: students doing cultural studies, who have varying amounts of prior knowledge about computers and cyberspace. In some cases, their knowledge outstrips mine, so I apologize for talking down to some readers.

The guide to further reading at the book's end is my attempt to suggest what I think are the best handful of books for that same imagined audience. These are the books I recommend to my students, as places to begin getting to grips with cyberspace and cyberculture. I've added in a little commentary on the titles I've selected, just to help you decide which of my 'top 20' might be interesting or useful to you. Like the websites at each chapter's end, this list is specific to the time and place of its compilation. Even if books don't disappear quite as dramatically as websites sometimes do, they do have their shelf-life – and, of course, new titles appear with quite alarming frequency. Again, like the websites, this list was put together by one person (me), from one set of resources (my book shelves and teaching experience), at a particular moment (January 2001). To echo David Hakken (1999: 227) again, this book represents a 'personal walkabout in cyberspace' – and it's a walkabout I think I'll be on for a long time to come.

# Chapter 2

# STORYING CYBERSPACE 1
## Material and symbolic stories

The experience of participating in a story, as teller or audience, is typically that of being caught up in it while it is being told. . . . Stories convey meaning about the social context and identity of the teller and audience. However, stories also have an *effect* on that identity and context.

John McLeod

I N  T H I S  C H A P T E R and the one that follows, I want to focus on the ways that cyberspace is talked about and written about. I shall pick out a number of ways of telling stories about cyberspace, and explore the kinds of stories that have been told. This assembling of stories is my attempt to sketch out an agenda for the rest of the book. What I want to stress is that any attempt to understand cyberspace and cyberculture must look at the stories we tell about these phenomena. Moreover, I want to suggest that we need to think about different modes of story-telling and different kinds of stories simultaneously, in order to understand how cyberspace and cyberculture are storied into being at the intersection of different knowledges and metaphors. The three strands of story-telling I identify as (1) *material stories*, (2) *symbolic stories* and (3) *experiential stories*. In similar moves, N. Katherine Hayles (1999b: 2) discusses 'virtual creatures' through what she calls three 'modes of interrogation': *what they are*, *what they mean* and *what they do*, and Michael Menser and Stanley Aronowitz (1996) use the terms *ontology*, *phenomenology* and *pragmatics* to discuss ways of thinking about technology. I shall provide my definition of what these three kinds of stories are about, sketch some of their narrative forms and contents, and highlight the ways that they intersect as the two chapters unfold. But before that, I need to attend to two further acts of definition: to define the terms *cyberspace* and *cyberculture* themselves.

'Cyberspace' is a complex term to define; indeed, its definition can be refracted through our three story-telling tropes to give us different (though often overlapping) definitions. We can define cyberspace in terms of hardware, for example – as a global network of computers, linked through communications infrastructures, that facilitate forms of interaction between remote actors. Cyberspace is here the sum of all those nodes and networks ('*what it is*'). Alternatively, a definition based partly on the 'symbolic' trope could define cyberspace as an imagined space between computers in which people might build new selves and new worlds ('*what it means*'). In fact, cyberspace is all this and more; it is hardware and software, and it is images and ideas – the two are inseparable. Moreover, the ways we experience cyberspace represent a negotiation of material and symbolic elements, each given different weight depending on the kind of experience ('*what it does*'). We can experience cyberspace mundanely, as where we are when we sit at a computer checking emails; or, we can experience cyberspace as an immersive realm where our 'real life' (RL) bodies and identities disappear – even if what we're doing in those two scenarios isn't, at one level of interrogation, that different.

In *The Cybercultures Reader* Michael Benedikt defines cyberspace along similar axes, pointing out a number of different ways of conceptualizing what turns out to be an elusive thing. Consider just a couple of his attempts at definition:

> Cyberspace: A new universe, a parallel universe created and sustained by the world's computers and communications lines. A world in which the global traffic of knowledge, secrets, measurements, indicators, entertainments, and alter-human agency takes on form: sights, sounds, presences never seen on the surface of the earth blossoming in a vast electronic light.
>
> Cyberspace: A common mental geography, built, in turn, by consensus and revolution, canon and experiment; a territory swarming with data and lies, with mind stuff and memories of nature, with a million voices and two million eyes in a silent, invisible concert to enquiry, deal-making, dream sharing, and simple beholding.
>
> (Benedikt CR: 29)

After ten such attempts, Benedikt states that 'cyberspace as just described does not exist' (30). In fact, I would argue that it *does* exist – maybe not in terms of hardware and software, but certainly in terms of story-telling. Attending to cyberspace through its stories makes definition harder, but that's a necessary thing if we are going to grasp the manifold places it occupies in the worlds of science and technology, business and everyday life, dreams and nightmares. So, in fact, I am deferring definition because to define cyberspace too rigidly at this point would shape the agenda of the ways we read the stories I want to introduce. Instead, it's more useful to *redefine* cyberspace in the context of each story, and then explore the overlaps and intersections of these definitions. As John McLeod (1997) remarks, stories are ways of making sense of the world and our place within it – so, what I want to do in these two chapters is to share with you a number of different stories, that taken together might give a broader picture of the relationships between cyberspace and everyday life.

What, then, of 'cyberculture'? Setting up a distinction between cyberspace and cyberculture is a false dichotomy, I think: cyberspace is always cyberculture, in that we cannot separate cyberspace from its cultural contexts. So, while Dani Cavallaro (2000: xi) writes of cyberculture as 'an environment saturated by electronic technology', we need also to read those technologies themselves as cultural – to look at 'ideas, experiences, and metaphors in their interaction with machines and material change', as Paul Edwards (1996: xv) puts it. So, in effect, cyberculture is a different way of saying cyberspace; one that emphasizes precisely that interaction which Edwards highlights, and which importantly sees the relationship as two-way: computers don't just give shape to metaphors, but are themselves shaped by metaphors. Moreover, the Internet and its related technologies spill over, to impact on everyday life in many different ways. Daniel Miller and Don Slater (2000: 14) argue that this means we need to disaggregate cyberspace, and they thus stress the need to look at 'a range of practices, software and hardware technologies, modes of representation and interaction that may or may not be interrelated by participants, machines or programs (indeed they may not all take place at a computer)'. This is part of the approach I shall be adopting in this book: to explore the multiple cyberspaces that we encounter. However, having separated out three strands of story-telling, I shall also work to mix them together again, and to see them as simultaneous, mutual and densely woven together. The story of cyberspace *as* cyberculture, then, is a hybrid of these different narratives. So, let's start the story-telling now.

## Material stories

Telling 'material stories' here means talking of the histories of the technologies that come together to make cyberspace as what Jordan (1999: 22) calls 'the really existing matrix' (as opposed to its imaginary versions) – the story of *how it came to be what it is*. But it also means making materialist readings of the world shaped by cyberculture – in what I shall refer to as a political economy of cyberspace. The histories that I want to lay out here are well covered in the existing literature, and so I shall concoct a version that blends a number of narratives. The most obvious history in this regard, then, is the story of computing and communications technologies, and then of their convergence – though this in itself has a whole series of prehistories, in terms of forms of human organization, communication, object-making and image-making, of which the computer is an offspring. Language, mathematics, writing, science, art . . . all of these can be written into a story of the emergence of cyber-culture (Benedikt CR). Here I want to concentrate on telling the story of computing, the Internet and virtual reality; for the parallel histories of communications media, see Levinson (1997) or Wise (2000).

## Computer stories

To tell the history of computing is itself a complex task, involving as it does a wide range of ideas, incidents and outcomes. Paul Edwards (1996) describes two genres of computing history, the first an 'intellectual history' in which 'computers function primarily as the embodiment of ideas about informa-tion, symbols, and logic', and the second an 'engineering/economic history' which sees computers as 'devices for processing information' (Edwards 1996: x–xi). He proceeds to list the key players and moments in these two versions, noting their intersections and divergences. Their co-existence is partly explained by the split between software and hardware, and also by the different disciplinary emphases placed on accounts written by different his-torians. However, Edwards notes that these kinds of stories are only partial; they are 'insider's accounts' that 'ignore or downplay phenomena outside the laboratory and the mind of the scientist or engineer' and therefore fail to take into account 'the influence of ideologies, intersections with popular culture, or political power' (xii). To counter this, Edwards sets these histories alongside his own, which concern the shaping of (and shaping by) metaphors and discourses – specifically the *closed-world discourse* of Cold War geopolitics and the *cyborg discourse* formed from cognitive psychology and cybernetics (also defence-related). This approach has a lot to recommend it, in its weaving together of material (technology), symbolic (strategy) and experiential (subjectivity) story-lines, and in terms of setting the evolution of computers in cultural and political context – in the case of Edwards' story, Cold War culture and politics.

The military origin of many of cyberspace's components is well known, and the subject of considerable ambivalence. It also contributes, as Jordan (1999) says, to a prevailing 'myth' of cyberspace – a myth that, for some critics, taints cyberspace to this day with militaristic overtones (see, for exam-ple, Sardar CR). The increasing technologization of war has brought more and more scientists into the military, and brought more and more military fund-ing to scientists. For example, the complex calculations involved in modern war (calculations that had once been done by people – the first computers were human), progressively became too complex; they required machines. The need for machines for computation in the fields of ballistics, ordnance, information management, battle control, training, military intelligence and command systems led to cornerstone innovations in post-war digital computing: the

electronic computer, integrated circuits, hypertext, computer display monitors, graphical interfaces, virtual reality simulations, artificial intelligence, networking and packet switching. As Richard Wise concludes, '[n]one of the
technologies that make multimedia possible – fast powerful computers, imaging and simulation techniques – would exist today had it not been for the Cold
War and the space race' (Wise 2000: 23). (Indeed, we need to see the space
race as part of the Cold War.)

Running parallel to the military history of computing is the story of
commercial computing – of the development and selling of machines to
business users and then to private users, taking computers out of their twin
environments of the laboratory and the battlefield and into the workplace
and then the home. Paul Ceruzzi's (1998) *A History of Modern Computing* lays
out these tales compellingly, tracking the growth and development of the
US computer industry since the Second World War. Crucial steps towards
cyberculture at the intersection of these two histories include the establishment of the US Department of Defense's Advanced Research Projects Agency
(ARPA) as a response to the Soviet's successful launch of Sputnik in the late
1950s. ARPA was created to fund research projects with potential military
applications (though much of the more direct military research was soon
hived off to NASA); it thus represents the consolidation of military funding
for scientific (and computing) research in the climate of the Cold War.
Subsequently, the migration of researchers from ARPA to the Xerox
Corporation's Palo Alto Research Center (Xerox PARC), following a down-
sizing of military funding for computer research in the late 1960s, shifted
the emphasis of computing research into the commercial sector.

Moreover, the personnel that moved from ARPA to Xerox PARC were
computer scientists embedded in the 1960s counterculture – indeed, they
were relieved to be released from DoD links in the context of the Vietnam
War. Richard Wise (2000: 32) thus writes that Xerox PARC was 'a key link
between military research, counter-culture computer idealism and the emergence of a commercial market in multimedia', giving it a central role in
rerouteing the history of computing in the 1960s. The role of the computing
counterculture is placed centrestage in many analyses, since it brought about
key innovations which sought to 'democratize' computing:

> In the 1960s and 1970s the vanguard of the computer revolution
> consisted of young men and women imbued with counter-cultural values
> who, recognising that microcomputer technology would eventually
> make unprecedented computer power accessible at low cost, wanted
> to create 'insanely great' machines. They saw computers as tools that
> might both aid the fight for social justice and trigger a spiritual renais-
> sance that would sweep away the technocratic state.
>
> (Wise 2000: 27)

Xerox PARC thus became a core site in the development of personal computing, giving us the Alto computer (complete with a mouse, a keyboard and a monitor), a prototype laptop called the Dynabook, and new forms of programming aimed at making computers more user-friendly. The personal computer (PC) entered a world where computers had previously been cumbersome, elite machines of corporate America (epitomized by IBM's continued faith in mainframe computers). Now DIY kit-computers such as the Altair were available to electronics hobbyists, many of whom were similarly influenced by the values of the US counterculture. For this computing counterculture, personal computers offered the possibility for both mind-expansion and cultural revolution, if they could be brought to the masses (the Dynabook was designed as a 'mass computer' with this intent). In that climate, amateur 'self-help' groups like Berkeley's Home Brew Computer Club sprang up (initially to support Altair users with software and peripherals); these clubs became training-grounds for many of today's computer gurus, including Bill Gates and Paul Allen of Microsoft and Steve Jobs and Steven Wozniac of Apple. Against the then-dominant computer giant IBM, the companies formed by these Home Brew alumni arguably retained (at least initially) some traces of that countercultural ethos while expanding rapidly into new markets, reshaping the industry, breaking-up IBM's hold on the sector, and continuing to innovate in hardware and software production (for example, through the development of programming language MS-DOS and the graphical user interface or GUI – both making computers more user-friendly and therefore 'democratic').

*Internet stories*

The Department of Defense's ARPA facility is, of course, most often associated with another series of key innovations towards cyberspace – innovations in decentralization and networking. While this was partly related to military needs – as we shall see – it was also a broader innovation in computer usage, based around the idea of time-sharing. Tim Jordan sets the scene:

> In the late 1960s computers were large, expensive, often specialised and different to each other. One would be very good at graphics, another at databases, but unfortunately the two might be thousands of miles apart and be too expensive for both to be bought for both locations. The obvious answer was to dial up using a phone line or a dedicated link and use them remotely. . . . As more and more defence contractors in the US asked for computers as part of defence research, the Department of Defense's Advanced Research Projects Agency (ARPA) decided it was time to find a way of allowing researchers to

use each other's computers from a single terminal, no matter where they were located and no matter what system each target computer was running.

(Jordan 1999: 33)

The project that evolved from this brief was ARPANET, a decentralized network linking a small number of supercomputers to remote terminals. In one of my favourite depictions of ARPANET, Dodge and Kitchin (2001: 108) reprint a hand-drawn sketch-map of the network (with only four nodes, at the University of California Santa Barbara, University of Utah, University of California Los Angeles and the Stanford Research Institute) in 1969 – quite a humble origin for the Internet. The time-sharing capacity of this kind of network – allowing one computer to process data from a range of terminals, thus maximizing the productivity of these hugely expensive machines – was also being thought about in Britain at this time, where the government was concerned with gaining competitive edge in the emerging information economy (Abbate 1999). The key innovation to successful time-sharing was packet switching – a method of breaking up information into individually-labelled 'packets' of a standard size, that could be sent down different routes on the network (depending on queues), and reassembled at the host computer in the correct sequence, to then be processed. Researchers in Britain and the US had been working on this idea for some time, the most notable being Paul Baran at the US's Rand Corporation, who had been commissioned by the US Air Force to work on a system for maintaining military command in the wake of a nuclear attack – the idea he came up with was a distributed network, made possible by packet switching (Slevin 2000). The distributed structure of ARPANET, making use of packet switching, thus offered itself up to such military applications – although, as both Jordan (1999) and Slevin (2000) note, this aspect of ARPANET has been blown up into a 'myth' that overstates the military origins of the Internet.

This linking of remote computers, through the capacity to time-share, also encouraged the linking of remote computer scientists, leading to the formation of a community of researchers who shared not only computing time, but also ideas – indeed the project leader who commissioned ARPANET envisaged it as a way of connecting people in a 'man-machine symbiosis' (Slevin 2000). The first applications developed for ARPANET were Telnet (remote log-on – to access other machines in the network), FTP (file transfer – to share programs on the network) and TALK (forerunner to email, which proved very popular). In retrospect, it is perhaps less surprising than it was at the time that one of the most widely-used applications on ARPANET was email – its appeal to users ensured its success and widespread adoption, making ARPANET a communications system as much as a computing system (Abbate 1999). As Tim Jordan writes:

The key point about email is that rather than people using ARPANET to communicate with computers, as the designers had expected, people used it to communicate with other people. This was despite the fact that email was not programmed into the system but was added unofficially in an ad hoc way. Email emerged spontaneously as the basic resource provided by ARPANET.

(Jordan 1999: 38)

The establishment of those initial four nodes in 1969 was rapidly followed by more connections within the US, as well as international connections, first to Norway and Britain and then elsewhere. By March 1977, there were 111 nodes connected up (Dodge and Kitchin 2001). The original ARPANET was split into two strands in 1983, with military uses sectioned off on to the more secure MILNET. The research-oriented ARPANET was itself gradually supplanted by the National Science Foundation's NFSNET. ARPANET was decommissioned in 1990, followed five years later by NSFNET, as the Internet 'backbone' increasingly became the domain of commercial enterprise – paving the way for the intensive commercialization of the Internet and the rise of e-commerce (Slevin 2000).

Important technical innovations that facilitated the spread of networking included the design of the Interface Message Processor (IMP), a computer dedicated to 'translating' between machines in order to remove problems of incompatibility. IMP was eventually superseded by the Transmission Control Protocol/Internet Protocol (TCP/IP) that both translated and 'managed' the flow of data between nodes. The invention of the modem made connection more accessible and straightforward, and gave rise to widespread PC-based Internet use, spawning bulletin boards, mailing lists, discussion groups and conferencing systems like Usenet, FidoNet and Internet Relay Chat (IRC), as well as more specialized applications such as Multi-User Domains (MUDs). Importantly, these were often cooperative networks, facilitated by the free circulation of software – though alongside these grew up commercial networks such as CompuServe. The growth and diversification of uses also gave rise to the need to standardize addresses, leading to the development of the Domain Name System (DNS) – 'ac' for academic institutions, 'com' for companies, and so on.

Rapid growth also created the need for ways to locate relevant information in the expanding network. The Gopher program was the first attempt to 'navigate' the Internet, but soon proved unsuitable for tracking the increasingly incompatible resources. The breakthrough that eased this problem was the World Wide Web, devised by Tim Berners-Lee and colleagues at the CERN (Coseil Europeen pour la Recherche Nucleaire) physics laboratory in Switzerland. Berners-Lee worked up the WWW as a solution to three problems at CERN: information loss accompanying staff turnover, the induction of new staff and the retrieval of stored information. The solution came from rethinking the ways that information is linked, stored and retrieved – instead of being hierarchical, it should be web-like, based on the ideas of hypertext and hyperlinks (which had already been considered, in military context, as a way of improving human effectiveness in data-handling; see Wise 2000). The WWW system, then, acts a multi-user system for searching and retrieving from an ever-expanding pool of information, and its usefulness ensured its speedy diffusion in cyberspace (Berners-Lee made his program freely available on the Internet in 1991). Its key tools are the universal resource locator (URL), a way of identifying information resources, hypertext mark-up language (HTML), which converts different forms of information into hypertext pages that can be read over the Web and located through their URL, and the use of Web servers (computers that supply the information as webpages), Web browsers (an interface that 'surfs' for information) and search engines (that provide access to databases of webpages). Recent developments in the Web have expanded the kinds of information available from text and still images to sound and moving images, creating a rich and diverse multimedia resource in cyberspace (Wise 2000). The Web has become so popular and successful, in fact, that 'it is *the* mode of cyberspace, particularly for the mass of users who only came online since the mid-1990s' (Dodge and Kitchin 2001: 3) – for many of us, the Web *is* cyberspace.

## VR stories

However, the story of the Internet and World Wide Web is only one branch of the material story of cyberspace. Running alongside it is the story of virtual reality, or VR (for a diagram of the 'merging timelines of cyberspace' showing the Internet alongside virtual reality, see Dodge and Kitchin 2001: 8). Attempts to produce 'virtual environments' can also be tracked back to military research, especially in the context of simulation as a method of training, and to the entertainment industry, via for example 3-D movies, Sensorama and the IMAX cinema system (Wollen 1993).

Flight simulators have been in existence since the early twentieth century, and were first combined with computers in the 1960s (Wise 2000). The work of Ivan Sutherland on head-mounted 3-D computer displays prefigured the model of virtual reality head-sets from that time, and were only substantially improved through VR research at NASA in the mid-1980s. NASA's involvement in VR research is seen as pivotal; at its Ames Research Center, scientists worked on telepresence technologies for use in space, and produced a Virtual Environment Workstation and a Virtual Environment Display System (Bukatman CR). Data-gloves were also being developed by NASA, though the break-through DataGlove system later developed by Tom Zimmerman at VPL was inspired by the 'air guitar' – the imaginary guitar rock fans play (Hayward 1993) – giving a further reminder of the role of countercultural forces in shaping cyberspace (Davis 1998).

Simulators developed more rapidly across the 1990s, finding applications in medicine, architecture, and notably in arcade games, where fantasy worlds can be experienced outside scientific and military contexts (Haddon 1993). In some critics' eyes, in fact, there has been a convergence of arcade games and military applications, making modern warfare seem like a game (Gray 1997). Moreover, VR came to be a major feature of sci-fi movies, with films like *Tron* or *Lawnmower Man* adding to the fantasy of a future life in immersive virtual environments (even if their narratives played out ambivalence towards new technologies).

Virtual reality has not, however, become as widely-accessible as the Internet – other than through arcade games and via cinematic narratives – and the hype around it witnessed in the early 1990s (embodied in books like Howard Rheingold's (1991) *Virtual Reality*) has subsided somewhat. Nevertheless, VR remains a key component of cyberculture, since it offers the promise of immersive and interactive environments that mirror cyberpunk's imaginings more closely than the Internet (on cyberpunk, see 'Symbolic stories' below). Indeed, as Richard Wise (2000) notes, the creator of Virtual Reality Markup Language (VRML), Mark Pesce, was inspired by William Gibson's work, which he merged with ideas from New Age countercultures. Erik Davis (1998: 192) describes Pesce as 'a technopagan, a goddess-worshipper, ritual magician and occasional partaker of psychedelic sacraments', tracing the 'magical' dimension of VR imagined through VRML (and very much part of VPL's technoshamanic project). VRML marks the convergence of virtual reality with the WWW, enabling navigable, 3-D hyper-linked spaces to be created in cyberspace: 'a VRML webpage is both the territory and the means to navigate this territory' (Dodge and Kitchin 2001: 30). The possibility of 'desktop VR' has been taken up as an extension of text-based MUDs, producing 3-D graphical virtual worlds accessible for synchronous interaction over the Internet, such as the commercially-run AlphaWorld (see Dodge and Kitchin 2001). These kinds of developments might, therefore, be seen to be moving us ever closer to the cyberspace imagined in cyberpunk.

What these stories suggest, I want to argue, is that '[t]he meaning of the Internet [and virtual reality] had to be invented – and constantly reinvented – at the same time as the technology itself' (Abbate 1999: 6): that the history of cyberculture told here is one that blends the linear narratives of technological progress with incidents of happenstance; moreover, it is a story woven from diverse threads, which have somehow come together to give us the 'really existing matrix' of cyberspace. However, as I shall argue in a while, it makes no sense to keep this story separate from other kinds of cyber-story – for the 'reality' of cyberspace and cyberculture always bears the imprint of the imaginary and the experiential. Moreover, as I hope to suggest now, we need to re-place cyberspace in its political-economic context, and rewrite its 'material story' as the outcome not only of technological development, but also of the interplay of technology with society, culture and politics.

### Political economy stories

Dodge and Kitchin (2001: 26) provide a useful definition of the 'political economic position' on cyberspace, describing it as an approach that highlights the fact that 'the relationship between technology and society is bound up with capitalist modes of production and the associated political, economic and social relations which underlie capitalism' – a particular way, then, of talking about 'what it is'. This mode of analysis has important implications for thinking about cyberspace, made even more pressing by what many commentators see as the progressive colonization of cyberspace by corporate capitalism. Arturo Escobar (CR) sets out an agenda for researching the 'political economy of cyberculture', focusing on issues such as the relationship between information and capital, the role of institutions in managing the flow of information in cyberspace, the broader impacts of biotechnology (especially in the Third World context), and the restructuring of relations between rich and poor under the regime of 'cyber-capitalism'. Some of these issues are taken up elsewhere in this book, but here I want to visit a few of them, starting with the basic political-economy question of Internet use and users: how many are there, and who and where are they?

These are important questions to ask, since getting a sense on the size, shape and spread of the online population begins to give us an indication of broad political-economic issues; it also grounds the 'hype' about cyberspace in facts and figures. It is, however, a difficult task to find answers – as Timothy Luke (1999: 27–8) writes, '[a]n accurate census of Internet users needs to be updated daily or weekly, not monthly or yearly, to keep track of its exponential growth. . . . Numbers can be cited, but they become inaccurate even as they are reported.' In spite of this note of caution, surveys of use and users *are* being conducted – indeed, surveys of the Internet population are proliferating, as competing agencies attempt to get a definitive grip on the statistics, which increasingly have market value. Tim Jordan surveys the surveys, commenting on their methods and findings; he summarizes thus:

> The Internet is growing at exponential rates but is overwhelmingly located in the already industrialised world where users are wealthy, white and highly educated, while uses are essentially to communicate with other people whether for social, research or business purposes.
> (Jordan 1999: 49)

Beyond the certainty of that kind of summary, however, the stats exhibit considerable variability. Using a method of counting host computers and then multiplying by a projected number of users, Jordan states with reasonable confidence that there were between 40 and 70 million Internet users in mid-1998. James Slevin (2000), meanwhile, cites the figure of 150–180 million users in 1999, though he does not discuss the reliability of his sources. Whatever the number of users in total, however, what matters more to our analysis is their distribution *spatially* and *socially*. Here again, however, the numbers vary – though the overall picture is pretty clear. Jordan writes that, in July 1998, the US had 65 per cent of all Internet hosts; Slevin (2000: 40) states that 'almost 99 per cent of all Internet connections were in North America, Western Europe and Japan' by the late 1990s. So, those millions of users are geographically concentrated into particular parts of the world. Striking concentrations and inequalities are also revealed elsewhere: of the 145,000 hosts in sub-Saharan Africa in 1998, more than 96 per cent were in South Africa – take away South Africa, and the stats for sub-Saharan Africa show only one user per 5,000 people. More than three-quarters of the 115,000 hosts in the Middle East and North Africa in 1998 were in Israel. The cost of Internet access in Vietnam in 1999 was one third of the average annual salary. In Indonesia, Internet access costs twelve times more than it does in the US. Moreover, between one third and one half of the world's population lives more than two hours away from the nearest public telephone. And so on – the pattern that emerges is of huge disparities globally, all of them exacerbating what Sean Cubitt (1998: 149) calls, in a telling phrase, 'the excommunication of the developing world' (see also Holderness 1998). These inequalities are also reflected lower down the spatial scale, too, within nations, regions, cities and neighbourhoods (Loader 1998), although we must also be mindful of generalizing here, since empirical work at particular locations suggests that context-specific patterns emerge locally (Miller and Slater 2000).

What, then, of the *social* characteristics of the online population? Jordan (1999: 53–4) again usefully summarizes from a range of survey data: 'users are white, have professional or managerial occupations, higher than average incomes and are likely to be located in the developed world'. The gender breakdown of users is seen to be gradually equalizing, the age profile is stable at early- to mid-thirties, 'race' remains around 90 per cent white, and household incomes of US$60,000 are commonly cited in surveys. More than 75 per cent of users in a US survey had attended college (compared with only 46 per cent of the total population). Problematically, we do not have comparable surveys of the social characteristics of the offline population. As Robins and Webster (1999) discuss, data on excluded populations have not been collected, principally because there is no commercial interest in those people – all the surveys of Internet users are driven at least in part by the imperatives of the market, as a component of the broader contemporary process of the commodification of information.

Users and non-users are only part of the equation, of course. We need also to think about questions of *ownership* and *control* — crucial material questions often forgotten when cyberspace gets imagined as a dematerialized 'dataspace':

> [Cyberspace] has an immense material base underpinning its operations, which depend upon complex wired and wireless systems of transmission via microwave towers, communications satellites, fibreoptic networks and on-line services. Consequently, who designs, owns, manages or operates all of the hardware needed to generate cyberspace is a key question. . . . [T]here is an elaborate and expansive political economy driving cyberspatial development.
>
> (Luke 1999: 31)

Cyberspace is, in summary, owned, managed and controlled space — Luke names it 'hyperreal estate' (46). And this feature of cyberspace is, some commentators argue, becoming both more complete and more obvious, as a result of what Saskia Sassen (1999: 52) calls 'the mass discovery by business of the Net':

> This is a particular moment in the history of digital networks, one when powerful corporate actors and high-performance networks are strengthening the role of private electronic space and altering the structure of public electronic space. Electronic space has emerged not simply as a means for communicating, but as *a major new theatre for capital accumulation and the operations of global actors.*
>
> (Sassen 1999: 49; my emphasis)

Luke's essay on the emerging political economy of cyberspace is, in my opinion, particularly insightful, and raises a number of significant issues regarding the morphing of cyberspace into this 'theatre for capital accumulation', which rewires the social strata in terms of new binaries: 'inside/outside, access-granted/access-denied, platform-compatible/platform-incompatible, operational/inoperable' (Luke 1999: 27). Crucially, this rewiring distorts the vision of cyberspace as a democratic realm of universal access, which had been central to the utopian rhetoric of 'cyber-hype' (see Ross 1998). Luke names this new political-economic realm 'dromoeconomics', defined as 'modes of production organized around controlling the speeding flows of capital, labour, information, products, resources and techniques coursing through global modes of production' (32). Dromoeconomics impacts on all spheres of online life, as well as offline life (either by drawing it in, or rendering it invisible).

## Work stories

One sector that Luke highlights, and that I would like to look at here, is forms, modes and patterns of work. Again, in terms of a material reading of cyberspace, this focus is a crucial counter to the fantasy of free-flowing data conjured in visions of cyberculture: it reminds us that computers have to be made, and data inputted. As Andrew Ross (1998: 12) writes, '[m]asses of people work in cyberspace or work to make cyberspace possible. It is not simply a medium for free expression and wealth accumulation; it is a labor-intensive workplace'. Dromoeconomics thus brings with it a new cyberspatial division of labour:

> The cyberspatial resources of global computer nets permit virtual enterprises to employ thousands of poor women in Jamaica, Mauritius or the Philippines in low-paid, tedious data entry or word-processing jobs for firms in London, Paris or San Diego. Cyberspace permits dromo-economic entrepreneurs to virtualize segments of a core workplace at these peripheral locations, while porting the telepresence of peripheral labourers into the productive systems of a core-based company.
>
> (Luke 1999: 37)

Global corporations have made extensive use of cyberspace technologies to disaggregate their activities, exploiting the substantial cost-benefits of 'off-shore data processing' in peripheral economies. This is an ambivalent process. On the one hand, it provides a means for those economies and their workers to get 'wired'; against this, issues of low-pay (especially pay-per-keystroke piece-work), health hazards (RSI, problems associated with overuse of VDUs), non-unionization and casualization reveal the risks of this kind of work (Pearson and Mitter 1995). In his excellent essay 'Jobs in cyberspace', Ross (1998) details this 'low-wage world of automated surveillance, subcontracted piecework, crippling workplace injuries, and tumors in the livers of chip factory workers' (33–4). Even in 'core' economies, regimes of what Ross calls 'low-wage HTML labor' (18) work to sustain cyberspace – reminding us again that there is a material reality as the flipside to the cyber-hype. America Online, for example, is sustained through the free labour of some 15,000 volunteers, some of whom went public with their dissatisfactions in early 1999 (Terranova 2000). Cyberspace doesn't just *happen*; data do not *grow* from some digital primordial info-soup. Computer hardware has to be built somewhere, by someone; software has to be written, data have to be inputted, websites maintained, and so on. The stuff of cyberspace isn't the spontaneous uploading of consciousness for and by 'jacked-in' console cowboys – it is the product of labour:

> Simultaneously voluntarily given and unwaged, enjoyed and exploited, free labor on the Net includes the activity of building Web sites,

modifying software packages, reading and participating in mailing lists, and building virtual spaces on MUDs and MOOs.

(Terranova 2000: 33)

Terranova's and Ross' work thus reveals what we might call the 'dot.com underbelly': the new economic miracle isn't just – as the folk stories would have us believe – a happy tale of Great Ideas, venture capitalism and instant riches; it's also a tale of this new world economic order, of digital sweat-shops and virtual 'alienated labour'.

However, Terranova complicates this analysis by setting it alongside argu-ments that see cyberspace as operating like a 'high-tech gift economy' (36) where labour is freely given, where ideas and products can be freely circulated (as in, for example, shareware, freeware and the open source movement) – in ways that are profoundly anti-capitalist. The open source movement makes the source code of its software freely available, and its ideals were used by Netscape in 1998, when it launched its new web browser. Making the source code open also brings advantages to the supplier, in terms of letting users check the code, sort out bugs and glitches and improve the software. Netscape's dalliance with open source prompted considerable debate, which Terranova outlines; as she concludes, this particular story tells us that 'the Internet is always and simultaneously a gift economy *and* an advanced capitalist economy' (Terranova 2000: 51). Moreover, she writes, this should not be seen as a benign and unproblematically equivalent coexistence. The tendency for capital appropriation of cyberspace seems inexhaustible, even in the light of the volatilities of the high-tech stock market in the wake of the e-commerce boom. As Sassen (1999) notes, strategies like open sourcing or free access to the Internet are *tactical* acts, aimed at gaining strategic advantage and keeping us online. This, then, is the ambivalence of 'free labour' in cyber-space – labour that is freely (willingly) given, but also given for free (without remuneration).

These political-economic versions of our material story all work to remind us of the realities of cyberspace, then – of the work of cyberspace, the dromoeconomics that work through cyberspace, the ways in which infor-mation is both the product of labour and made over as a commodity. These are, I think, among the most important stories to tell about cyberspace, since they demand that we track our own relationship to global processes that have immense material impacts. The dream of uploaded consciousness has to be tempered by reminders of those for whom cyberspace isn't a consensual hallucination, but a source of minimal wages or crippling injuries. Setting that 'imaginary' cyberspace alongside these material realities leads us into the next type of storytelling I want to engage with in this chapter – the symbolic stories that emerge and merge on page and screen to produce versions of the consensual hallucination of cyberspace.

As a bridging move to the realm of fantasy, I want to highlight Jordan's (1999) use of the neat distinction between two forms of cyberspace, *Gibsonian cyberspace* and *Barlovian cyberspace*. Gibsonian cyberspace, named after cyberpunk guru William Gibson, is the purely symbolic version of cyberspace found in fiction and film; Barlovian cyberspace, however – named after cyberspace guru John Perry Barlow (who first used Gibson's term to describe computer-mediated communications) – represents the mediation of image and reality: 'joining together the visions of cyberpunk to the reality of networks creates a concept of cyberspace as a place that currently exists' (Jordan 1999: 56). This idea – that we experience cyberspace at the intersection of reality and fantasy – will form the bedrock for part of the experiential storying that comes in the next chapter. I wanted to signal it here, however, as an early indication of its centrality to my overall argument. I will be back in Barlovian cyberspace later, then; for now, I want to shift the focus to symbolic story-telling, and journey into Gibsonian cyberspace.

## Symbolic stories

> Cyberpunk fiction has become a self-fulfilling prophecy in which we understand cyberspace through its fantasies but then we find that cyberspace is in fact like cyberpunk.
>
> (Jordan 1999: 33)

As we have already seen, central to my argument in this chapter is the role of the 'symbolic' in giving us another way of thinking about cyberspace. There is, therefore, a tale to tell here about *representations* of cyberspace in popular culture – their production, circulation and consumption has profound impacts on how we come to envision and experience cyberspace. Absolutely crucial in this context is the role played by cyberpunk fiction. Cyberpunk is widely cited as a key influence on the evolution of cyberculture; as Tim Jordan notes, we understand cyberspace through cyberpunk, and also try to square our experiences of cyberspace with the way it is imagined in cyberpunk. So, we need to have a look at cyberpunk here, highlighting elements of the genre that are centrally-placed in constructing a symbolic cyberspace.

### Cyberpunk stories

Cyberpunk is best understood as a subgenre of science fiction; it is sometimes seen as a distinctly 'postmodern' take on sci-fi (Cavallaro 2000). Its central concerns are summarized by Douglas Kellner (1995: 320) as 'the intensities, possibilities, and effects of new modes of technologically mediated experience'. Writers associated with cyberpunk include Bruce Sterling, Pat Cadigan, Samuel Delaney, Neal Stephenson – but its best-known author is William Gibson, whose 'Sprawl Trilogy' (*Neuromancer* (1984), *Count Zero* (1986) and *Mona Lisa Overdrive* (1988)) is widely-seen as defining the genre, as well as defining the cyberpunk version of cyberspace (Kneale 1999). Other key publications include two anthologies of cyberpunk writing, Bruce Sterling's (1986) *Mirrorshades* and Larry McCaffery's (1991) *Storming the Reality Studio*. McCaffery's collection importantly contextualizes cyberpunk by including work by writers seen as influential upon the genre, such as William Burroughs, J. G. Ballard, Don DeLillo and Thomas Pynchon, as well as critical commentaries and theoretical work from, among others, Jacques Derrida, Jean Baudrillard, Arthur Kroker and Fredric Jameson.

Gibson's centrality to cyberpunk's writing of cyberspace itself contains a story which has grown to almost mythic proportions – the story of how he coined the term 'cyberspace', defined the cyberpunk genre and provided a model for imagining cyberspace that has ghosted it ever since. Widely cited in this tale are these 'facts': (i) that Gibson was only dimly aware at best of work in the area of virtual reality when he wrote *Neuromancer*; (ii) that he wrote *Neuromancer* on a cranky old manual typewriter; and (iii) that his inspiration for imagining cyberspace came from watching kids play arcade games (see Bukatman 1994; Davis 1998; Dodge and Kitchin 2001). It's a coincidence, then, that *Neuromancer* 'hit the cultural cortex around the same time that personal computers invades the home, and world financial markets launched into twenty-four-hour orbit' (Davis 1998: 191) – though the serendipity has since come to be seen as prophetic rather than merely lucky.

Here's Gibson's own famous account of coining the term:

> Assembled word *cyberspace* from small and readily available components of language. Neologic spasm: the primal act of pop poetics. Preceded any concept whatever. Slick and hollow – awaiting received meanings. All I did: folded words as taught. Now other words accrete in the interstices.
>
> (Gibson 1991: 28)

That's one of two key quotations from Gibson, recited like incantations in virtually every discussion of cyberspace, framing the story of cyberpunk and cyberculture. The second is, of course, his definition of 'cyberspace' from *Neuromancer*:

> Cyberspace: A consensual hallucination experienced daily by billions of legitimate operators, in every nation, by children being taught mathe-matical concepts. . . . A graphical representation of data abstracted from the banks of every computer in the human system. Unthinkable

complexity. Lines of light ranged in the nonspace of the mind, clusters
and constellations of data. Like city lights, receding.

(Gibson 1984: 67)

Gibson therefore described (and thereby defined) cyberspace as the sum of
the world's data, represented graphically, and accessible by 'jacking in'
through computer consoles (see Tomas CR). Jacking in involves the uploading
of one's consciousness into cyberspace, leaving the 'meat' of the body behind
(see Chapter 7). Once 'inside', users ('console cowboys') can 'fly' through
the data, which is assembled in ways that resemble the urban landscape, with
flows of data like traffic and banks of data like skyscrapers – a way of depicting
cyberspace that has endured, featured in films, comics and adverts:

> The city is a digitised parallel world which from 'above' might appear
> as rationally planned, . . . but from 'below' reveals itself as a . . .
> labyrinth, in which no one can get the bird's eye view of the plan, but
> everyone effectively has to operate at street level in a world which is
> rapidly being re-structured and re-configured.
>
> (Burrows 1997a: 242)

This aesthetic is neatly captured in the following passage from *Mona Lisa
Overdrive*:

> All the data in the world stacked up like one big neon city, so you can
> cruise around and have a kind of grip on it, visually anyway, because
> if you didn't, it was too complicated, trying to find your way to a
> particular piece of data you needed.
>
> (Gibson 1988: 22)

Cyberspace is a datascape, then; in cyberpunk, it has come to exist as
an imagined merger between the Internet and virtual reality, populated by
console cowboys' uploaded consciousnesses, avatars, artificial intelligences,
personality constructs – unthinkable complexity at 'street' level, with gangs
forming around 'technophilic' identities (Tomas CR). It's also simultaneously
corporatized and militarized; it is cross-cut by ICE (Intrusion Counter-
measures Electronics) that have to be 'hacked' through to access corporate
data systems (Kellner 1995). As Dodge and Kitchin describe it, then, cyberpunk imagines

> a future dominated by libertarian capitalism, where global wealth and
> power are the preserve of multinationals and nation-states are weak or
> gone; where a dual economy flourishes and is enforced through corporate
> modes of governance and surveillance; where society is increasingly

urbanised within fragmented, divided, simulacra cities; where the body is enhanced through the use of genetic engineering and technical implants.

(Dodge and Kitchin 2001: 206)

Against this backdrop, the genre's 'heroes' are often ambivalently located as working *within* and *against* the system, trading their 'machine skill' (hacking) across markets both legal and illegal. As Leary (CR: 535) writes: 'Cyberpunks are sometimes authorized by governors. They can, with sweet cynicism and patient humour, interface their singularity with institutions. They often work within "the governing systems" on a temporary basis'. Like the hackers Andrew Ross (CR) discusses, this makes the cyberpunks ambiguous and threatening figures – the enemy within.

The term 'cyberpunk' has – as we can see in the preceding paragraph – come to refer not only to a genre of fiction, but also to the characters depicted in the work, and subsequently as a term to describe assorted subcultural formations clustering around cyberculture (see Chapter 8):

> *Cyberpunk* is . . . a risky term. Like all linguistic innovations, it must be used with a tolerant sense of high-tech humour. It's a stop gap, transitional meaning-grenade thrown over the language barricades to describe the resourceful, skilful individual who accesses and steers knowledge/communication technology towards his/her own private goals. For personal pleasure, profit, principle, or growth.
>
> (Leary CR: 534–5)

As many critics note, sci-fi generally and cyberpunk particularly have to be read as tales about the present as much as about the future (Cavallaro 2000). Moreover, the works can only be understood by *locating* their authors – to get a handle on the resources they have at their disposal; resources which come to shape their imaginings. Cyberpunk narratives are thus described as 'fast-paced, full of bizarre characters, twists of plot, and weird surprises – *just like life in high-tech society*' (Kellner 1995: 302; my emphasis). And Bruce Sterling (1986: xi) points up the 'real life' (RL) social setting from which cyberpunk burst forth: 'The cyberpunks are perhaps the first SF generation to grow up not only within the literary tradition of science fiction but *in a truly science fictional world*' (my emphasis). Larry McCaffery concurs, noting the writers' simultaneous embeddedness in popular culture and technoculture:

> The cyberpunks were the first generation of artists for whom the technologies of satellite dishes, video and audio players and recorders, computers and video games (both of particular importance), digital watches, and MTV were not exoticisms, but part of a daily 'reality matrix'. They

were also the first generation of writers . . . who had grown up immersed in technology but also in pop culture, in the values and aesthetics of the counterculture associated with drug culture, punk rock, video games, . . . comic books, and . . . gore-and-splatter SF/horror films.

(McCaffery 1991: 12)

What this means for some readers is that cyberpunk can enact a kind of social criticism of the future, read through the circuits of contemporary culture. Roger Burrows (1997a: 237–8), for example, says it is 'possible to decipher, within . . . cyberpunk, a *sociologically* coherent vision of a very near future which is, some argue, about to collapse into the present. . . . Whether Gibson intends it or not, his fiction *can* be systematically read as social and cultural theory.' In a second essay, Burrows cranks up this comparison: 'The themes and processes which a symptomatic reading of cyberpunk reveal are a good deal more insightful than those offered by what now passes for the theoretical and empirical mainstream' (Burrows 1997b: 38). Indeed, some commentators have suggested that a 'recursive' relationship has evolved, with 'fact' (or 'theory') and 'fiction' informing each other. So, when Allucquere Rosanne Stone (CR: 513) describes *Neuromancer* as a kind of source code for 'the technologically literate and socially disenfranchised', she is also remarking on it as a 'massive intertextual presence not only in other literary productions of the 1980s, but in technical publications, conference topics, hardware design, and scientific and technological discourses in the large'. Kevin Concannon argues from this recursivity that the border between scientific and literary space is now the site of merging, and that cyberspace

has taken on a life of its own, its science fictionalization overcome by its real world possibility. . . . [S]cience is creating an alternate space of possibility that at once diverges and reinforces its fictional representation. . . . The border not only divides the two but also draws them together, making any distinction between the fiction of cyberspace and its fact impossible to determine: all seems fact and fiction.

(Concannon 1998: 441)

James Kneale's (1999) work is worth signalling here. What's important about it for us is that he adds *readers* in his project on cyberpunk fiction, rather than relying solely on textual analysis. While the readers he talked to often found Gibson's descriptions of cyberspace 'vague', they fleshed this vagueness out by referring to their own experiences of information technology. In light of this, Kneale's interest is in 'the intersection of . . . writing technologies and virtual technologies' (206) – how readers rewire Gibsonian cyberspace into Barlovian cyberspace, by adding in their contact with 'the really existing matrix'. Tim Jordan makes this point, too:

whatever science fiction imagines may be possible, some of its fantasies have limped into real lives. Text[-based CMC] may be deeply impoverished, compared with Gibson's cyberspace . . . but it is enough, more than enough, for Barlovian cyberspace to blossom and grow.

(Jordan 1999: 57–8)

In these accounts, the interplay of cyberpunk and CMC is signalled as productive – cyberpunk is seen as providing a 'cognitive map' of human-computer interaction, tinged with critical warning signs. However, other critics argue that cyberpunk has had a negative impact, propagating myths that obscure the reality of cyberspace. For instance, McBeath and Webb (1997: 249) write that '[t]here are many confusions haunting cyberspace. Primarily the confusions can be located at the level of metaphors which are invoked to characterise the nature of cyberspace' – cyberpunk is here equated with generating *mis*understanding, even with misleading us. Gibson has himself criticized the appropriation of his ideas, arguing that the irony in his writing often gets erased by those who over-enthusiastically and over-simplistically embrace his vision of the cyberfuture (see Dodge and Kitchin 2001).

## Pop culture stories

Of course, cyberpunk is only one of the cultural sites where symbolic stories around cyberspace get produced – and though it is often held up as central in terms of its themes and visions, it is perhaps less central in terms of its mass exposure. While there have been some attempts to make cyberpunk movies (such as the Gibson-derived *Johnny Mnemonic* or the Gibson-inspired *The Matrix*), and while sci-fi movies have also evolved a cyberpunkish aesthetic and narrative style (embodied in the 'tech-noir' of *Blade Runner*, for example), a lot of the discussions of 'symbolic' versions of cyberspace tend to neglect the other genres and forms of what we might call 'popular cybercultures'. Dodge and Kitchin (2001: 184), for example, quickly dismiss 'mainstream cyberfiction' – typified by 'the spate of 'cyberthrillers' and romantic 'You've Got Mail' novels' – as lacking 'the dark, edgy style that characterises cyberpunk'. And where these mainstream works are discussed, they are often read as relatively simplistic (and conservative) indicators of technophobia and social anxiety (Kuhn 1990). While that may be true, we need to remember the cultural work that those kinds of representations do, rather than simply analysing them textually (in the way that Kneale engages with cyberpunk). Crucial to this is acknowledging the role played by the diversity of representations of cyberspace in providing a portfolio of meanings that audiences piece together. So 'You've Got Mail' romances *can* give us particular insights into cyberculture, and more importantly, can be used as a symbolic resource in the on-going process of meaning-making.

The increasing visibility of aspects of cyberculture in 'mainstream' contexts might be seen as unproblematically normalizing them, but I think this reading obscures the complexities of representation. Let's take an example from my own on-going meaning-making. One night a while back I was at home, finishing reading Dani Cavallaro's (2000) *Cyberpunk and Cyberculture*, with the US Country Music Awards on as background TV. Alan Jackson came on, and began singing a song called 'www.memories' – I looked up to see Jackson and his band on stage, surrounded by computers on haybales, the song's lyrics full of lost love told through cyberspace metaphors, of 'Clickin'' on me' and surfing for memories, of the heart-broken cowboy-as-website (giving a whole new meaning to Gibson's 'console cowboy'). There was, at that moment, something acutely resonant for me in these images and sounds, of a way of thinking about cyberspace as it might be squared with a cowboy's life, and how the cyberspace of memory isn't just the kind of space Cavallaro describes at the end of her book (where the idea of 'prosthetic memory' gets interrogated through the standard texts, *Blade Runner* and *Total Recall*). Jackson's song is equally about prosthetic memory, it seems to me, but framed in a particular cultural context that can extend the ways we (*or at least I*) now think about the concept (for a broader discussion of 'high-tech rednecks', which also resonates with 'www.memories', see Fox 1997). The song hyperlinked intertextually for me with the melancholy of Deckard in *Blade Runner*, sat at the piano, looking at old photos, and made me pause for thought about the personal memories a computer might hold – both in its memory, and in the memory of past scenes played out around it.

It's that kind of intertextual moment that I think makes 'mainstream' depictions of cyberspace in popular culture important to consider. It raises some interesting particular questions, too: in what ways is the discourse of cyberculture legible within something like Country and Western music? (Jackson is not alone – I've since heard a Randy Travis song about email, too, and Fox (1997) mentions a George Jones song called 'High-Tech Redneck'.) What kinds of metaphorical or cultural work are computers-on-haybales doing in the setting of the CMA? What kinds of connections are being made by the people sitting in the audience, either in Nashville or at home? In acknowledging the multiplicity of symbolic sites where we encounter cyberspace – and the multiplicity of cyberspaces we encounter there – I'm trying to highlight the continuous work of thinking cyberspace, of adding into the mix new images, new ideas. This can be at banal levels (so, after Alan Jackson, whenever I say 'www-dot' it's with his cowboy drawl), but it can also be more profound, shifting our overall perspective on cyberspace and our place (or potential place) within it.

Logging the symbolic resources as we log on to them also gives us insights into the ways we each make a version of Barlovian cyberspace, folding the images and ideas in with our experiences of contact with cyberspace. While

Jordan (1999: 56) defines Barlovian cyberspace only in terms of 'the visions of cyberpunk' meeting 'the reality of networks', I'd like to enlarge the definition to encompass all the places where experience and imagination intersect. That's the trajectory of my final segment of story-telling, which is concerned with what I've called experiential stories – stories of what happens when we encounter cyberspace, of 'what it does' and 'what we do' with it. That is the story in Chapter 3.

## Summary

This chapter has focused on two different ways of thinking and talking about cyberspace. I began by recounting the histories of the Internet and World Wide Web, in order to produce a materialist account that emphasizes the material culture of cyberspace – the development of hardware and software that makes cyberspace possible. To this account was then added a second material perspective, which I named the political economy of cyberspace. Here, we examined the demographics of Internet users, in order to establish who is in cyberspace and who is not, and then considered questions of power and ownership, as a reminder of the implication of the Internet in broader webs of economics and politics. This was followed by a discussion of what Jordan (1999) refers to as 'the cyberspace imaginary' – the ways in which cyberspace is depicted in fiction and film. Prominence was given here to cyberpunk fiction, for its powerful visions of the future – and William Gibson's work was highlighted for its pivotal role in providing one of the most important fictional writings of cyberspace. However, I also discussed what we might call 'mainstream' imaginings of cyberspace, in order to show that we get access to ways of thinking about the Internet and computers from a wide range of sources in the mass media. Finally, as a link between this chapter and the next, I introduced the concept of 'Barlovian cyberspace', understood here as the mediation of material and symbolic stories. Barlovian cyberspace is a way of naming and describing the ways we experience computers and the Internet, in recognition that our experiences sit at the intersection of material and symbolic understandings.

# Hot links

## Chapters from The Cybercultures Reader

Michael Benedikt, 'Cyberspace: first steps' (Chapter 1: 29–44).

Scott Bukatman, 'Terminal penetration' (Chapter 9: 149–74).

Arturo Escobar, 'Welcome to cyberia: notes on the anthropology of cyberculture' (Chapter 3: 56–76).

Timothy Leary, 'The cyberpunk: the individual as reality pilot' (Chapter 33:
529–39).

Andrew Ross, 'Hacking away at the counterculture' (Chapter 16: 254–67).

Ziauddin Sardar, 'alt.civilizations.faq: cyberspace as the darker side of the west'
(Chapter 48: 732–52).

Allucquere Rosanne Stone, 'Will the real body please stand up? Boundary stories
about virtual cultures' (Chapter 32: 504–28).

David Tomas, 'The technophilic body: on technicity in William Gibson's cyborg
culture' (Chapter 10: 175–89).

## Further reading

Jenny Abbate (1999) *Inventing the Internet*, Cambridge MA: MIT Press.

Dani Cavallaro (2000) *Cyberpunk and Cyberculture: science fiction and the work of
William Gibson*, London: Athlone.

Paul Ceruzzi (1998) *A History of Modern Computing*, Cambridge MA: MIT Press.

Erik Davis (1998) *TechGnosis: myth, magic and mysticism in the age of information*,
London: Serpent's Tail.

Martin Dodge and Rob Kitchin (2001) *Mapping Cyberspace*, London: Routledge.

Tim Jordan (1999) *Cyberpower: the culture and politics of cyberspace and the Internet*,
London: Routledge.

Richard Wise (2000) *Multimedia: a critical introduction*, London: Routledge.

## Websites

http://www.eff.org/~barlow/barlow.html

John Perry Barlow's home(stead) page, within the Electronic Freedom Foundation's website – way in to Barlovian cyberspace.

http://www.isoc.org/internet-history/

The Internet Society's huge resource on histories of the Internet, and much more.

http://www.georgetown.edu/irvinemj/technoculture/pomosf.html

Site dedicated to postmodern science fiction, with lots of links, including to
William Gibson's homepage.

http:///www.MappingCyberspace.com

Website running alongside Dodge and Kitchin's book, with an amazing gallery
of maps and depictions of cyberspace.

# Chapter 3

# STORYING CYBERSPACE 2
## Experiential stories

As the Internet increases in importance and pervasiveness, it will simply become part of the mundane fabric of social and cultural life.

*Jonathan Sterne*

I N TELLING EXPERIENTIAL STORIES, my focus in this chapter will be on Barlovian cyberspace – on the ways in which the material and symbolic aspects of computer-mediated communication (CMC) or the human-computer interface (HCI) are worked through in terms of cultural practice and everyday life. My concern is to explore the places where we encounter 'cyberspace', and here I want to take a broad sweep, to think about computers, their applications, and their close kin. So, I shall look at stories of the Web and email, but also consider text messaging on mobile phones; PCs more generally (and especially applications like word processing, and the 'screen aesthetic' of the interface), as well as thinking about computer viruses and computer games. But I shall also visit other sites where something akin to cyberspace can be witnessed – in the hospital, for example, where new medical imaging technologies (NITs) use digital machines to reveal the body's innards; and in the cinema, where computer-generated imagery (CGI) immerses us in digital worlds.

Part of my motive here is to think about cyberspace as, in Steve Jones' (1999a: x) words, 'a medium that intersects with everyday life in ways both strange and omnipresent', and to attempt what's seen by some writers as a difficult task: as James Costigan (1999: xviii) writes, 'the Internet is often experienced but difficult to translate and express'. Later, he makes a point of central relevance to my argument here, when he writes that '[e]very user takes a slightly different approach to his or her use of the Internet, and each has a slightly different expectation' (xxi). We have a lot to deal with, moreover, because experience of cyberspace is enmeshed not only in the Web but also the webs of production and consumption and the webs of meaning and metaphor that we have already explored. Jones sums up the breadth of this agenda:

> In regard to the Internet, it is not only important to understand audiences – people – and what they do with media, it is important to understand what audiences think they do, what creators and producers think audiences do and what they think audiences *will* do, what venture capitalists think about audiences and producers, what software and hardware makers think and do, and so on.
>
> (Jones 1999b: 9)

Now, this is a *huge* agenda – too huge for me to cover in one chapter of this book. My aim is, rather, to make a modest contribution to that agenda, by telling some stories about cyberspace that add to a much bigger picture. The stories are everyday ones, too – and that's an important arm of Jones' agenda, picked up more fully by Jonathan Sterne (1999) in his provocative and productive discussion, 'Thinking the Internet'. Sterne's sketch for how Cultural Studies might 'do' the Internet is discussed more fully in my next chapter, but here I want to signal his insistence on grounding the Internet in the fabric of everyday life – for stressing its banality or mundanity. As Miller and Slater (2000: 43) note, in their excellent ethnography of Internet users in Trinidad, 'much of the novelty has worn off, and the main usage is seen as mundane'. To start this story-telling, I want to shift into autobiographical mode, to think about my own experiences of cyberculture – you can't get more mundane and banal than that!

## Personal computing

Since 1995, I have been talking with Cultural Studies students about computers and cyberspace, and have always been interested in hearing their personal computing stories, which are very varied and always fascinating. Their story-telling inevitably provokes my own, and we compare our encounters – those students who have come straight through the education system, and are in their late teens and early twenties when they get to me, have an interesting nonchalance towards computers by and large – they've grown up in parallel, and so they don't think that much about them. My own story, by contrast, as someone born in the mid-1960s, is of being part of the last generation (in the UK) to just miss out on mass computing – at school and at university, computers appeared *en bloc* just as I was leaving. *Not* growing up in a computer culture has been a similarly interesting process, and that's my first story for this section. This may seem like an indulgence – but I was struck when reading the stats on uses of cyberspace by the fact that I pretty-much fit the profile of the 'typical' Internet user, as a white male in my mid-thirties, with an above-average education and income, and a job that gives me access to computer technology. So yes, it is an indulgence to write my own computer history, but it has uses beyond the confessional, in pointing up the many places of computing in everyday life. In this respect, I was particularly struck by Mike Michael's discussion of the use of the anecdote in academic writing. As he puts it:

> The anecdote acts as a focal point in which a described event adds some flesh to what might otherwise have been the dry bones of an arbitrary example. As a fairly detailed episode, it allows us to glimpse mundane technologies in use, in a particular time and place, and to witness how the meanings and functions of these artefacts are ongoingly negotiated.
> (Michael 2000: 14)

Deborah Lupton and Greg Noble (1997) also make the point that there are important insights to be gained from the ways that 'lay' people ('those people who perhaps know little about the technical features of personal computers but use them regularly as part of the routines of their working lives') make use and sense of these things – and that's certainly another description fits me. More-over, Miller and Slater (2000) show how computer use and experience changes across the lifecourse, in their discussions of cyberspace with Trinidadian schoolkids, which tracks distinct 'phases' passed through – phases also written into their biographical narratives. So, writing my own cyber-autobiography is a way to lead into the broader issues in the human–computer interface.

Last night I lay awake, scouring the recesses of my human memory, trying to remember my first contact with cyberspace – or, more accurately, my first use of email and my first surf of the Web. It's perhaps a testament to the banality of cyberspace that these landmark moments weren't retriev-able – they're not imprinted in my brain in the way that watching moon landings on TV or the first time I drove a car is, for example. Anyway, that started me on a broader trawl for computer memories, to see if I could trace any autobiographical story of key moments. Here's what I found.

I do remember the first time I saw a digital clock – marker of my entry into digital culture. I had a friend, whose father was a classic techno-tinkerer, always making machines and devices. I think I was about ten years old, and I went round to their house to play. In the living room, proudly displayed, was a large brushed-metal box, with a simple red LED display, showing the time in the now-familiar digital format. As someone schooled in telling time from a round clock face with hands, I found this strange new representation of time fascinating, watching the minutes click by, time moving in a line rather than a circle. To be honest, it took me ages to get used to time told that way, and even now I convert digital time back to analogue in my head. The two new proposals for 'Internet time' I've recently discovered – Swatch's New Universal Time and New Earth Time – thus have me really flummoxed. Anyway, that's digital memory number one: the clock made by my friend Kevin's dad. (It was at Kevin's house that I first met up with a video recorder, too – but that's another story.)[1]

I suppose that digital memory number two is to do with calculators – though this has been re-energized by recently finding my first calculator tucked away in a drawer in my mother's living room. It's a very primitive machine, bulky and very limited in its processing power. But it was a badge of pride, a Christmas gift from my parents that marked my status as someone embarking on a scientific training. It was with my calculator that I learnt about processing power, speed, reliability – but also about dependency (the anxiety of losing the calculator, or its batteries running out in the middle of a test) and redundancy (of the machine, quickly superseded by a thinner, fancier, newer one with LCD display and countless functions; and of skills, as I no longer needed to know how to perform algebraic contortions in my head). In that way it signalled my entry into technoscientific culture, marking me as 'good' at maths, and therefore equipped for physics and chemistry – the 'hard sciences' boys were groomed for at the time. (It's interesting that once we'd proved we were good at something, we were then allowed to use a machine that makes it easier.) It was also a playful object (we spent many lessons 'writing' and reading the digital numbers on the display upside-down, 0.7734 transposed to 'hELLO' in the strange, futuristic font of the LED display) and a fantasy object (calculators became *Star Trek*-like gadgets on the playground). Like the digital clock, it also had a mystery about it – it was an object I could not understand. How did it work? An analogue clock was easy to understand, with its cogs and weights and springs – it could be taken apart, and even mended, without dense technical knowledge. And maths was logical brain work – governed by rules and formulae that could be 'understood'. Digital clocks and calculators, however, truly were black boxes of magic – they were no longer 'transparent' (on kids and machine transparency, see Turkle 1999). So, entry into technoscientific culture also means trusting in machines we don't understand, and delegating tasks to them – quite an anxious combination (see Lupton CR) on anxious or 'risky' computing).

## Computer memories

Pinning down my first computer memory is more elusive. When I was about seventeen, I was taking a course at school called General Studies – a bit of everything – and was introduced to programming languages in a vague way then. My school had a few rudimentary machines, but access to them was privileged, and my privileges didn't extend that far (once it had become clear that I didn't, in fact, have the aptitude for those 'hard sciences'). Computing was an adjunct of maths and physics, something that only 'hard' scientists could aspire to access. Again, as with the calculator, the school computers carried particular status-based meanings, as elite machines out of the reach of everykid. At roughly the same time, however, computer games began to appear in my world – or, more accurately, in some of my friends' worlds. And here comes my introduction into another moment of computer-status marking – for computer games were illicit, even forbidden pleasures. My friend Ian had the equipment and games, and I could occasionally get access to them, though I had to then lie about my leisure time, since my parents were *against* things like computer games, just as they were against watching TV in the day, or hanging around shopping malls, or going to McDonald's (and for pretty similar reasons). My fear of being found out limited my game-playing, and to this day I have to admit to retaining some discomfort around computer games, even as I marvel at their creativity and their players' skill. Those early games – Pong, Pacman, Space Invaders – had a wonder to them that has now become commonplace; they also played a vital role in reconfiguring 'lay' computer use, as we shall see later (see also Bolter and Grusin 1999).

Just as I was a year or two ahead of computers settling into school, I similarly missed out on computers at university. Sure, the campus had a proud, new-built Computer Centre, but again this was an elite space, for computer scientists only. Other than there, however, computers were still largely absent. The university's huge library was still catalogued manually, for instance, with hundreds of little books full of slips of paper on to which were typed bibliographic details – something that made searching very difficult, at least until we became familiar with the physical layout of the shelves, and could perform our own embodied hyperlinks across the stacks. Some academic staff had computers, but most still had secretaries to do their typing. I do remember one palaeontology teacher telling us excitedly about JANET (the Joint Academic Network – an offshoot of the Internet linking universities), but as a tool for the likes of him, not the likes of us. We did, however, receive one very portentous introduction to the future of computing, though this was marked by a similar ambivalence to that which shaded the arrival of the calculator in my palm years before. It was during a first year undergraduate class on statistics. We had spent the term wrestling with different statistical techniques, calculating by hand assorted averages and variances. In the last two classes, we were shown the power of computers – we made punch cards to carry our data to a mainframe machine, and a week later were proudly presented with reams of printouts, our stats calculated for us. This was the future – a future where social scientists no longer had to number-crunch, but could dedicate their time to analysing the numbers crunched by a computer. To be honest, I was most interested in the punch cards themselves, with their random patterns of holes and their curiously old-fashioned, player-piano aesthetic (the picture of one published in Ceruzzi's (1998: 17) *A History of Modern Computing* brought back these memories vividly). And that was that – I never again had access to computers, until the word processor began to appear in the workplace, and I became a worker.

When I returned to academia, university life was still undergoing a technological transformation – something as yet unfinished. PCs were more widely available, even for students, and the workplace was getting progressively more wired. It was around this time – in the late 1980s – that I bought my first computer (it is to date, in fact, the only computer I've ever bought and owned). I was doing doctoral research, and lived fifty miles from the university, so worked mainly from home. Suddenly, a computer became essential – an 80,000-word thesis was just too big to hand-write – so I borrowed some cash off my parents and bought a word processor. Learning to use it was a painful and protracted process, without today's army of online support. Trial and error, make-do and my own scribbled 'user's manual' were the only tools I had for the job (plus a partner with an electronics background who often had to bail me out). That purchase re-introduced me to the accelerating world of computers, with its limited memory, incompatible software and obsolete disk-drive soon rendering it virtually useless – in the end, after it had been unused for some time, I gave the computer to a friend, who thought she might be able to upgrade it.

Since then I haven't owned a computer, and don't have one at home – I think this is explained by the fact that I see computers as work tools, and want some way of curbing the encroachment of work into my home. I've had a succession of machines at work, all cast-offs from up-grades elsewhere in the university. Computers are now *everywhere* at work, and more and more of the business of university life takes place through, on or in them (see Lupton and Noble 1997). Student files, for example, are held on computer, and student photographs are scanned into these. Central university administration communicates with students over email. 'Distributed learning' packages make teaching materials available on-line. Memos are virtually a thing of the past – through the ease of email has upped the amount of communication between workers here (more on this in a while). The computer in my office is a writing aid, a memory aid, a filing cabinet, an administration machine. . . . Despite the fact that it's only since the mid-1990s that I've had regular access to a decent computer at work, it's already become so enmeshed in the way my work life works, that doing all I have to do without it is inconceivable (see also Lupton CR). Actually, when I say '*the* computer in my office', I should actually say *this computer*, because there are four others in here, too – one belongs to my room-mate Tim, and the other three are cast-offs that nobody wants, victims of previous rounds of up-grading. They're especially melancholic objects, like the old calculator stuffed in my mother's sideboard – inanimate fossils, their memories still full of codes and programs, and of files of mine and Tim's stuff, the detritus of previous years of computing.

## Writing on computers

So, what about my day-to-day computer use? As Deborah Lupton (CR) so vividly demonstrates, there's a lot to learn from looking at the habits of everyday life in cyberculture. For me, as should be clear by now, the computer is first and foremost a work tool. I have my own rituals around it, then, that structure my working day. When I come in in the morning, the first thing I do is turn the machine on (then go and make coffee while it 'warms up' – a hangover from the days when it took some time for a computer to boot up. These days my machine is always ready and waiting in the time it takes a kettle to boil; sometimes, in fact, it's logged me back off the network because I haven't put my user name and password in in time). First to get a look-in is email, which then stays open all day – my in-box flashes with each new message, and I look what it is and who it's from before deciding whether to open it now, or later – or, as a way to get through what Luke (1999: 44) calls the 'blizzards of email', that I'll delete without having opened. The most frequent use of the computer, however, is still for word processing (especially in the past few months of writing this book!). And word processing, as a mundane yet remarkable practice, needs to detain us a wee while here, since there's lots of interesting things to say about it.

One of the avenues of enquiry I pursue with students is the ways in which word processing has altered the ways they write and think. Their responses vary massively, from those who still only use the computer as a glorified typewriter – as a presentational tool for typing-up their final, polished work – to those who use it like a notebook, jotting things down, moving them around, tinkering with ideas, sentences, words, quotations. Writing practices enabled by word processing have without a doubt changed the way some of us think – how we organize information, for example. As we shall see later, the programs that now commonly run on machines like mine – Windows, for example – have been seen to have similarly affected how we think.

The possibility for endless tinkering and revision is, I think, one of the most remarkable consequences of word processors – though its outcome in terms of the quality of written language is contestable. Various features of recent word processing packages seem to be ushering in a standardization of the written word – things like spell-checkers and grammar-checkers. It's become one of my favourite games, trying to satisfy the grammar-checker on my machine (tips: short sentences, simple punctuation, minimal poetic flourishes). It's underlined two transgressions in this paragraph so far, one for spelling (it would prefer 's' to 'z' in 'standardization') and one for grammar (ironically, it keeps highlighting 'grammar-checker' as a grammatical error!). Since I haven't bothered to customize the spell-checker by adding words it doesn't recognize but which I use regularly (something that I once used to do), I can keep an eye on the limits of its lexicon – and also log some interesting effects of the reshaping of language implicit in word-processing programs. So, while it doesn't recognize the words 'postmodern' or 'cyberculture', it does recognize 'CompuServe'. Says it all, really. (On the entry into common language of new words associated with cyberculture, see Shortis 2001.) The fact that my computer takes such a position on spelling and grammar also means that I tend to ignore its warnings, and only later spot mistakes that I concur with – making the programs redundant (though I've yet to figure out a way to shut them off). But the point I want to make about word processing is the way it encourages the quest for perfection – endless rewrites would be unthinkable with pen and paper, but can be requested if it's a simple matter of fiddling on screen (just ask those students who bring in drafts of essays for me to read).

To return to my own rituals for a moment, the next one I want to think through with you is what we might call the 'fetish of the hard copy'. The ritual runs like this: before I go home at night, I save the document(s) I've been working on that day, and then print them out to take home and read (this contrasts with Deborah Lupton's (CR) 'confession' of not printing out until the penultimate-draft stage – something that also causes her anxieties). Now, for me this is part practical – I don't have a computer at home – but only part, I think. While computers have, for me, become easy to write with, I still find them less agreeable reading partners; moreover, I find copy-editing to be a task that I can only do with pen and ink – so I read through what I've written over the day when I get home at night, mark up any corrections or alterations, and then retype and amend the document the next morning, before I start writing anew. (So much for cutting down on the amount of work I do at home!)

Even in the days of 'paper-free' workplaces, paper and print has something authorial and authoritative about it that pixels on a screen don't have, it seems – witness the way that an email that doesn't solicit a response gets followed up by a paper-and-print memo. (More to follow on email in a moment.) I also have to confess to always printing out useful things off websites, rather than just 'bookmarking' them. I like to have something *material*, in my hand. (I think this also goes some way to explaining my unenthusiastic response to on-line shopping.) One thing I never print out, however, is email. This lets us see my own personal hierarchy of computer-mediated communications, I think, as well as telling us something about human data-handling as an everyday practice. Let's stick with email a moment longer.

Email is a complex phenomenon, simultaneously a gift and a burden. As one of the most prominent offshoots of the Internet, its role has been to profoundly restyle communication in all kinds of ways. It has relatively quickly become assimilated into the fabric of everyday life, especially of everyday work life. Here I want to focus on a number of aspects of this. Before I had access to email in my office at work, my first daily ritual would be to check my post tray – this has been shifted down the hierarchy, and its contents thinned out, replaced by emails. Email has certainly reconfigured the way we talk to each other at work. In some cases, it's diminished social contact – it's quicker to send an email than go to someone's office for a chat (they might not be in, for one thing). But it's also enlarged the sphere of 'public' conversation within our workplace – I am recipient of far more emails than I was a participant in 'RL' discussions at work. But what I'm especially interested in here is not the volume of traffic, but its form, content and effects. Judith Yaross Lee (1996) has made some insightful observations about email, a communications medium that she locates 'midway between the telephone call and the letter': 'email converts correspondence into a virtual conversation, [allowing] literate and oral codes [to] mingle and swap juices' (Lee 1996: 277, 279). While it owes something of its format to the memo (its 'to-from-date-subject' template, for example), it has also its own codes, norms and etiquette. For example, Lee cites John Seabrook's (1994) discussion of his email exchanges with Bill Gates, noting how Gates would start and end messages abruptly, but also that his emails were more informal than other communications (since Gates replied to emails himself, without the mediation of a secretary). Douglas Coupland's 1995 novel *Microserfs* also features (and plays with) the 'email culture' at Microsoft, showing its distinctive norms and features.

Moreover, Lee correctly identifies email as a *performative* communication at many different levels. The sender's address, for one, carries with it social meaning (hence some people have different accounts, hosted by different systems, to use for different mailing activities). The 'subject' header that appears in your in-box provides space to grab the attention of potential readers, like a headline in a newspaper – and correspondingly, the chance for the receiver to make a choice about when (or whether) to open a particular message. The possibility for any one participant to 'reply to all respondents' on a mass-circulated email also offers the opportunity to make public their active participation in discussion – although this can be read negatively, as a sign of self-importance. Emails within an organization bring further questions of etiquette, too. There's certainly a strange protocol about email discussion and 'RL' discussion – while many conversations now begin with 'Did you get my email?' (which actually means 'Have you read my email?') – sometimes emails are not talked about in RL, but exist in a parallel realm: emails replied to by emails, RL conversations never spilling over. So, the answer to 'Did you get my email?' becomes 'Yes – I've sent you a reply' – end of conversation. To return to deleting email a moment, the proliferation of emails, blizzarding in, brings a daily dilemma: to save or delete? My own machine acts as a virtual archive of emails, even though I fastidiously delete anything deemed ephemeral. It keeps a virtual 'trail' of conversations, memories and lost contacts, an interesting artefact of the status of bits of information and communication in cyberspace. The role of the computer as a personal archive is, perhaps, worthy of a further comment or two. Upgrading brings another significant dilemma for the computer user: which files have to be transferred, and which can be left to die with the old machine? As a trace of past activities, the computer memory-as-archive is a similarly resonant artefact, therefore.

Lee's focus on the 'rhetoric' of email picks out other novel aspects of email performance and etiquette, such as the quotation of one message in the body of its reply, and the lack of closure of individual conversations (endless strings of thank-yous and so on). While these aspects have received less attention than other forms of linguistic and paralinguistic play in email (most notably the use of 'emoticons' or 'smileys' such as :-) or CAPITALS to suggest shouting), these minor moments of evolving communications norms that I've traced here are equally revealing of the ways that email-use is an adaptive and culturally interesting phenomenon. Tim Shortis (2001) discusses many of these 'emailisms', charting the impact that email has on how we write and read – things like the lack of 'conventional' punctuation, capitalization, and 'non-standard' spelling, all of which reinforce the idea of email as more informal, more conversational, than other written communications. It's also interesting to log at this point the incredible rise of text messaging on mobile phones, as an email-like phenomenon (Benson 2000). Text messaging (also known as texting, or even txtg) was a small afterthought to mobile phone technology, an add-on that has taken the industry by surprise. Its economical and playful use of written language resonates with that found in email, but the added feature of mobility and portability has expanded its range to all kinds of social settings, and put it to imaginative uses. As Richard Benson (2000: 25) jokingly enthuses: 'Text messages are like little sugar-rushes of contact, postcards from the people's cyberspace, the real reason God gave us thumbs and the capacity for language' – they have certainly been phenomenally successful, quickly becoming part of our expanding communications resources. The convergence of computers and mobile phones, promised in recent adverts, is now focused more on txtg merging with email than WAP technology giving Web access to phone-users, testifying to the success of txtg in rewiring mobile phone communications.

## At the interface

So far, I've concentrated primarily on content, on messages and files. Now I want to shift my focus to the *look* of computers, and the aesthetics of the interface – the latter can be defined as 'software that shapes the interaction between user and computer', or the way in which 'the computer represents itself to the user . . . in a language that the user understands' (Johnson 1997: 14, 15). As a bridge, I have a dimly-remembered anecdote: during the making of the movie *Disclosure*, a little animation to represent sending an email had to be concocted, in order to render the act of emailing more 'cinematic'. The animation consisted of the screen of text folding itself up, like a letter, slipping itself into an envelope, and then winging its way off to its addressee. The need for an animation on the interface, in this case for the benefit of a movie audience, takes us into the whole question of the look of the interface – how the computer screen is laid out for us, how it works, and how its look impacts on us as users. Julian Stallabrass (1999) makes this point in his discussion of the multimedia operating system Microsoft Windows, which he reads as epitomizing a 'rational' aesthetic common to software interfaces:

> Think of its particular features which have become so familiar that we tend to take them for granted; and how familiar it is all designed to be – the files and folders, those little thumbnail sketches which so appropriately bear the name 'icons' (and these little pictures are often of familiar objects), the sculpted 3-D buttons, the pop-up notices, decked out with instantly recognizable, if not comprehensible, symbols warning of hazards or admonishing the user's mistakes.
>
> (Stallabrass 1999: 110)

In the guise of 'user-friendliness', Stallabrass argues, the interface 'throws an analog cloak over digital operations' (110), effectively dumbing-down computer use rather than democratizing it, irritating rather than enamouring us with its 'constant cheerfulness' (110) and joky, matey demeanour. (Lupton (CR) asks why other pieces of domestic technology that people find hard to use – such as video recorders – haven't also been made-over with icons and general user-friendliness; something she reads as evidence of the profundity of our anxieties about computers.) Outside of the specifics of Windows as Microsoft's interface platform, moreover, the general interface practice of 'windowing' has received others' attention, too. Sherry Turkle (1999), for example, discusses the Windows interface as a tool designed for more effective computing, since it allows users to have a number of applications open simultaneously, stacked up one behind the other, so that we can move from one to the other easily – so, for example, at this moment I have my email open (so I know if I've got mail), and two word-processing files: this one, and the book's bibliography, so I can add in references as I write about them, rather than having to compile the entire bibliography later. What interests Turkle, however, is how the *metaphor* of windows has leeched into the 'life practices' of computer culture:

> [W]indows have become a potent metaphor for thinking about the self as a multiple and distributed system. . . . The life practice of windows is of a distributed self that exists in many worlds and plays many roles at the same time.
>
> (Turkle 1999: 547)

Probably my favourite story of human-computer interfacing is in Sean Cubitt's (1998: 88) *Digital Aesthetics*, particularly his discussion of the mouse, the cursor and what he calls 'the nomadic I-bar/arrow' (or 'pointer tool') on the (Macintosh) word-processing program he was writing with. Both the cursor and the pointer, Cubitt argues, locate the 'I' on the interface – showing *where I am* on the screen. But the presence of these two 'I's is confusing, too: 'where am I?' cannot be simply answered if there are twin possibilities (plus the third, of course, the 'I' written into the text). Where I am on the screen is therefore not the same as where I am in the text (or where I am in 'RL').

The mouse, moreover, is partly an extension of the machine, and partly an extension of the self – it comes to occupy a central position in the interface, performing many roles and taking many shapes on screen, controlling all. But it, too, exhibits schizophrenic or decentred tendencies in Cubitt's reading, which is worth quoting at length here:

> Under the myriad guises it takes as it roves across the screen – wristwatch, spinning ball, arrow, fingered hand, gunsight, magnifying glass, pen – the mouse pointer's mobility and its function in shifting modes – pulling down windows, opening files, driving scroll bars, dragging icons, clicking buttons – seats it at the head of a hierarchy of subject positions voiced in the Macintosh HCI. . . . In some ways, the mouse enacts the schizophrenic subjectivity credited with cultures of the 'post' [postmodern, poststructuralist]: it changes form and function as it wanders across the screen and from screen to screen through stacks, files, documents and programs. Restless and unstill, it skitters according to a logic of browsing, a tool and a toy, named for a pet proverbial for its quietness and timidity, a modest instrument . . . renowned as intuitive design, an extension of the pointing finger [see Wise 2000].
>
> (Cubitt 1998: 88)

The mouse is, then, for Cubitt a particular concentration of the logics and aesthetics of the interface, as well as a metaphorical device for thinking about computing subjectivity; the restless, nomadic mouse is figured as a cursor-tourist, wandering the screen, pointing but never finding a home – and ultimately as a melancholic creature: '[t]he mouse in the hand is blind, responds to a braille signage of taps, runs its errands tail-first' (Cubitt 1998: 90).

In terms of aesthetics, we also need to consider the 'objects' that circulate in cyberspace – the look of emails, websites and so on. As computer programs have grown in sophistication, so the products that we produce and consume have grown in 'style' – from the range of fonts available for word-processing, to the aesthetic processes of web design (see below). In their ethnography of the Internet in Trinidad, Daniel Miller and Don Slater (2000) look at the huge popularity there of 'egreetings cards' and 'egifts' such as virtual bouquets and virtual chocolates – users can select these off websites, and send them to each other (though there has, in this country at least, been some discussion of the etiquette of sending ecards as against 'real' cards). As a mundane artefact in cyberspace, Miller and Slater urge us to pay close attention to these cards, both for their 'look' and for their uses:

> These new electronic gifts are . . . new material forms that constitute relationships in new ways: that is to say, they should be treated seriously as mediations of material culture. . . . Apparently quite mundane new media, such as virtual postcards, can both transform older gifting practices and materially reconstitute the relationships in which they are embedded.
>
> (Miller and Slater 2000: 65, 82)

What we need to take from this is the sense that even these commonplace virtual objects do immense social and cultural work, reshaping friendships as they also reshape computer use. Similarly, we can reread the role of email in transforming communication and sociality in complex ways. Artefacts like egreetings cards produce a particular experience of cyberspace, then, at least in part as a result of their aesthetics – the coolness of computer technology matched by humour and sentimentality.

So far we have only looked at the look of computers and interfaces in isolation. We now need to ask some further questions, about what we might call networked aesthetics – how has the Internet brought about a restyling of the HCI? As we saw when telling symbolic tales, the 'matrix' imagined in cyberspace brings with it all kinds of imaginary images, of cities of data and so on. How have these impacted on and intermingled with the form and style of websites, network interfaces and so on? At the level of aesthetics, are we getting the cyberspace we imagine? Cubitt's got an interesting point about the impact of networking, which he equates with the *disappearance* of the computer:

The machines themselves have been urged into a background, their networks eliminating the sense that each terminal is a stand-alone device. Peering into the screen, the browser interface invites you to enter not the internal workings of one machine, but the composite assemblage of all linked terminals. The facilitating hardware, increasingly transparent as user-friendly, icon-driven designs become second nature to synergistic subjects, has loosened its grip on materiality to present itself as a vast virtual playground.

(Cubitt 1998: 83)

Certainly the bland, grey outer casing and functional form of most PCs lends itself towards this disappearance – at least until the arrival of the iMac on the scene (McIntyre 1999). But Cubitt's point is more to do with the allure of what's *between* the machines – the imagined cyberspace, rendered visible in media productions like websites. Considering websites aesthetically, therefore, throws up some interesting insights into Barlovian cyberspace (issues we might also consider through the lens of virtual art; see Stallabrass 1999). Daniel Miller (2000) has an intriguing reading of websites, which he sees as 'aesthetic traps' designed to snare surfers, a place to show one's skills in HTML, one's creative use of technology, and a place, in Miller's words, to 'grow' one's fame. There's a lot to commend in this analysis, and the aesthetic appeal of different sites is certainly something that does work to ensnare passing surfers – a well-designed site can be quite a draw in itself, regardless of content. While 'how-to' guides often stress navigability as equally important to good web design, Jason Whittaker (2000) includes navigation as *part of* the process of producing an aesthetically pleasing site, reflecting the centrality of the 'look' of the website as a measure of its success. As David Rieder (2000: 102) writes, it's wrong to argue that form must follow function in web design: 'it is important to realize that there are a lot of great websites that are designed to be non-functional and impractical'. Here I'd like to introduce an idea that I shall explore more fully later, in my discussion of computer generated imagery (CGI) in the cinema: the idea that a good website is appreciated for its own sake, *as a website*, rather than for its content, in the same way that audiences view special effects in films. Following Miller's webs-as-traps argument, then, we can see how the aesthetics of the site are indeed a way of showing programming skill, and that that is what impresses (or fails to impress) surfers who judge sites as sites in the same way they judge special effects *as special effects*. It is, I think, an example of what Stephen Heath (1980) calls 'machine interest', where an audience is wooed by the technology more than the product itself (his analysis is of early cinema, where content was purely secondary to the wonder of the technological accomplishment of making movies). Similarly, the quality of links to other websites, highlighted by Rushkoff (1997) as

43

central to a site's success – can be read as a way of demonstrating web-savvy, of knowing the cool sites to link to, and knowing what it is that makes other sites cool.

As we saw when we were telling material stories of the Internet and virtual reality, the devising of VRML by Mark Pesce was heralded as bringing the Web one step closer to the immersive virtual environments promised in cyberpunk. Dodge and Kitchin (2001) focus on the use of VRML and other programs to produce 'Web landscapes' or datascapes that in some ways mirror cyberpunk's version of cyberspace, such as the 3D Trading Floor of the New York Stock Exchange or the fly-through interfaces produced using HotSauce, which enables the browser to swoop through data ranged in three dimensions – a bit like the console cowboys Gibson depicted. These kinds of developments in networked interfaces are seen by some as a glimpse of a fast-approaching future where interfacing becomes fully immersive and interactive (Johnson 1997). One area of digital culture where immersivity and interactivity have evolved with particular intensity is in the world of computer games, to which we shall now turn.

## Computer play

> Video games . . . serve as excellent flight simulators for cyberspace.
>
> (Rushkoff 1997: 182)

Video, arcade, PC and Internet-based computer games have all had a profound effect on the place of the computer in everyday life since they were first introduced in the early 1970s. They are widely credited with reorienting the experience of computing away from a 'serious' scientific enterprise and towards a leisure activity. Crucially, it is through games-playing that *immersion* and *interactivity* first became foregrounded as part of the experience of the human–computer interface. Leslie Haddon (1993: 123) writes that games 'were certainly the earliest forms of interactive software to find a mass market', adding that they 'provide the most common introduction to the principles of interactivity' for computer users. Moreover, Vivian Sobchack (1987) describes the evolution of 'video game consciousness' as spreading out from games per se to provide a framework for experiencing all digital media products. Games thus have important things to tell us about developments in computer technology and use – we need to go back to telling material stories here, therefore, to set out the evolution of computer games, and then move into the experience of gaming.

As Douglas Rushkoff argues, the form and content of games has been continuously evolving in parallel with innovations in computing, always exploiting the new capacities of machines:

The advancement of video games over the past three decades was based on the emergence of new technologies. It was less a consciously directed artistic development than a race to utilize new computer chips, imaging techniques, and graphics cards. Every time a new technology arrived, game developers would redefine the essence of their game around the new hardware. . . . The style and content of the games is based on the specific qualities of the new machines as they become available.

(Rushkoff 1997: 172)

There are distinct but intersecting stories to tell here about arcade games, video games and microcomputer games. Haddon (1993) tracks the early history of games back to the early computer science departments of universities, particularly the artificial intelligence (AI) department at MIT (Massachusetts Institute of Technology), founded in the late 1950s. The role of hobbyists is important in this context. For hobbyists associated with the emerging computer science culture at places like MIT, games were a way to learn about programming, and to expand the capabilities of machines through software innovation. The 'hackers' that emerged from the convergence of MIT's model railway club and the AI department began experimenting with programming, devising early games programs (for chess and solitaire, for example). They took a *playful* approach to computing, and wrote exploratory software – partially to demonstrate the machines' potential, and to experiment with forms of interactivity. Out of this culture emerged many key innovations in computing, as we have seen; games were among the most influential.

Interestingly, early games were incorporated into computers as much as a sales device as anything else – they were a way of demonstrating the computer, and of showing its 'accessible and friendly face' (Haddon 1993: 126). Games also performed a diagnostic function, for testing if machines were in full working order. However, before developments in microprocessors made computers widely available, games on computers remained elite applications. The mass appeal of games only became more fully realized when they migrated to a new location – the amusement arcade. Nolan Bushnall, co-founder of Atari, combined his working knowledges of computer games and of amusement parks, producing the highly successful arcade game Pong (modelled on table tennis, but inspired by the arcade success of pinball). Other popular games such as Space Invaders and Pacman secured the place of coin-operated arcade games on the leisure landscape, particularly prominently with the young. It's interesting to note that the co-option of computer games into amusement arcades was an attempt by the arcades to shake off their 'sleazy' image; these new games conferred upon the arcades a 'modern' look, with the scientific or educational lustre of computers remaking arcades as spaces for 'family' entertainment – this being prior to the 'moral panic' around computer games, of course. The placing of computer games in arcades slotted them into specific forms of youth sociality, giving rise to what Haddon (1993: 138) describes as 'video games culture' – a phenomenon soon tainted by fears of delinquency, addiction and desensitization to violence. Interestingly, it was these concerns that spawned the first large-scale social science inquiries into computing and its effects, making the computer an object of social-scientific scrutiny. Moral panics about compulsive and anti-social games-playing have stained the place of computing in the popular consciousness ever since, as witnessed by similar panics around the Internet – panics founded on the computer game's two key features, as immersive and interactive media. In this kind of reading, 'immersive' gets rewritten as 'addictive', and 'interactive' as 'anti-social', since kids were assumed to interact with machines rather than each other – though this argument has been disputed by work focused on gaming culture (Haddon 1993). Indeed, the sociality of games-playing developed in arcades can be seen as emerging in cybercafés; Miller and Slater (2000: 72) discuss the dense 'relationships around the computer' they witnessed in Trinidadian cybercafés. Similarly, Nina Wakeford (1999) details the spatial relationships and modes of social life played out in cybercafés, reminding us of the importance of thinking about where computers and users are located in 'RL' while they are in cyberspace.

Back in the gaming world, meanwhile, the next migratory move of games was into the home, and on to television: home video game technology provided an alternative use for the television set – and, what's more, this new use offered greater opportunities for interactivity. Popular arcade games like Pong thus entered the living room. Although primitive by today's standards, Pong was a radical departure from previous ways of experiencing the computer interface:

> It was a genuine surprise to watch a dot on the screen behave like a ball, bouncing off each striking paddle or ricocheting off the side of the screen and returning on an appropriate trajectory. There was a vast difference between this graphic behavior and the operations of a traditional computer, which manipulated symbols and presented its results only in rows of alphanumeric characters on the screen or on perforated printer paper. The game suggested new formal and cultural purposes for digital technology.
>
> (Bolter and Grusin 1999: 90)

Of course, for an entire constituency of users, Pong was their very first contact with computers, so their sense of marvel wasn't a comparative one with other computers – it was a comparison with other toys and games, and with the passive consumption of conventional television. This too was then fed into moral panics about young people being given another form of 'couch-potato' technology; again, however, this was despite evidence to the contrary, which suggested that 'communal practices were carried into the use of domestic machines – despite the image of the isolated games-player in the home' (Haddon 1993: 140; on the couch potato, see Michael 2000).

The first home games were pre-programmed devices, each one delivering only one game. Later came the facility of using programmable cartridges to deliver different games through the same hardware – and the console was born. This splitting of hardware (consoles) and software (games) also facilitated the rapid growth of the games industry, and the proliferation of games on the market, thus establishing computer games as part of the entertainment economy. Console games boomed in the late 1970s, but their position in the market came under threat from the microcomputer, where games found another home. Hobbyists had an important role to play here, too, in both consuming and producing games software for micros – and games-writing became the principal entry-point for learning about programming. The use of audio cassettes to store software enabled the circulation of home-made games, creating a cottage industry that would also be absorbed into the games business. And although the industry's marketing strategy for home computers stressed their multi-purpose remit, games became a prominent part of that remit – until the reintroduction of dedicated games platforms through the Nintendo and Sega consoles in the late 1980s.

Sony's PlayStation and its later upgrade Playstation 2 (which includes DVD and Internet capabilities) and the Nintendo 64 have since emerged as market leaders, virtually defining the console games market into the twenty-first century, while the Nintendo GameBoy brought portability to games-playing – although this has lost some of the prominence it had in the mid-1990s, it retains a place in the market. Back on the personal computer, both CD-ROM technology and then the Internet have opened up new possibilities for gaming. Networked gaming has also appeared on consoles, most prominently in the UK via Sega's Dreamcast and the Playstation 2 platforms. The Internet has also developed a 'help' function for games-players, since websites give hints on how to play games successfully; it is also possible to download 'patches' of software that reconfigure games (most notoriously, those patches that make the players on games appear naked). The current situation seems to be a settled market, with a variety of platforms and gaming environments co-existing – although there is a steady stream of innovation and repurposing in the games sector. The games software business remains diverse, with many companies supplying games to play on the most popular platforms (and, indeed, providing different versions of the same game for different platforms). As Haddon (1993) adds, innovation has also extended to the retailing of games, with software especially being sold through a wide range of outlets, including record shops, newsagents, supermarkets and even petrol stations. In arcades, meanwhile, games have become more diverse, more interactive, and more immersive – especially through their incorporation of 'real' objects alongside virtual environments (so a soccer game can now involve kicking a real football that translates its movements on to the screen, for example). Some arcade games also have Internet capabilities, making networked play possible here, too.

## Looking at games

In the light of our previous focus on the role of interfaces in human–computer interaction, it's important to highlight the ways in which games have reshaped that interaction; as Jay Bolter and Richard Grusin (1999) suggest, the computer game is an interface which demands the players' intimate involvement – the story here is, then, of the morphing of the interface in order to facilitate the game's two key aims, immersion and interactivity. For example, Pong had only one 'point-of-view' (from above) and very simple movements – it was soon superseded by similar games that made use of graphics and scrolling technology and then 3-D rendering, making games look more 'realistic'. So, although similar in basic structure, games like Street Fighter and Mortal Kombat emerged, with a look very different from Pong.

Rushkoff (1997) classifies computer games into three archetypes, based on content: *duel games* (including Pong, Street Fighter and Mortal Kombat), *quest games* (such as Adventure, Zelda, Déjà Vu and Myst), and *apocalypse games* (Asteroids, Space Invaders, Pacman, Super Mario, Sonic the Hedgehog, Doom) – a classification later augmented by *simulation games* (Balance of Power, Sim City, Civilization). Duel games are relatively simple; their narrative is based on 'defending your side of the screen and penetrating your adversary's' (Rushkoff 1997: 173). Quest games, which evolved from text-based 'stories' somewhat like real-life role-playing games (such as Dungeons and Dragons), involve the player exploring a simulated world, often in search of something, and undertaking tasks along the way. Both kinds of games changed over time at the level of the interface, largely as a result of advances in programming:

> The evolutionary path of the quest and duel games was the same: they moved from overhead-view, iconized graphics to side-viewed cartoon graphics and ended with rendered three-dimensional worlds seen from close to the point of view of the character.
>
> (Rushkoff 1997: 175)

A similar set of moves can be traced in apocalypse games, which involve players in an escalating series of battles, increasingly through quest-like narratives, in a bid to either defend or re-establish the 'status quo' of the world within the game (Bolter and Grusin 1999). In tracking the shifts in the look of computer games, and especially in the changes made to point-of-view and perspective (so the player becomes a participant rather than a spectator), we can see a change in the experience of game-playing: games are transformed 'from stories told or observed into stories experienced' (Rushkoff 1997: 178). Games morph into 'interactive film', utilizing cinematic conventions and aesthetics to heighten immersion. The simulation games add to this, by putting the player in the position of 'god', controlling rather than merely reacting to the action. Moreover, the networking of games facilitated by the Internet has further reshaped the experience of playing, restating the collectivity of gaming as interaction between people, as well as between people and computers. The networked simulation game Civilization enacts what Rushkoff (1997: 180) calls 'shared world building', a powerful rendering of Gibson's 'consensual hallucination', bringing immersion and interactivity at a (potentially) global scale:

> Fully evolved video game play, then, is total immersion in a world from within a participant's point of view, where the world itself reflects the values and actions of the player and his [sic] community members.
> (Rushkoff 1997: 180–1)

The computer chip has also migrated to other toys and games, producing some interesting hybrids in recent years. The most notable of these are a family of so-called 'cyber-pets', including the Tamagotchi, Furby and its kin, and cyber-dogs. I'd like to think about these for a moment or two here; although they are not 'computer games' in the strict sense, they are fascinating instances of the production and consumption of computer technology in a play context; they belong to a class that Sherry Turkle (1999) names 'computational objects'. The virtual pet, or Tamagotchi, emerged in the late 1990s, originally produced by Japanese company Bandai – it was conceived, so the folklore goes, by a Japanese mother who didn't have space at home for her kids to have a 'real' pet (Bloch and Lemish 1999). The Tamagotchi comes in the form of a small plastic casing with a LCD display in the centre and tiny push buttons on the sides – it's a bit like a digital watch. Once activated, the cartoon egg of the screen hatches out, and the Tamagotchi is born as a simple digital image, vaguely animal-shaped. Once it comes to life, the Tamagotchi has to be looked after by its owner, who can press buttons for feeding, cleaning and disciplining the growing pet. If it is neglected, it 'dies'. Its health and development can be monitored, and it undergoes a series of transformations in its limited lifecourse:

> [Tamagotchi] demand of their owners to feed them, play games with them, inquire about their health and mood, and, when they are still babies, clean up their virtual 'poop'. Good parenting of a Tamagotchi will produce a healthy offspring; bad parenting will lead to illness, deformity, and finally, to the pet's virtual death. The Tamagotchi are

only the first in a projected series of computational objects that seem destined to teach children a new lesson about the machine world: *that computational objects need to be related to as another life form.*

(Turkle 1999: 552; my emphasis)

For a brief time, here in the UK (and elsewhere), Tamagotchi were a very visible craze, especially among the pre-teens. According to estimates, up to 40 million were bought worldwide, and there were frenzies of panic-buying – and shortages in shops – at peak periods (Bloch and Lemish 1999). Of course, as is increasingly the case, their stay in the toy limelight was relatively brief; but while they were with us, they enabled some adults and lots of kids to think about things like artificial life and the domesticating of technology. (Lots of adults, predictably, were perplexed by Tamagotchi, unable to understand their appeal.) As Turkle (1998) insists, children have often led the way when it comes to using 'computational objects' to think with, settling into ways of relating to them that differ radically from they ways that grown-ups experience them. So, while adults were bemused by and dismissive of Tamagotchi, kids were able to *enjoy* them as boundary objects blurring the distinctions of what counts as 'alive' – children did not naively relate to Tamagotchi as alive (they knew how to cheat death for their cyberpets, for example), but nevertheless engaged with their needs and growth with a depth of immersion that grown-ups usually found incomprehensible.

The success of Tamagotchi has inevitably led to a proliferation and diversification of virtual petting. One interesting turn that the toys took was their migration off the screen, into 'RL' – toys such as Furby use computer technology, but come cased in fur, like cyborg teddies (Furbies resemble the Gremlins from the 1980s movie of the same name). Furby has a number of technological implants to make its 'aliveness' manifest: its eyelids and ears move; it can talk, initially in its own language (Furbish), and then by 'learning' from its owner; it has light, touch and motion sensors, so that it reacts to being tickled, turned upside down, or left in the dark. Like the Tamagotchi, it needs caring for, feeding (though, as the manufacturers warn, *not* with real food – it's satisfied by suckling on its owner's finger) and educating. Two Furbies can interact with each other, if placed face-to-face, chattering and dancing, fluttering their eyelids and giggling. As sophisticated computational objects, then, they rewire a whole range of pet, toy and playmate behaviours. Of course, kids already have a greater flexibility when it comes to the boundaries between these kinds of classifications, and are adept at fantasy play, in scenarios where different kinds of objects (or *what adults would consider different kinds of objects*) get brought together in a playful heterogeneity. Furbies are able, therefore, to find a comfortable home among close and distant kin – they are now joined by other cyber-pet/toys, such as the robot dogs that rose to prominence in the Christmas build-up in the UK in 2000. We need to look to these toys, and their owners, therefore, for what they can tell us about the role of play in the experience of computers, bringing them into the fold along with the more familiar classes of computer games.

Now, as I confessed earlier on in telling tales of my computing past, I've inherited an ambivalent stance towards computer games, and have only very rarely (and very ineptly) played them. By and large, they're an area of computing that remains quite alien to me – though there is, I have to admit, a dormant Furby 'asleep' on the bookcase in my living room. However, one game that I once read about (though haven't played) did particularly attract my attention: Virus. This game stages our anxieties about computer viruses, enabling players to both experience the horror of viral attack and to attempt to defend their machine. The game renders a facsimile of your computer's hard drive, remade as a gaming landscape, and then lets loose viral agents that attack all the stored data and programming, destroying it before your eyes. However, unlike the 'real' experience of viral attack, you are given the opportunity to fight back, to duel with the virus, and maybe even to save your computer (and by implication, yourself). What I like about this game is the way that it taps into, but simultaneously domesticates, what must be seen as the greatest source of panic around computing, and especially networked computing: the threat of the computer virus. If Tamagotchi or Furby aim to convince us that computers are our friends, Virus stages the computer as both threat and saviour. With this in mind, then, it is to viruses that our attention now turns.

## Panic computing

What scares you most about getting the virus?

Is it the prospect of witnessing your system's gradual decay, one nagging symptom following another until one day the whole thing comes to a halt? Is it the self-recrimination, all the useless dwelling on how much easier things would have been if only you'd protected yourself, if only you'd been more careful about whom you associated with?

(Dibbell 1995)

Computer viruses have long fascinated me, and for a number of reasons. For one thing, they are part of hacking culture, showing the role of computing subcultures as 'enemies within' – as performing a critical function on the power of computing, and on our dependence on computers, by subversive or unorthodox use of computing skill (Ross CR). They make very visible most people's anxieties about that power and dependence, as well as revealing how poorly we understand the insides of our machines. As such, they are good objects to think about computing with. The surge of viral panics in the wake of the 'Love Bug' in 2000, which overshadowed anxieties about the Millennium or Y2K Bug (a programming glitch rather than a virus, of course) has a lot to tell us, I think, about those issues. While the Y2K Bug revealed our latent technophobia – concretizing an ambient fear of over-reliance on computers matched by a lack of understanding of their workings (hence all the 'educative' PR work by governments, assuring us of compliance) – the Love Bug brought home forcefully the possibilities for putting the Internet to malicious use, revealing our defencelessness. The bug showed the exposure of the net, subverting its decentralized character – which simultaneously facilitated the rapid networked spread of the virus and allowed its writer to hide, at least for a while.

Reading computer viruses (and the virus warning messages that endlessly circulate in cyberspace) is, therefore, a particularly telling way to think about computers in everyday experience. Let me start by showing you a fairly recent and fairly typical virus warning that came into my in-box:

Three Serious WARNINGS

WARNING No. 1
If you receive any CELCOM Screen Saver, please do not install it!!!!!! This screen saver is very cool. It shows a NOKIA hand phone, with time messages. After it is activated, the PC cannot boot up at all. It goes very slowly. It destroys your hard disk. The filename is CELL-SAVER.EXE

WARNING No. 2
Beware! If someone named SandMan asks you to check out his page. DO NOT! . . . This page hacks into your C:?drive. DO NOT GO THERE . . . FORWARD THIS MAIL TO EVERYONE YOU KNOW.

WARNING No. 3
If you get an E-mail titled 'Win A Holiday' DO NOT open it. Delete it immediately. Microsoft just announced it yesterday. It is a malicious virus that WILL ERASE YOUR HARD DRIVE. At this time there is no remedy. Forward this to everyone IMMEDIATELY!! PLEASE PASS THIS ALONG TO ALL YOUR FRIENDS AND PEOPLE IN YOUR MAILBOXES. AOL HAS SAID THIS IS A VERY DANGEROUS VIRUS AND THERE IS NO REMEDY FOR THIS YET. FORWARD IT TO ALL YOUR ON-LINE FRIENDS A.S.A.P.

Now, before we get into thinking about viruses in general, let me tell you one thing about this particular warning message: I have edited it slightly here, because the warning I received included the URL (address) for the SandMan homepage. When I typed this on to my machine just now, the address became 'live' – the software on my word processor is trained to recognize the form of URLs, and turns them into hyperlinks in the document. One mis-aimed click, therefore, and I'd be at SandMan's site, my hard drive corroded. I left the live link there, on screen, for a few moments, then decided to delete that part of the virus warning from my on-screen manuscript just to play it safe – to protect my machine, and also Routledge's systems *(What if the copy-editor or typesetter clicked on it? How would I deal with that guilt?)* This is, I think, an incredibly telling anecdote about viruses. I have no way of knowing for sure that the 'threat' posed by SandMan is in any way 'real' – the message could just be a hoax. As Sean Cubitt writes, a virus warning like this is itself viral:

> a message that has become, through its constant forwarding from list to list, a self-replicating piece of code that preys on [newbies]. The explanation has itself become part of the virus, the inevitable secondary infestation, like the sore throat after the cold.
>
> (Cubitt 2000: 129)

Moreover, while the warning states that SandMan will be able to hack into my hard drive, it doesn't say what will result from that hack. Nevertheless, I can't afford to ignore the warning, just as anyone receiving that message dutifully forwards it on to all their friends. Virus warnings are objects of anxiety in themselves, then: will I *remember* that a message proclaiming 'Win A Holiday' shouldn't be opened? When I open my in-box, I often habitually click through all unopened messages, just to clear them off the system – in which case it might be too late. Half asleep, first thing in the morning, on a dull, wet Stoke-on-Trent day, the chance to win a holiday might be just enough to tempt me . . .

This kind of trick – of sending a virus clad in something appealing – came to prominent public attention in May 2000, thanks to the Love Bug, an email virus coming with the header 'I Love You' and promising a seductive attachment: the message read 'kindly check the attached LOVELETTER coming from me'. *A love letter? For me?* . . . Like the promise of a holiday, who could resist opening up such an email? From the evidence of those few days in early May, not many people: the Love Bug caused upwards of US$1bn worth of 'damage' before the warnings came out (Meek and Tran 2000). Its effects were felt all around the wired world, and it spread with amazing rapidity:

> Billions of pulses raced through the world's phone lines, splattering the virus in all directions. It was the fastest-spreading bug ever, infecting five million machines within 36 hours. Everyone from the Pentagon to the House of Commons to New Zealand universities was hit. An

estimated 20 per cent of the world's computers were affected and half of all machines in the UK.

(Burke and Walsh 2000: 19)

The panic surrounding the Love Bug was obviously very real; computers were infected and affected, business was halted, money was lost, lives were disrupted. It was a particularly 'nasty', 'aggressive' bug (Meek 2000). More-over, the media coverage around the Love Bug reanimated debates about hackers and viruses, and about security and anxiety in computer culture. Deborah Lupton has taken apart previous media coverage of viruses, reading them as traces of 'panic computing'. For her, the designation of rogue programming as a 'virus' has a lot to tell us:

> The nomination of a type of computer technology malfunction as a 'virus' is a highly significant and symbolic linguistic choice of metaphor, used to make certain connections between otherwise unassociated subjects and objects, to give meaning to unfamiliar events, to render abstract feelings and intangible processes concrete.
>
> (Lupton 1994: 557)

For Lupton, the use of the term virus carries a moral agenda with it – the morality of danger, risk, trust and protection, spilling over from the other global viral crisis, HIV/Aids. Tracking parallels in public health discourse and computing discourse, she identifies the same logic at work: imperatives about safe sex become rewritten around safe software (see also Ross CR). The Love Bug reinforces that motif, by tempting us into 'risky' behaviour on the promise of romance.

To return to SandMan briefly, one reason that the live link in my text caused me an anxious moment was because I had read in one newspaper report about new strains of so-called superviruses. One, called Bubbleboy, also arrives by email – but the recipient doesn't even have to open its attach-ment to unleash the virus: 'by the time it was in your inbox it was too late' (Burke and Walsh 2000: 19). Although Bubbleboy does no real damage, other than clogging up email systems, it powerfully demonstrates one devel-opmental trajectory in viral programming – it's hyper-contagious, spread by the most minimal of contact. Other notorious viruses in the post-Love Bug spotlight include Chernobyl, which destroys the basic programming in computers that enable them to start up – it most devastatingly 'kills' machines. Virus-watchers, moreover, predict the cross-fertilization of Love Bugs, Bubbleboys and Chernobyls, breeding superviruses that are highly contagious, very quickly spread and immensely destructive. The possibility of viral cyberterrorism is thus activated – a theme also played out in the movie *The Net*. In such a climate, it is perhaps inevitable that there has emerged a 'new kind of hypochondria among computer users', as Mark Ludwig (1996a: 27) describes it.

Against this increasingly panic-stricken scenario, it was with mixed feelings that I read Ludwig's advocacy of virus writing, and Julian Dibbell's (1995) essay 'Viruses are good for you'. Dibbell attempts to offset panic computing by recasting viruses as 'autonomously reproducing computer programs', as artificial life-forms existing and mingling in the 'ecology' of computer networks. As he says, the aim of this move is to refute the 'mix of bafflement and dread' that marks our current response to viruses: 'Overcoming our fear of computer viruses may be the most important step we can take toward the future of information processing'. As Ludwig (1996a: 19) puts it, 'I am convinced that computer viruses are not evil and that programmers have a right to create them, possess them, and experiment with them', adding that 'viruses can be useful, interesting, and just plain fun'. His expanded definition of viruses works to shed them of their malevolent image:

> *computer viruses are not inherently destructive*. The essential feature of a computer program that causes it to be classified as a virus is not its ability to destroy data but its ability to gain control of the computer and make a fully functional copy of itself. It can reproduce. When it is executed, it makes one or more copies of itself.
>
> (Ludwig 1996a: 29; emphasis in original)

In order to similarly broaden out the world of computer viruses, Dibbell introduces us not only to the complex ecology of viruses, but also to the ecology of programmers, sketching their motives – motives a long, long way from the popular image of twisted or vengeful hackers. He reminds us that the moral panic around hackers covers over the central role of hacking in the evolution of computing, and also notes that most viruses have no destructive aim – they are a way of demonstrating programming skill, and testing current systems. Destructive applications or 'jokes' embedded in viruses often only really serve to give the virus 'character' (Ludwig 1996a: 33), adding to its aesthetics or reputation. One hacker Dibbell talked to described viruses as 'electronic graffiti' – sometimes prankish, sometimes malicious, but more often just a powerful way to display subcultural skill and inventiveness in cyberspace, to show who you are, that you're there, and that you know what you're doing.

Other virus writers have different motives, of course. There are those with an interest in artificial life (A-Life or AL), for whom viruses are a first step towards other life-forms in cyberspace – revealing, in a weird kind of way, their kinship with Furby and Tamagotchi. Collecting and observing computer viruses 'in the wild' thus gives these virus hunters insights into computing, into evolution and into the possibilities of A-Life. Others breed viruses, letting them mix and mingle in quarantined machines (like virtual safari parks, maybe), watching the programming solutions that evolve in these ecologies, looking for evolutionary leaps that might be harnessed to create 'intelligent agents', such as those that might do our on-line searching on our behalf, or sort our emails to save us the trouble (on A-Life, see Hayles 1999b; and Chapter 7).

Dibbell's and Ludwig's arguments are important, then – though quite difficult to pitch to someone who's just lost their hard drive to the SandMan, or whose computer won't even come on, thanks to the Chernobyl virus. As a counter to the prevailing popular image of viruses and virus-writers, these essays ask us to take a more *generous* definition (and therefore a fuller understanding) of computer viruses. Malevolent viral hacking *does* happen, and can be catastrophic; but that's only one part of this strange new ecology in cyberspace. As we shall see in Chapter 7, there are arguments that stress a more inclusive view of the potential joint kinship between humans and A-Life – with viruses slotted into this emerging technobiodiveristy.

However, in another essay on computer viruses and evolution, Ludwig (1996b) presents a slightly more pessimistic scenario about the outcome of creating self-replicating, evolving programs in cyberspace. As he asks: 'What would a virus that had become what it is primarily by evolution be like?' (Ludwig 1996b: 243). Applying a Darwinian logic to computer viruses, Ludwig suggests that self-serving viruses could easily destabilize the matrix of computers in the same way that biological viruses can over-run their hosts. Using the analogy of the Cambrian 'explosion' in bio-life, Ludwig concludes:

> Right now there is no reason to believe . . . that a similar flowering will not take place in the electronic world. If it does, and we're not ready for it, expecting it, and controlling its shape, there's no telling what the end of it could be. . . . We often imagine that computers will conquer man [*sic*] by becoming much more intelligent than him [*sic*]. It could be that we'll be conquered by something that's incredibly stupid, but adept at manipulating our senses, feelings, and desire.
>
> (Ludwig 1996b: 246)

Learning from the Love Bug, then, a computer virus could find the emotional buttons it needs to push to get a needed response out of humans, just as bio-viruses ingeniously utilize our foibles to create opportunities for replication and transmission.

Part of Lupton's (1994) argument that is particularly significant, as we have already seen, is her focus on the symbolism at work here: the designation of these programmes as *viruses* taps into images and metaphors of illness, embodiment, mortality. Anxieties over viruses in computers and in bodies thus come together, bound by the logic of contagion and vulnerability. In this way, the rise to prominence in popular discourse of the virus metaphor in computing re-emphasizes the body's permeability to viruses at the same time as the computer's; moreover, it brings the body and machine together, as twin sites of panic. In other domains, too, the body–machine relationship gives us insights into experiences of cyberspace – in the dream of disembodiment that stages the body as useless 'meat', for example (see Chapter 7). Another area to interrogate this relationship is in the field of medical imaging technologies, which reveal the insides of the body, and sites of disease, through an application of computer-aided visualization techniques, producing what we might describe as distinct medical cyberspaces.

## Medical cyberspaces

The medical cyberspaces that I want to focus on here are those produced in and by new imaging technologies (NITs), rendered as 'scans' from techniques such as computed axial tomography (CT), magnetic resonance imaging (MRI), ultrasound and positron emission tomography (PET). Through these machines, Sarah Kember (1999: 29) writes, 'medicine can now simulate, capture and seemingly re-create the human body in cyberspace'. These technologies fall into a lineage of medical imaging that Lisa Cartwright (1995) names 'medicine's visual culture' – something that begins with anatomical drawings and ends (at the moment) with this array of techniques and their representations. When we encounter these as patients, then, they offer us simultaneously a new, mediated access to our own body's interior, and an experience of what we might call 'cyber-embodiment'. The result can be profoundly disorienting, letting us glimpse all the guts and goo that makes us up (see Gromala CR). Despite this strangeness, however, some of the products of these technologies have become commonplace, such as ultrasound sonograms of foetuses proudly shown round by parents-to-be as 'baby's first photo' or 'baby's first video' (Mitchell and Georges 1998; Petchesky 2000). Images from medical cyberspace thus enter the public domain, often as the site of biological and technological marvel – read as more-or-less transparent 'pictures' of the body's interior, which then shape 'lay' understandings of embodiment, health and illness, and also affirm the health benefits of medical technoscience (Beaulieu 2000). However, the sphere of popular representation uses these images in particular ways, to tell particular stories. As Kim Sawchuk writes:

> Images of interior body space come to us through major capital investments in high technology medical instruments, but they are not only encountered in a hospital or doctor's office. The representations of the body produced within medical culture have intersected with representations in popular culture since their invention.
>
> (Sawchuk 2000: 9)

The resulting spectacles, which Sawchuk calls 'anatomical entertainments', produce a new pastime that she names 'biotourism', where the body is displayed as an object for the public's gaze. The field of medical technoscience stages the body as the site for productive technological interventions, and these anatomical entertainments replay that motif in a manner that is popularly legible – though in the process of translation between medical and popular domains, the images and what they are made to represent may be radically transformed (Beaulieu 2000). Moreover, as feminist analyses of new imaging technologies suggest, we need to be mindful of the *politics* at work in all of these representations, so that critique of medical technoscience is not effaced. Images from foetal sonograms, for example, can become a 'weapon of intimidation against women seeking abortion' (Petchesky 2000: 181), as the sonogram is 'read' not only for medical information, but also to construct a notion of foetal subjectivity. Lisa Mitchell and Eugenia Georges discuss this process in their work on the 'fetal cyborg' produced through the sonogram:

> The uncertainty about fetal subjectivity is . . . erased in the cyborg. Awareness of surroundings and of being distinct from other selves, intention, moods and emotion on the part of the fetus are included frequently in the explanation of the image for parents. Fetal movement which impedes the process of conducting the examination is described as evidence that the fetus is 'shy', 'modest', or 'doesn't like' something. . . . Conversely, a clear, easily attained fetal image may be offered as evidence that the fetus is 'being good' or 'very cooperative'.
>
> (Mitchell and Georges 1998: 109)

New imaging technologies are therefore implicated in *constructing* rather than merely representing images of the body. At the level of experience, these kinds of images thus produce a way of thinking about bodies and technologies that, I would argue, has a powerful bearing on ideas about cyberspace, for example by reminding us of the power and politics of images.

Diana Gromala documents her own experiences of medical technoscience, and then her subsequent attempts to rewire that experience through art practice, similarly foregrounding these issues:

> I came to my first virtual reality experience in a research hospital, subversively catching glimpses of the interior of my body. . . . [P]hysicians used microvideography to explore my viscera, projecting it on television and larger screens to other physicians and interns. Drugged but conscious, I was nonetheless consistently and vehemently discouraged from viewing my own body, though I thrilled in the abject pleasure it produced when I caught glimpses of its enormous and animate projections.
>
> (Gromala CR: 602)

In her work *Dancing with the Virtual Dervish: Virtual Bodies*, Gromala reuses and reworks images of her body's interior, in connection with dancers and virtual reality technology, in order to produce a contested set of representations and experiences of medical cyberspace. While still working as a form of biotourism, Gromala's project suggests new agendas that intervene critically in the process of cyber-embodiment (see also Chapter 7).

The most spectacular instance of biotourism in cyberspace to date is the Visible Human Project (VHP) – the construction of two complete, 3-D digital renderings of adult male and female human bodies, accessible over the Internet (see Waldby 2000b). The VHP receives fuller attention in Chapter 7, but for now I wanted to mention it here, in order to signal its importance both to medical technoscience and to critiques of medical technoscience. The VHP produces a very distinct medical cyberspace – rather than the glimpses of live flesh seen on CT or PET scans, here we have two corpses offered up for virtual dissection (and even reanimation). Moreover, the VHP establishes these bodies as biomedical benchmarks – as 'normal' bodies against which others' 'abnormalities' might be assessed. The virtual bodies produced by the VHP also capture that sense of technological marvel that I introduced earlier in this section, making them objects of intense public scrutiny, while the stories of their journeys into cyberspace get luridly retold with a mixture of fascination and disgust. They have come to occupy a very distinct place in medical cyberspace, therefore, but one nonetheless that links them with 'baby's first photo' and other examples of medicine's visual cyberculture. It also links them to broader discussions of the future of embodiment in cyberspace, and issues of 'posthumanism'. We shall return to these themes in Chapter 7.

The VHP produced a 'data set' of mappings of the human body, which are available for subsequent and eternal manipulation. While the principal intention was that medical researchers could utilize the data for simulation work – and there are a growing number of examples of this kind of use emerging – the data has also been used to produce more populist moments of anatomical entertainment. The most notable of these was the use of the VHP data in a sequence of the sci-fi movie *The Fifth Element* (Waldby 2000b). Here the meeting of technoscience and popular culture produces an interesting commingling, suggestive of the uprooting of medical cyberspace and its circulation in parallel with other cyberspaces – in this case the cyberspaces of the cinematic special effect. In terms of sites where cyberspaces is encountered and experienced, I want to move on to argue now, the cinema occupies a particular and very significant position on the landscape of everyday life.

## Cyberspecial effects

The use of computer-generated imagery (CGI) to produce special effects in films has received a lot of critical attention across a range of perspectives. As I want to suggest, the cinema can be thought of as a site for the experience of cyberspace through contact with CGIs. As Michele Pierson (1999: 158) writes, cinematic special effects 'put the display of the digital artefact – or computer-generated image – at the centre of the entertainment experience'. Moreover, as film theorists argue, we need to see cinema itself as a special effect (Metz 1977; Bukatman 1995) – or, to recycle William Gibson, as a form of 'consensual hallucination'. Our willing immersion in the images on the screen might be seen as a tutoring in the possibilities of cyberspace, there-fore – even as giving us a commonplace site to experience 'cyborgization', as our bodies and minds interact with the technologies of the screen (Parker and Cooper 1998).

In terms of thinking about CGIs, most work to date has focused on science fiction cinema, exploring the role of special effects in the construc-tion of imagined futures – for example, in debates about the tension between narrative and special effects in the sci-fi movie, and of the role of effects in producing the experience of sci-fi viewing (King and Krywinska 2000). In this argument, sci-fi films are all about CGIs, with the filmic narrative merely shaped around key effects sequences – producing an experience of 'marvel at the capabilities of the medium itself' analogous to the experience of tech-nological marvel in cybermedicine (Cubitt 1999a: 129). So, the CGI in sci-fi plays a double marvel: marvel at the future it depicts, and marvel at the technologies used in that act of depiction: '[a]s well as representing the techno-scientific wonders demanded by science-fiction narratives, they are also presentations of the techno-scientific achievements of the filmmaking and special effects industries to cinema audiences' (Pierson 1999: 161). So, special effects must be legible *as special effects* – if they were invisible, they could not capture the audience's wonder, which comes from our enjoyment of effects as effects (Hockley 2000). Pierson suggests that GCIs thus produce 'hyperreal' rather than 'real' images, with their hyperreality serving to rein-force their status as effects. 'Too bright and shiny by far, the hyper-chrominence and super-luminosity characteristic of the CGI effects produced over this period [1989–95] imbued the digital artefact with a very special visual significance' (Pierson 1999: 173). Cubitt (1999a) compares this CGI aesthetic with *trompe l'oeil*, a clever visual trick whose cleverness comes from exposing itself as a trick.

This need to make plain the effects is also manifest in the tendency for effects-heavy films to be increasingly accompanied by 'making-of' documen-taries that reveal the technical secrets of those effects sequences. Like the tech-nomedical objects from the previous section, then, special effects promote

Heath's (1980) 'machine interest' – something which, as we have already seen, he tracks back to the experience of early cinema (often referred to as 'the cinema of attractions'). Explaining to audiences the process of constructing effects sequences works to expand our repertoire of what we might call 'CGI-savvy', preparing us for the delights of watching future special effects. Reading this from a political economy perspective, Luke Hockley (2000) suggests that CGIs 'add value' to films, providing a further marketing device – effects are therefore commodified (birthing an entire CGI industry). I can anecdotally confirm the role of special effects in adding value to movies: last week, in a supermarket queue, a fellow shopper asked if the video of *Gladiator* she was about to buy was 'the one with all the computer effects in'.

That anecdote is interesting for another reason, too – as it reminds us of the migration of CGIs from their original home in science fiction. Films that have recently been promoted very heavily through their effects sequences also include historical dramas (*Forrest Gump*, *Titanic*, *Gladiator*), computer-animated features (*Toy Story*, *Antz*, *A Bug's Life*), disaster movies (*Volcano*, *Deep Impact*), 'meteorological dramas' (*Twister*, *The Perfect Storm*), and here in the UK natural history documentaries like *Walking with Dinosaurs*. One way of reading 'making-of' documentaries is that the technical complexities of CGIs mean that they have to be explained to audiences if we are going to fully appreciate and marvel at the images on screen – as I think we can see in the documentary accompanying the video/DVD release of *The Matrix*. However, these explanatory add-ons perform other functions, too. In the 'making-of' documentary that preceded the broadcast of *Walking with Dinosaurs*, for example, the virtual Brontosaurs and Pterodactyls also 'acted up', playing for the camera in a sequence of mock 'out-takes'. This facet of CGI-based films recurs at the end of *Toy Story 2* and *A Bug's Life*, where computer-generated characters on computer-generated sets fluff their lines, talk off-camera, and play practical jokes on one another (see Byrne and McQuillan 1999). This playfulness lets us revel in our GCI-savvy, producing a simulation of behind-the-scenes activity to complement the stories of effects-generation – reminding us that special effects don't make mistakes, but can be made to make mistakes.

This kind of argument can be linked back to the one I made earlier about cinema as 'consensual hallucination'. The pleasures of viewing the cinematic special effect involve the suspension of disbelief in combination with using CGI-savvy, so recognition of the special-effect-as-trick doesn't diminish our enjoyment, but rather doubles it: while the narrative might pause to allow us a moment to contemplate the effects sequences, as Bukatman (1995) argues, we soon pick the thread up again, and enjoy the film at two levels (at least). As an immersive medium, too, film can facilitate something akin to the dream of experiencing Gibsonian cyberspace – in fact, it may be that there are important lessons to be learnt in movie theatres for prospective cybernauts. And even in the living room, video-watching can produce the same (or at least similar) experiences of immersion, but with the addition of interactivity (in the form of the remote control, and the rewind/fast-forward and pause buttons). New media technologies such as DVD (digital versatile disks) increase the opportunities for interactivity, bridging film and computer technology in a new way, by opening up control of the cinematic narrative and turning passive 'film watching' into active 'film playing' (King and Krzywinska 2000). The increasing synergies between film and computer games in fact show cross-overs in multiple directions: games made from films, films made from games, and the mixing of cinematic and digital aesthetics – as games use 'camera angles' in depicting their narratives, while films use stylizations derived from computer games (as in the fight sequences of *The Matrix*, for example).

The idea of cinema as special effect or cinema as consensual hallucination can be expressed another way: cinema can be thought of as a process of *cyborgization*, as producing a 'cyborganic' space between the screen and the viewer (Parker and Cooper 1998). Cinema can thus be seen as a form of cyberspace, the movie theatre as a place where we encounter and experience cyberculture (doubly so, of course, if we are watching an effects-heavy sci-fi movie). As interactivity ups the ante for experiencing the cinematic in new ways, moreover, we shall no doubt see emergent cultural forms and practices in multimedia futures that expand the sites for our experiential stories; all I have been able to do here is gesture towards some of the most prominent tales.

## Summary

My aim in this chapter has been to explore some of the places where we encounter cyberspace, and to therefore highlight the Internet's impacts on everyday life. To do this, I used particular modes of story-telling, beginning with the autobiographical – recounting anecdotes on my own experiences in digital culture as a way to begin thinking through what these stories mean. In recognition of the existence of many different (but overlapping) cyber-spaces, my stories have roamed around the digital landscape, taking in many moments of contact with a range of cybercultural artefacts, from cyberpets to digital clocks, from websites to viruses, from cinematic special effects to digital images of the human body produced in technomedicine. My aim here has been to expand the ways we think about cyberspace, and to explore the cumulative resources we might have at our disposal, all of which contribute to our on-going meaning-making processes. I have also sought to emphasise the role of the 'look' of cyberspace and computers, in order to think about images and representations we also encounter. Added together, the series of stories I have told in this chapter work to produce a complex narrative of experiences of cyberspace, but one that simultaneously stresses the mundanity of many of these experiences.

## Note

1.  I lost touch with Kevin, the way kids do, and only met up with him again a decade or so later, when he was fronting a punk band called Terminal Boredom. I later heard that he died of cancer in his late twenties, and would like to remember him through this chapter.

## Hot links

### Chapters from The Cybercultures Reader

Diana Gromala, 'Pain and subjectivity in virtual reality' (Chapter 38: 598–608).
Deborah Lupton, 'The embodied computer/user' (Chapter 33: 477–88).
Andrew Ross, 'Hacking away at the counterculture' (Chapter 16: 254–67).

### Further reading

Jay David Bolter and Richard Grusin (1999) *Remediation: understanding new media*, Cambridge MA: MIT Press.
Sean Cubitt (1998) *Digital Aesthetics*, London: Sage.
Philip Haywood and Tana Wollen (eds) (1993) *Future Visions: new technologies of the screen*, London: BFI.
Daniel Miller and Don Slater (2000) *The Internet: an ethnographic approach*, Oxford: Berg.
Sherry Turkle (1997) *Life on the Screen: identity in the age of the Internet*, London: Phoenix.

### Websites

http://www.mimitchi.com/html/index.htm
Tamagotchi World website, with lots of info on virtual pets and the culture of their owners.

http://www.vmyths.com/
Excellent site focusing on hoaxes and myths around computer viruses, confirming their status as 'urban legends'.

http://www.pong-story.com/

Site dedicated to the history on Pong, the first video game, with some great photos of early games platforms.

http://www.VFXPro.com/

CGI site hosted by the Visual Effects Society, with news and reviews on special effects in film, plus cool downloads of trailers and effects sequences.

# CULTURAL STUDIES IN CYBERSPACE

Cultural studies has the pedagogical task of disentangling the Internet from its given millennial narratives of universality, revolutionary character, radical otherness from social life, and the frontier mythos.

*Jonathan Sterne*

**T**HUS FAR, THIS INTRODUCTION to cybercultures has told a number of different stories; stories about what cyberspace is, what it means, and what it does. In this chapter, I want to tell another story: the story of the emergence of distinct ways of thinking about the relationships between science, technology and culture. My aim here is to provide an outline for understanding some of the ways in which cultural studies approaches (or might approach) cyberspace, and I hope to accomplish that aim by exploring a disparate but interconnected set of themes. I shall begin by looking at how we think about science and technology, before focusing in on computers and cyberspace. I shall also be looking at the role cultural studies plays (or could play) in thinking about these things. I want to sketch a number of theoretical and methodological approaches to science and technology, in order to work towards a discussion of how, to use Jonathan Sterne's (1999: 264) phrase, 'cultural studies does the Internet'. I shall also attempt to show how particular ideas and theorists have been (or might be) used in this practice.

## Thinking about science and technology

Donald MacKenzie and Judy Wajcman (1999) note that the dominant 'common-sense' way of thinking about technology remains 'technological

65

determinism' – a mode of understanding that prescribes a one-way relationship between machines (technology) and people (society), in which
technologies change, and that change impacts on people. In this formulation,
technology and society are kept separate, even held in opposition to one
another: technology *causes* social change. MacKenzie and Wajcman are quick
to point out that this is too simplistic, and moreover 'promotes a passive
attitude to technological change' since it 'focuses our minds on how to *adapt*
to technological change, not how to *shape* it' (5; emphasis in original).
However, they are keen to retain the idea that technology does produce
social effects – it's more the case that these are more complex and contingent than a simple, deterministic cause-and-effect model suggests. Nevertheless, such straightforward determinism retains a powerful influence on
how people think and talk about things like cyberspace, for example in mass
media coverage. The task of critics, therefore, is to recast ways of understanding the technology–society relationship, adding complexity and contingency to the picture.

There have been a number of different ways of approaching this task,
emerging from academic disciplines such as philosophy, sociology, history and
cultural studies. Each has its own contributions to make, and these have, moreover, become fused and commingled in fields such as science studies, science
and technology studies (STS), and cultural studies of science and technology.
It is not possible for me to sketch the lineages of all these areas here; I shall
pick out significant aspects of each, and point towards sources that can provide the detail. Let me pick out one over-arching tenet of these studies, which
addresses the issue of contingency already highlighted: Andrew Webster
(1991) calls attention to the idea of 'epistemic relativism' in studies of science.
What this means is that scientific knowledge is located culturally, historically
and geographically. This draws our attention to the idea that science is made
at a particular time and place – it is not a universal entity, but the product of
people (scientists), who are themselves products of the setting in which they
do science. To put it another way, science is itself a social practice. The same
idea works with technology, too; if we look closely at the invention, development, production, consumption and use of a particular technological artefact (a computer, for example), we can see how each stage is overlain by
broader social processes, which it *shapes* but is also *shaped by*. Computers have
turned out the way they have because they are social and cultural as well as
technological objects – and, of course, they are political and economic objects,
too (Star 1995). The kind of historical work carried out by Paul Ceruzzi, for
example, combined with studies of computer scientists and computer users
*in situ*, adds together to provide a complex and contingent picture of what
computers are, what they mean and what they do – and why.

There are, as I have already hinted, complex stories to tell about the
evolution of these ways of thinking about science and technology. I can only

highlight selected aspects of these here, and I have chosen to look at the social construction of technology and cultural studies of science and technology. The social construction of technology (SCOT) perspective attempts to enlarge the framework for thinking about the technology–society relationship through its notion of the 'interpetive flexibility' of technology. MacKenzie and Wajcman (1999: 21) define this as 'the way in which different groups of people involved with a technology . . . can have very different understandings of that technology, including different understandings of its technical characteristics'. In the language of SCOT, these 'relevant social groups' can work together or be in conflict, but they all exert a particular influence on the form, use and meaning a technological artefact takes. In this way, SCOT recognizes that technologies have a social life that extends from the moment they're first thought of right through to the moment they're disposed of. In acknowledgement of the SCOT imperative to redress technological determinism, one volume of essays by SCOT researchers is called *Shaping Technology/Building Society* (Bijker and Law 1992), reversing the deterministic formulation that technology is built, and then shapes society. SCOT is a relative of the field known as the sociology of scientific knowledge (SSK), which has similarly sought to complicate our understandings of how science works. Methods including ethnography and discourse analysis are here brought in to provide descriptions of science in action (Webster 1991).

In the mingling of historical, sociological and cultural analyses of science, the domain of science studies has also emerged, marked by a rich and varied portfolio of approaches (Biagioli 1999). Science studies has been a controversial enterprise, especially with scientists, who are often hostile to the ways in which scholars from the humanities and social sciences have sought to deconstruct scientific knowledge and practice – a tension referred to recently as the Science Wars (Ross 1996; Segerstrale 2000). The Science Wars spilled out from academia into the mass media in the mid-1990s, following the publication of Alan Sokal's essay 'Transgressing the boundaries: towards a transformative hermeneutics of quantum gravity' in the US cultural studies journal *Social Text* (Sokal 1996). Following its publication there, Sokal elsewhere revealed that the essay was a 'hoax', cobbled together by namedropping trendy cultural theory and pasting in some science bits (some of these had intentional mistakes in, to prove his point that the *Social Text* editors didn't know their quantum physics). The furore caused by Sokal's article refocused attention on cultural studies, and the US 'academic left' more generally (for the full story, see Segerstrale 2000). It certainly muddied the waters for a great number of people working in cultural studies of science and technology, just as earlier controversies around SSK had challenged sociologists over their lack of scientific training (Ross 1996).

SSK and SCOT are also associated with actor-network theory (ANT), which makes an important contribution to thinking about science and technology by including non-humans (Michael 1996). In part, this addresses one criticism of the SCOT approach, which argues that SCOT simply replaces technological determinism with social determinism (Wise 1997). ANT maps the connections between humans and non-humans in scientific or technological practice, thus including non-humans (chemicals, components, artefacts, animals) in the class of relevant social groups, along with humans (at all scales from an individual scientist to a multinational corporation). It therefore seeks to stress the technological and the social as mutually determining. To get a flavour of ANT's approach, consider two titles of essays by one of its leading proponents, Bruno Latour: 'Technology is society made durable' (Latour 1991) and 'Where are the missing masses? A sociology of a few mundane artefacts' (Latour 1992). In the former, Latour suggests that social relations are always technological, since the task of perpetuating society has to be 'delegated' to non-human actors (the written word, tools). In the latter he argues that sociology has to consider technology as social; sociology's 'missing masses' are those artefacts with whom we share our everyday lives (Michael 2000). In order to pursue this agenda, ANT has evolved its own way of thinking and talking about networks and actors, which I do not have time to share with you here. Moreover, its approach has been subject to criticism, even from within (Law and Hassard 1999; Woolgar 1996). In particular, in its attempt to flatten the distinction between human and non-human, ANT has been accused of being dispassionate towards difference, failing to account for those excluded from its networks (Wise 1997). It is, however, an important attempt to shift away from simplistic and deterministic formulae for understanding science, technology and society.

Part of the criticism emanating from within ANT concerns the problem of the name and the problem of what ANT has become – a field of academic knowledge in its own right, with its own baggage. As Bruno Latour (1999: 15) puts it, in his view 'there are four things that do not work with actor-network theory; the word actor, the word network, the word theory and the hyphen!' A similar uneasiness circles around the area of research variously known as cultural studies of science and technology (Balsamo 1998) or cultural studies of technoscience (Reinel 1999). As with ANT, part of this unease concerns the shoe-horning of diverse work and ideas into a recognizable 'field' or 'area'. This problem resonates with the history of cultural studies as a cross-disciplinary and inter-disciplinary enterprise; a site of mixing, hybridizing and shape-shifting: 'cultural studies proceeds by way of a cutting-out and stitching-together of various theories and theorists (and experiences and narratives)' (Menser and Aronowitz 1996: 24). Marked equally by anti-determinism, cultural studies of science and technology has become an important site for rethinking the complexities of what Balsamo (1998: 291) terms 'the cultural embeddedness and the cultural circulation of scientific and technological knowledge'.

In terms of cultural studies of technology – or technocultural studies, maybe – a key part of the emerging agenda has been to redress both the overblown celebration of technology's promise, and the equally overstated technophobia. Balsamo (2000: 272) refers, instead, to technocultural critics as 'anxious technophiles', and offers up the following 'morals' for cultural studies of science and technology: don't leave science and technology to the technocrats, and don't leave the education of technocrats to academics in science and technology. This concern chimes with the call for cultural critics to encourage scientific and technological literacy (or 'technoliteracy') through the education of future scientists and non-scientists alike (Balsamo 1998, 2000). In 'Hacking away at the counterculture', Andrew Ross (CR) similarly calls for critics to adopt a hacker-like approach to new technologies: to critique from a position of knowledge, rather than ignorance. As a way of countering the hype either for or against new technologies, such technoliteracy provides a way of navigating an informed yet critical path (Sterne 1999). 'Wary, on the one hand, of the disempowering habit of demonizing technology as a satanic mill of domination, and weary, on the other, of postmodernist celebrations of the technological sublime', technocultural studies instead offers 'a realistic assessment of the politics – the dangers *and* the possibilities – that are currently at stake in those cultural practices touched by advanced technology' (Penley and Ross 1991: xii):

> All kinds of cultural negotiations are necessary to prepare the way for new technologies, many of which are not particularly useful or successful. It is the work of cultural critics, for the most part, to analyze that process, and to say how, when, and to what extent critical interventions in that process are not only possible but also desirable.
>
> (Penley and Ross 1991: xv)

So far, we have addressed cyberculture from one particular angle – that of science and technology. Of course, this is only part of the story, since computers (and the Internet) need to be looked at from other angles, too. This complexity makes computers good objects to think with:

> Because computers are simultaneously communication media and product, objects of analysis and infrastructure for analysis, intimate and formal, they form good occasions to study a variety of basic processes: the development of material culture, the formation of practice-based networks, the fallibility of language, the relationship between power and infrastructure.
>
> (Star 1995: 6)

While by no means exhaustive, Susan Leigh Star's list of ways of thinking about computers is a useful reminder of their multiple uses and meanings.

To get a sense of the location of culture in this multiplicity, I want to briefly turn attention to work on a different — but no less significant — technocultural artefact: the Sony Walkman. The Walkman personal stereo has, I think, many resonances with the Internet, in terms of its story — in terms of the way it enables us to think about technology and culture:

> The Walkman . . . is a typical cultural artefact and medium of modern culture, and through studying its 'story' or 'biography' one can learn a great deal about the ways in which culture works in late-modern societies such as our own.
>
> (Du Gay *et al.* 1997: 2)

In their book *Doing Cultural Studies: the story of the Sony Walkman*, Paul Du Gay and his colleagues introduce a way of grasping the complexity (and simultaneous mundanity) of the place the Walkman occupies in everyday life. Their focus is on 'the articulation of a number of distinct processes whose interaction can and does lead to variable and contingent outcomes' (Du Gay *et al.* 1997: 3), and to establish a framework for analysing this they have devised a model of 'the circuit of culture'. This circuit has five nodes, each a significant cultural process: representation, identity, production, consumption and regulation. Their model stresses the complex linkages between these processes, building up a web of connections whereby each process is linked to every other in a two-way relationship. So, rather than a deterministic model of cause and effect, the circuit of culture seeks to understand the on-going and shifting interplay between these processes, which together produce the Walkman as a cultural artefact:

> To study the Walkman culturally one should at least explore how it is represented, what social identities are associated with it, how it is produced and consumed, and what mechanisms regulate its distribution and use. . . . We have separated these parts of the circuit into distinct sections but in the real world they continually overlap and intertwine in complex and contingent ways. However, they are the elements which taken together are what we mean by doing a 'cultural study' of a particular object.
>
> (Du Gay *et al.* 1997: 3–4)

As Du Gay *et al.* suggest, the Walkman is both part of our culture and has its own distinct culture, built up from the cultural practices and meanings clustered around it. It is woven into the fabric of and has profound impacts upon everyday life — not least in the way that users consume music. It is also a very mundane, everyday thing that, even if we don't own or use ourselves, is all around us; it is in every sense a cultural object:

It belongs to our culture because we have constructed for it a little world of meaning; and this bringing of the object *into* meaning is what constitutes it as a cultural artefact. . . . We can talk, think about and imagine it. It is also 'cultural' because it connects with a distinct set of *social practices* . . . which are specific to our culture or way of life. It is cultural because it is associated with certain *kinds of people* . . . [and] . . . *places* . . . – because it has been given or acquired a social profile or *identity*. It is also cultural because it frequently appears in and is represented within our visual languages and media of communication. Indeed, the *image* of the Sony Walkman – sleek, high-tech, functional in design, miniaturized – has become a sort of metaphor which stands for or represents a distinctively late-modern, technological culture or way of life.

(Du Gay *et al*. 1997: 10–11; emphasis in original)

It is not difficult to see how we could substitute the computer or the Internet for the Walkman, and use the circuit of culture framework to do a 'cultural study' here. From an ANT perspective, of course, the circuit of culture is inadequate, in that it fails to include those non-human actors. The story of the production of the Walkman that Du Gay *et al*. tell, for example, is very much a *human* story – so, while we hear about the engineers and accountants, we don't hear about the ferric molecules on audio cassette tape or the headphone socket. On balance, I would have to say that the circuit of culture model works better for us in this context, though I would not want to forget the interventions that ANT has made to the theorizing of technology and society. In this respect, I agree with J. Macgregor Wise's argument that 'technology is intimately bound up with the social [or cultural] but, at the same time, is not reducible to it' – which leads him to look for a theory 'that recognizes objective material constraints as well as socially constructed constraints on the form and function of any technology' (Wise 1997: 58). As we shall see later in this chapter, Wise turns to the work of French philosophers Gilles Deleuze and Felix Guattari to formulate the theory he wants.

## Cultural studies of the Internet

If we are to begin to understand culture in cyberspace, we . . . need to adapt our analyses, . . . by rethinking articulations of culture and power.

(Jones and Kucker 2000: 222)

In this section I want to look at another discussion of how we might do a 'cultural study' on the Internet which I think is particularly insightful: Jonathan Sterne's (1999) essay 'Thinking the Internet: cultural studies versus the millennium'. Sterne is keen to stress the banality of the Internet, and to think it through as a mundane technology as a counter to what he calls 'millennial scenarios' – which come in both technophilic and technophobic hues (Sterne 1999: 258). He begins with an anecdote about a student user of the Internet, sketching a 'banal scenario' of how computers are stitched into the fabric of this student's daily life. Like my own attempts at storying the experiences of cyberspace, Sterne's anecdote brings this into perspective. This importance essay therefore intervenes in the evolving shape of what David Silver (2000) tags 'critical cyberculture studies', an emerging domain marked by an emphasis on *contextualizing* cyberspace and on challenging the 'common-place' assumptions about what takes place there.

Sterne's take on cultural studies defines its particular 'intellectual strategies', and then seeks to explore these in the context of the Internet: 'attention to the political character of knowledge production, an orientation towards the analysis of context, a commitment to theory, and a theory of articulation' (Sterne 1999: 261). This brings him to a working agenda for a 'cultural study' of the Internet which seeks to address these issues:

- Why study the Internet?
- What is at stake in how the Internet is studied?
- Where does the Internet fit into social and cultural life?
- What counts in a study of the Internet?
- How should we think about and represent the Internet?
- What theories are useful to describe the Internet?

Stressing cultural studies' experimental approach to theory and method, and critical of academics' ignorance of the Internet, Sterne asserts that 'theorizations of the Net require the same level of specificity as other objects one might theorize, such as literature, music, politics, globalization, or the relationship between time and space' (265). As a model of good practice, he singles out Raymond Williams' (1974) *Television: technology and cultural form*, highlighting what he considers to be its key features:

> It engages the dominant discourses about a medium without taking them at face value; it provides innovative descriptive material that allows other scholars to further reconceptualize the medium; it considers the past and present historical and institutional conjunctures shaping the medium; and finally, it considers the politics and the *future* of the medium without, again, taking available discourses on their own terms.
>
> (Sterne 1999: 268; emphasis in original)

However, as Sterne notes, a lot has changed since Williams wrote *Television*, and moreover there are significant gaps in Williams' account. The cultural landscape has changed, as have our modes of analysis. In place of such grand projects as *Television*, Sterne finds much more localized cultural studies of the Internet, which he groups into two categories: studies of 'subjectivity, textuality, and experience' (both on-line and off-line analyses, often based on a mix of ethnography, discourse analysis and autobiography) and 'episodic studies' in which 'the Internet becomes one site among many in everyday life or a particular inflection of virtuality, cyberspace, or computer-mediated communication' (271). The former category includes essays we shall visit elsewhere in this book, such as those by Dibbell (1999) and Branwyn (CR), and writing about cyberpunk. The 'episodic studies' include studies of the impacts of information technology on work and leisure (e.g. Brook and Boal 1995), work on cyborgs (largely set in motion by Haraway CR), studies of the discourses around the Internet (such as Ross CR) and critiques of the 'frontier myth'. The work Sterne focuses on here as 'the most developed cultural studies work to date on the Internet' (274) is Wise's (1997) *Exploring Technology and Social Space*. Wise simultaneously reads the development of technology and the development of ways of thinking about technology, including a critical discussion of ANT, and end up going to Deleuze and Guattari for assistance. Despite the fact that Wise opens his book by declaring 'This book is not about the Internet, at least not entirely. Likewise, it is not a book about cyberspace, at least not centrally' (Wise 1997: xiii), his broad-ranging, theoretically-informed and critical approach offers up some particularly useful directions to move in and towards.

Ultimately, Sterne evolves a manifesto for cultural studies of the Internet, which begins by calling for cultural studies to be a 'third voice outside the technophilic/technophobic dichotomy' (Sterne 1999: 276), adding in an emphasis on the mundanity or everydayness of the Internet (which also helps to dampen the hype surrounding it) and on treating the Net like other media, other technologies and other commodities. Finally, he returns to Williams' *Television*, suggesting that someone should write a similar volume called *The Internet*. We can thus summarize Sterne's essay as calling for:

- Seeing the Internet as 'a productive cultural site and element of social relations'.
- Moving beyond 'the commoplaces of Internet discourse'.
- Thinking beyond 'the technophilic–technophobic' dichotomy.
- Treating the Net as 'one site among many in the flow of economcs, ideology, everyday life, and experience'.
- Recognizing the 'banality of the Internet'.

(Sterne 1999: 282)

I've worked through Sterne's essay in quite a lot of detail because I think it is an important intervention in the development of a possible agenda for cultural studies in cyberspace. Importantly, it is not about the *study of Internet culture* (where what happens on-line is cordoned off from 'RL'; see Porter 1997), but advocates *cultural studies of the Internet*, which it locates both on-line and off-line (see Jones and Kucker 2000).

It's not the task of this book, however, to follow all the paths Sterne highlights, though I shall be returning both in this chapter and elsewhere to some of the key issues raised. For a start, what I'd like to do now is take what Sterne calls a 'detour through theory' (264), and have a look at some particular theorists whose work has been used to think about cyber-space and cyberculture. The list is by no means exhaustive – it's not even that extensive – but my aim is merely to suggest one or two potentially fruitful places to go to for help in the task of theorizing cyberspace. There are so many theories and theorists out there, and a large number have been (or could be) used to think about some aspects of cyberculture. The ones I've chosen to feature here are those that I have found particularly insightful or provocative.

## Theory in cyberspace

> Understanding the logic of technology requires an open mind.
> (Armitage 1999a: 7)

Sherry Turkle's (1999: 545) investigation of the ways in which cyberspace enables participants to 'play' with identity – in particular the use of computers to build 'multiple selves' – leads her to reminisce about and then redeploy theory, which she refers to as her 'French lessons' (since the theories she encountered were largely French poststructuralist accounts of the 'decentred' self). As she says, when she first heard these ideas about self-identity, they interested her but seemed abstract:

> These theorists of poststructuralism, and what would come to be called postmodernism, spoke words that addressed the relationship between the mind and the body but from my point of view had little to do with my own. . . . This disjuncture between theory . . . and lived experi-ence . . . is one of the main reasons why multiple and decentred theories have been slow to catch on – or when they do, why we tend to settle back quickly into older, centralized ways of looking at things.
> (Turkle 1999: 545)

Now, this is a fairly common problem with theory – it can be so abstract, so seemingly disconnected from 'real life', that it can be hard to do anything with other than read and attempt to understand. However, some years later,

Turkle found herself in an environment where these ideas suddenly made sense: 'When, twenty years later, I used my personal computer and modem to join on-line communities, I experienced my French lessons in action, their theories brought almost shockingly down to earth'. Here, in MUDs and virtual communities, Turkle experienced dencentring for herself, and theory started to make sense. I like the way Turkle tells this story, because it shows a good way of making use of theoretical material; like Sterne (1999: 264) says, a detour through theory enables us to construct 'a new analysis or description of a concrete problem'. There's a more thorough discussion of the decentred subject and its implications for identity in cyberculture in Chapter 6; my point in mentioning it here is to illustrate the way that theory can be incredibly useful in understanding the processes that take place in cyberspace – but also that we need the right approach to theory. Like technoliteracy, I think that 'theory-literacy' is one of the best tools we have (and should encourage in others) if we are going to navigate a critical path through cyberculture. Cultural studies is often either praised or condemned for a kind of theoretical promiscuity (and likewise a methodological promiscuity) – with poaching ideas from all kinds of places, and using them in new ways. For purists this is sacrilege, but for those of us simply wanting to make sense of the world by any means neces-sary, pluralism is a much better tactic that purism.

As Turkle notes, her 'French lessons' brought her into contact with post-structuralist and postmodern theories and theorists, and ideas emanating from postmodernism and poststructuralism remain important for theorizing tech-nology and culture (for an introduction to these theoretical terrains, see Sarup 1993). However, John Armitage (1999a: 1) suggests that more recently 'mod-ern and postmodern cultural theories [are] yielding to new "hypermodern" and "recombinant" cultural theories of technology'. Reviewing this 'new cultural theory', Armitage reiterates the point that we need 'an approach to the study of technology in the present period that is eclectic and open-minded', offer-ing 'recombinant' theory as 'a perspective that is based on [the] contemporary cultural experience of everyday life' – this theory, then, is pulled together by 'scavenging among the remnants of modernism and postmodernism' (Armitage 1999a: 2–3). There are, for Armitage, two key domains in which to deploy this body of theory: in theorizing the importance of technology in the determination of new cultural practices and of new political practices. Note his use of the word *determination*, which immediately raises the issue of technological determinism. Armitage addresses this by acknowledging 'fatal' and 'apocalyptic' strands in the new cultural theory, arguing that it is wrong to reject technological determinism; instead, he insists, we must 'work *with*, or at least around, the seductions of technological determinism for radical cultural and political purposes', *relativizing* rather than rejecting it (12). Indeed, he goes on to suggest, we need to move beyond a knee-jerk reaction to technological determinism, in part as a recognition that the charge relies on continuing to effect a separation between technology and culture (or politics) — a separation that is increasingly untenable:

> Today, many new cultural and political theorists react to these developments by asking whether the charge of technological determinism is either worth making or worth answering.
>
> (Armitage 1999a: 12)

As we shall see, some of the theories and theorists I shall be highlighting in the next section do take a particularly fatalistic or apocalyptic view on new technologies; it is therefore worth keeping in mind Armitage's argument as we explore them. But that's enough about 'theory' in the abstract; what I want to do now is provide some snapshots of theories and theorists, pointing out where I think they are useful for the project we've set ourselves. I will have to be fairly brief, and so cannot give a full exposition of the different writers I've chosen. Those unfamiliar with their work might need to have a handy guide nearby; good places to start include Peter Brooker's (1999) *A Concise Glossary of Cultural Theory*, Ellis Cashmore and Chris Rojek's (1999) *Dictionary of Cultural Theorists*, and Steven Best and Douglas Kellner's (1991) *Postmodern Theory*. Finally, to avoid privileging one over the others, I will work though them in alphabetical order. Time to start our own French lessons, then.

### Baudrillard

Jean Baudrillard is one of the key thinkers associated with postmodernity. In the 1970s, he began to theorize the notion of simulation — an effect of the proliferation of media images in society, through which our sense of what is 'real' gets progressively eroded. We ourselves become mediatized, seduced by the 'ecstacy of communication', living through screens or as screens. The resulting culture of 'hyperreality' is one in which the distinctions between real and imagined, surface and depth, or reality and illusion can no longer be used. Drawing on the theory of semiotics — about the relationship between the sign and what it represents — Baudrillard suggests that in postmodernity signs have become disconnected from reality; instead of representation, we have simulation. His notion of the simulacrum (a copy of a copy with no original) embodies this process, and the procession of simulacra outlines how this has come about. First, signs straightforwardly represent reality; second, signs distort reality, or misrepresent it; third, the sign disguises the fact that there is no underlying corresponding reality — signs become representations of representations; and fourth, the sign no longer bears any relation to reality — images have replaced reality. In his most famous discussion of simulation, Baudrillard looks at Disneyland, arguing that the purpose of Disneyland is to make us believe that the rest of America is real, when in fact everything is Disneyland (Baudrillard 1983). Equally well-known is Baudrillard's provocation that the Gulf War did not take place – that the intense mediatization of the war and the use of 'smart' weapons made it seem more like a video game (see Norris 1992). In both examples, simulation is an ideological tool:

> It is an illusion, yet its principal aim is to make us forget that this is the case. It constructs us as passive consumers of assorted false promises and manages to keep us in its thrall by making us forget that we are the world's inmates rather than free agents.
>
> (Cavallaro 2000: 212)

These kinds of ideas can be applied to cyberspace, then, to argue for an intensification of the process of simulation – that the new media and communications technologies further disconnect us from reality, creating for us instead a virtual reality. This use is playfully hinted at twice in the movie *The Matrix*: first, as the central character Nero keeps his contraband computer disks hidden in a hollowed-out copy of a Baudrillard book; and second, when Nero is shown what reality really is by Mobius, who says 'Welcome to the desert of the real', a term from Baudrillard's (1983) *Simulations*. In that movie, the 'real world' that people experience and live in is one huge computer-generated simulacrum.

While his pronouncements are simultaneously pessimistic (even apocalyptic), Erik Davis (1998: 278) concludes that Baudrillard's 'dour prophecy certainly resonates' – though Davis argues that there might be ways to avoid domination-by-simulation. One place where this dour prophecy certainly resonates is with cyberpunk fiction – indeed, Baudrillard's work on simulation and hyperreality has been described as science fiction:

> Like Baudrillard, cyberpunk fiction problematizes the notion of the subject; concepts of reality and time and space are called into question with notions of cyberspace; implosion between individuals and technology subverts the concept of the human being; and the erosion of traditional values raises questions concerning which values deserve to survive and what new values and politics could help produce a better future. Indeed, both Baudrillard and cyberpunk call into question the very nature of contemporary society, culture, values, and politics, and thus force us to confront key theoretical and political issues.
>
> (Kellner 1995: 304)

However, while noting the resonances between the two, Kellner ultimately finds cyberpunk (especially Gibson) as producing a less pessimistic futurology than Baudrillard, in that it includes the possibility of resistance and transgression. Nevertheless, the similarities Kellner traces suggest that Baudrillard's ideas can give us critical insight into the workings of cyberspace (certainly at the level of symbolic stories, as in cyberpunk). His work, however, is not without its critics. Mark Poster, for example, accuses Baudrillard of failing to define his key ideas, of using hyperbole in place of systematic analysis, of totalizing his insights and of ignoring evidence that counters his pessimistic proclamations. Moreover, Poster argues that:

> Baudrillard's work remains infused with a sense of the media as unidirectional, and therefore does not anticipate the imminent appearance of bidirectional, decentralized media, such as the Internet, with its new opportunities for reconstructing the mechanisms of subject constitution.
>
> (Poster 1995: 19)

Despite all this, though, Poster concludes that Baudrillard's work is still important, not least in that it 'represents the beginning of a line of thought, one that is open to development and refinement by others' (113) – and among those 'others', Poster points to work by Gilles Deleuze, Felix Guattari and Donna Haraway, particularly in their reconsideration of the human–machine relationship. An infuriating aphorist to some critics, a postmodern sage to others, Baudrillard has been responsible for providing an important foundation for thinking about images, ideas and identities – even if, at the end of the day, his work 'takes us en route to developing a theory of postmodernity, [but] it ultimately fails to deliver the goods' (Best and Kellner 1991: 143).

### Deleuze and Guattari

> [T]he machines don't explain anything, you have to analyze the collective arrangements of which machines are just one component.
>
> (Deleuze 1995: 75)

Individually and together, Gilles Deleuze and Felix Guattari (who describe themselves as 'sorcerers') have created a new way of thinking and a new set of terms to describe the world that has many possible implications for looking at cyberspace. In their two most famous collaborations, *Anti-Oedipus* (1984) and *A Thousand Plateaus* (1988), they discuss rhizomes, machinic assemblages, flows, lines of flight, deterritorialization and reterritorialization, becomings, bodies without organs, nomadism – all concepts which can be (and many have been) applied to cyberspace and cyberculture. These concepts are difficult to define outside of Deleuze and Guattari's own terms, and can be highly abstract. To get a handle on their use, I will focus on two texts that provide 'Deleuzoguattarian' perspectives on aspects of cyberspace:

J. Macgregor Wise's (1997) *Exploring Technology and Social Space* and Charles Stivale's (1998) *The Two-Fold Thought of Deleuze and Guattari* (specifically the chapters 'The rhizomatics of cyberspace' and 'Mille/punks/cyber/plateaus: becomings-*x*').

Wise's project is to find a new 'episteme' – a way of thinking about the world – more useful than the outmoded 'modern' episteme to the world we now live in (the world of new media and communications technologies). Deleuze and Guattari provide Wise with this (actor-network theory falls short, though it does provide some insights); we are, he contends, living in a Deleuzian world. In this world, technology is 'a socially active hybrid that connects with others and bends space while being at the same time coded by abstract forces' (Wise 1997: 57). Following Deleuze and Guattari's discussion of technology and language as the two fundamental strata of human existence, Wise refers to technology as machinic assemblages (content) and language as assemblages of enunciation (expression), focusing on the ways in which these assemblages relate to one another in social space ('the space created by the actions of multiple humans over time' (Wise 1997: xiii)):

> As social space, the Internet – or, rather, its communities – is produced through habit, both the linguistic habits of repetitive characteristic phrasing or shorthand (BTW, LOL, FYI) and technological habits of typing, of the hardware and software 'preferences' of configuration, of bodily posture, and so forth. To grasp this space is to address both of these dimensions: the articulation of the machinic assemblage to the assemblage of enunciation, *the machines we use and how we talk about them or think about them.*
>
> (Wise 1997: 73; my emphasis)

To track this articulation, Wise looks at popular representations of new communications technologies, and the ways in which these then feed into other visions of cyberspace – specifically, those embodied in discussions around the Information Superhighway or National Information Infrastructure (as promoted in the US by Al Gore, when he was Clinton's VP), and in *Wired* magazine's 'corporate individualism or capitalist libertarianism' (151). Witnessing the centralization and corporate colonization of cyberspace, Wise looks for productive political possibilities to stall these processes – or, to use the Deleuzoguattarian phrase, he looks for 'a minoritarian deterritorializing machine' (162), finding it is grassroots Internet use (bulletin boards) and some formulations of the cyborg (inspired by Haraway). Ultimately, Wise returns to those two fundamental strata, technology and language, arguing the need to critically examine both, in all their interrelationships: 'there are never technology questions that can only ever be answered by technology answers' (189). Deleuze and Guattari assist Wise, it seems, by freeing his mind from the modern episteme, enabling him to look anew at the world and the place of technology within it. It is the assemblage that ultimately appears to be most useful here, and the idea of technology and language as strata.

Stivale provides a somewhat different take on cyberspace through Deleuze and Guattari, beginning with their notion of the rhizome:

> The 'rhizome' constitutes a model of continuing offshoots, taproot systems that travel horizontally and laterally, constantly producing affective relations/becomings that themselves contribute to the dynamic multiplicity of creation and existence.
>
> (Stivale 1998: 71)

To explore the rhizomatics of cyberspace (or cyberspace as rhizome), Stivale follows a thread on an online discussion list dedicated to Deleuze and Guattari, so that these rhizomatics are two-fold: the discussion that moves on- and off-line is rhizomatic in form and content, as discussants on the list argue about whether, for example, flaming can be thought of as rhizomatic. A similar tactic moves back and forth from an account of a conference to discussions of the conference (and of his on-line account of the conference) on the discussion list. In their shifting, multi-perspectival shape, these sections attempt a hypertext-like structure, giving a neat illustration of the rhizomatics of/in cyberspace.

Deleuze has made some comments about cyberspace directly, in particular in stressing that computers have ushered in 'control societies' in place of the previous 'disciplinary societies' described by Foucault (see below). Like Baudrillard, Deleuze seems pessimistic about control societies, though Stivale spots productive possibilities in Guattari's (1995) *Chaosmosis*, in a discussion of the 'ecology of the virtual'. Then, as Kellner did with Baudrillard, Stivale turns to cyberpunk, in particular to consider the Deleuzoguattarian idea of becomings, from *A Thousand Plateaus*. This is a complicated notion, with becoming set against being — becoming is not about finally arriving at having become something (else), but an ongoing process. *A Thousand Plateaus* introduces a number of such becomings: becoming-woman, becoming-animal, becoming-imperceptible. Out of becoming, new alliances come into being; not hybrids exactly, since Deleuze and Guattari point out that becoming is not merging. In two of their famous examples, they discuss 'the wasp and the orchid' and *Moby Dick*. In the case of the former, the orchid takes on some patterning from the wasp, in order to attract it, and the wasp then fulfils the role of pollination for the orchid. The wasp and the orchid haven't become one, but each is in process of becoming the other; this is a process of 'involution' rather than evolution, more akin to contagion than procreation, in that heterogeneous elements are brought together: 'these combinations are neither genetic nor structural; they are interkingdoms, unnatural participations' (Deleuze and Guattari 1988: 242). In the discussion of becoming-animal, Deleuze and Guattari see becoming in relation to the pack, reminding us of the importance of multiplicity:

> A becoming-animal always involves a pack, a band, a population, a peopling, in short, a multiplicity. . . . The wolf is not fundamentally a characteristic or a certain number of characteristics; it is a wolfing. . . . [E]very animal is fundamentally a band, a pack. . . . It is at this point that the human being encounters the animal. We do not become animal without a fascination for the pack, for multiplicity.
>
> (Deleuze and Guattari 1988: 240)

In *Moby Dick*, Captain Ahab's becoming-whale introduces a second idea: along with the pack, or in the pack, there is also always an exceptional individual, a loner, which they refer to as the anomalous: 'every animal swept up in its pack has its anomalous', and it is 'by means of this anomalous choice that each enters into his or her becoming-animals' (243–4). The anomalous is a 'phenomenon of bordering', at once part of the pack and apart from it.

Becomings in cyberpunk, therefore, can be seen to take shape in certain types of cyborgs, artificial intelligences (AI) and artificial life-forms (A-Life). In fictional writings by cyberpunks such as Rudy Rucker, John Shirley and in Gibson's 'Sprawl' trilogy, Stivale looks for becomings, such as the 'becoming-sentient' of the AI Wintermute in *Neuromancer*, concluding that 'the very possibilities of diverse and merged subjectivities prevalent in the cyberpunk novels suggest affective relations quite difficult to enunciate, yet potentially quite real as a field of "becoming" in daily life' (Stivale 1998: 132; see also Land 1998). *Mona Lisa Overdrive* (1988), the third part of Gibson's 'Sprawl' trilogy, is, Stivale writes, 'truly the novel of "becomings", in which all the characters undergo various degrees of transformation brought about by the sentient "becoming-imperceptible" of AI' (137–8). Like Haraway's (CR) description of the cyborg as a potentially 'powerful infidel hetero-glossia', Stivale finds in cyberpunk the possibility for becomings, although he also sees in figures such as the clone and the 'posthuman cyborg' a merging at the level of filiation rather than alliance (just as Haraway warns that cyborgs can become part of the 'informatics of domination' rather than resisting it).

Like Wise and Stivale, my attempts to explain or describe 'Deleuzo-guattarian' theory end up reiterating the words of the sorcerers themselves; the ideas seem simple, but can be difficult to talk about outside of their own language and logic. Of course, a bit of sorcery comes in handy, given the many 'magical' aspects of cyberspace – don't forget that the Internet is the place *Where Wizards Stay Up Late* (Hafner and Lyon 1996; see also Cubitt 2000; Davis 1998). And, to be sure, terms like rhizome, becoming, machinic seem almost ready-made for cyberspace, just as Baudrillard's thesis about simulation was waiting for virtual reality to happen (for a broader comparison of Baudrillard with Deleuze and Guattari, see Kroker 1992). Stivale achieves the best *illustration* of their ideas, I think, in his readings of cyberpunk (doubly useful as it can be read alongside Kellner's essay on Baudrillard and cyberpunk).

## Foucault

The work of Michel Foucault contains a number of important theoretical insights useful to the analysis of cyberspace, though his writings never significantly addressed either the media or computers. However, from his study of the disciplinary society and the architecture of the panopticon to his work on discourse, power/knowledge and the subject, there are ideas and concepts in Foucault's work that can help us think about a number of different aspects of on-line life. As David Lyon (2001: 114) states, it is 'ironic that Foucault, who had almost nothing to say about computers, should inspire some radically new approaches to digitized surveillance'. I want to have a look at two essays dealing with this aspect of Foucauldian theory here, since they illustrate very well the ways in which we can use different theoretical perspectives in the project of developing a critical understanding of cyberculture.

Foucault was interested in the propagation of discourses – bodies of 'expert' knowledge and writing – that have given shape to modern societies and subjects. In a series of writings about particular discourses and institutions, including prisons and insane asylums, Foucault elaborated the idea that discourses do more than describe a society and its subjects: they *define* them – discourses constitute subjects. Thus, the discourse of criminology defines the criminal, legitimating punishment (which, depending on the prevailing discourse, might be execution, incarceration, or rehabilitation). The so-called human sciences (such as psychiatry and criminology) have evolved to name and classify individuals and groups, in an attempt to normalize populations (by defining those who may be classed as 'abnormal' – the mad, the criminal, the homosexual). These discourses and institutions therefore *discipline* human subjects, and this disciplinary function is achieved in part through techniques of surveillance. While his work has been criticized for taking liberties with historical method, the insights from Foucault's research have attracted considerable attention and support from cultural critics.

The best-known work on surveillance by Foucault is to be found in *Discipline and Punish* (1979), a book about prisons – and especially his discussion of the panopticon. The panopticon was a design for a prison building from the late eighteenth century, in which the cells are arranged around a central guard tower, clustered according to the 'class' of criminal (all murderers together, all burglars together). The lighting in the cells means that the prisoners cannot see into the tower, but the guards can see into the cells. In this way, the prisoners could never know if they were being watched by the guards (or if, in fact, there were any guards in the tower at all); instead, they had to monitor their own behaviour, just in case they were being watched – so discipline becomes internalized. This idea of a potentially all-seeing institution that might be monitoring our actions – and through which we therefore come to police ourselves – has obvious implications for other modes of surveillance, such as closed-circuit television (CCTV) in city centres, speed cameras on roads, and forms of worker-productivity monitoring (Lyon 2001). Computer technologies have also been discussed in this way, for example in Mark Poster's (1995) work on databases, to which I now want to turn our attention.

Central to Poster's argument is a conceptualization of databases as 'configurations of language' – and that we need therefore to think about databases using a theory of the social effects of language (Poster 1995: 79). Not surprisingly, the place to head for this is poststructuralism, where the relationship between language and subjectivity is elaborated:

> Poststructuralists make a number of salient points about the interaction of language and subjects [remember Turkle's 'French lessons']: (1) that subjects are always mediated by language; (2) that this mediation takes the form of 'interpellation'; and (3) that in this process the subject position that is a point of enunciation and of address is never sutured or closed, but remains unstable, excessive, multiple.
>
> (Poster 1995: 79)

So, language names us (or gives names to the things that we are: teacher, middle-aged, homosexual), and this naming occurs through the ways we address one another, and accept the way we are addressed by others. However, this is not a once-and-for-all process, since our identities are multiple (so a middle-aged, homosexual teacher is also a son, a lover, a taxpayer). The role of discourse here is to produce certain subject positions and to naturalize them – in an effort to facilitate the domination of the subject. In the context of this broad poststructuralist understanding of the subject, then, Poster elaborates his thesis on databases as 'super-panopticon':

> Databases are discourse . . . because they effect a constitution of the subject. . . . In its electronic form, the database is perfectly transferable in space, indefinitely preservable in time; it may last forever everywhere. . . . The database is a discourse of pure writing that directly amplifies the power of its owner/user.
>
> (Poster 1995: 85)

As a result of the digitization and virtualization of more and more activities of everyday life – shopping, banking, working – databases can be compiled with ever more detail, building up distinct 'profiles' of our habits, values and tastes. In this way, our personal data becomes a component of our social identities, redefining and reconstituting who we are in terms of the database's uses: 'databases are nothing but performative machines, engines for producing retrievable identities' (87). In contrast to the disciplinary regimes Foucault investigated, Poster argues that a distinctive feature of database surveillance is that we willingly submit to it, providing the information necessary through our credit card purchases, loyalty cards, phone banking, web searches and so on: 'the phone cables and electric circuitry that minutely crisscross and envelop our world are the extremities of the super-panopticon, transforming our acts into an extensive discourse of surveillance, our private behaviors into public announcements, our individual deeds into collective language' (87). Moreover, databases produce a kind of hyperreality – a simulacrum of the individual or population derived from the data stored and retrieved. And the subject thus produced is, Poster argues, very different from that produced in Foucault's panopticon through the process of subjectification (the internalization or interiorization of disciplined subjectivity). Instead, the super-panopticon works through objectification, 'producing individuals with dispersed identities, identities of which the individuals might not even be aware' – identity is located *outside* the subject (93).

In line with his argument about our willing submission to database surveillance, Poster notes that we live in a climate of increasing 'database anxiety', aware of the fact that we are lodged in countless databases, and that the data we surrender can be put to all kinds of future uses. At the level of social control, databases provide governments with raw materials for policy formulations, and Poster argues that the aim of policy is to produce stability in the population (drawing again on Foucault, this time via his notion of governmentality). In this way, databases are critical objects for exploring, as Armitage (1999a) implores us to, the impacts of technology on cultural and political practices.

A second working-through of Foucault's ideas about discourse and discipline in relation to cyberculture is provided by Kevin Porter. His starting-point is to argue that 'it is in the interests of power . . . that computers be as thoroughly integrated into society as possible' (Porter 2000: 44). Why is this? It's because the aim of current systems of power is to *make people accessible to computers* (rather than vice versa), since computers are 'perfect' disciplinary (and disciplined) machines:

> It is hard to imagine better exemplars of perfect vigilance than computers, which ceaselessly track countless financial transactions, global weather conditions, satellite broadcasts, online chatroom conversations, etc. And their panoptic gaze extends to the labor of employees,

such as data processors and telephone representatives, whose every keystroke or utterance is (or is potentially) recorded, timed, and assessed.

(Porter 2000: 52)

So, computers do the work of supervision (or surveillance). They also produce three other effects of discipline: individuation (through databases that provide profiles of our habits, for example), docility (transforming the body to perform its tasks more 'effectively', through ergonomics for example), and segmentation of time and space (through timetables, schedules, planners and so on – as we see in computerized personal organizers). Moreover, while recognizing that computers cause us problems – the proliferation of data, our surrender into databases – we simultaneously look to computers to solve our problems; the computer helps us cope with the quickening pace of modern life, even though it is computers that are speeding things up! (see Virilio 1995.) In the end, this means for Porter that humans have to be usurped by machines in all spheres of data-handling, as we're just too slow. Our only role, therefore, is as *subjects of data*.

In the course of his life, Foucault wrote about a large number of different things, and his work should not be reduced to the ideas of discourse and surveillance played out here. To signal other aspects of his work that have been used to think about cyberculture, I'd like to refer briefly to an essay by Alan Aycock (1995), which uses Foucault's (1986) discussion of 'the care of the self' to explore postings on a Usenet news group, rec.games.chess. Aycock's focus is on the use of the Internet among the news group's users as a resource for 'fashioning' an identity (specifically as either 'romantic' or 'modern') through communicating with each other about chess and computing. Although sketchy, Aycock's essay reminds us that Foucault, like many of the theorists presented here, turned his attention to a number of questions – and that the answers he found might prove useful for examining distinct domains of cyberculture.

## Virilio

Another postmodern French huckster to some, yet a prescient techno-savvy strategist to others, Virilio's writings always provoke his readers to reason beyond their inherited and conventional ontologies.

(Luke and O Tuathail 2000: 364)

Theorist of war, speed and vision; theorist of military power, knowledge and technology; virtual theorist – Paul Virilio has attracted these and countless other appellations. Like the other theorists discussed here, Virilio is hard to categorize (not that this is a problem, bearing in mind Armitage's call to be 'open-minded'). While he might be said to share some concerns and characteristics with these theorists, his work is better described as a theory 'the cultural logic of late militarism', rather than as postmodern or poststructuralist theory (Armitage 1999b: 9). Moreover, his work crosses a number of domains: 'He is, at one and the same time, a historian of warfare, technology and photography, a philosopher of architecture, military strategy and cinema, and a politically engaged provocative commentator on history, terrorism, mass media and human–machine relations' (Luke and O Tuathail 2000: 361). As we shall see, to his critics his work is marred by a 'pessimistic liberal anarchism' (Cubitt 1999b: 132) and, as with Baudrillard, a tendency for hyperbole, totalization and generalization. To his fans, however, he is *the* theorist we need to understand contemporary technoculture, with 'lament as his chosen form of mediation' (Kroker 1992: 22):

> He is, perhaps, the world's first virtual theorist, the writer who understands the universe of technology and politics, not by standing outside of its violent logic, but by travelling inside its deepest interstices with such speed, such 'apparent' theoretical force, and such insistent moral concerns that the virtual world of technology is finally compelled to disclose its secret, to finally say that 'real power is not knowledge-power or the accumulation of wealth, but "moving power" . . . [S]peed is the hope of the west'.
>
> (Kroker 1992: 21)

Virilio's thesis on speed – or 'dromology' – is of central importance in thinking about new technologies, since these are, as we have already seen, all about speed, acceleration – or even better, instantaneity (Armitage 1999b). This acceleration is, for Virilio, a portent of apocalypse, as well as an effect of the intensifying militarization of contemporary societies and media cultures. As Luke and O Tuathail suggest, Virilio's thesis is not unlike David Harvey's (1989) 'time-space compression', although for Virilio the process is driven as much by military as by capitalist imperatives (Armitage 1999b).

In his essay 'Red alert in cyberspace!', Virilio (1995) engages with this 'tyranny of absolute speed', as well as discussing what he refers to as 'the great accident of the future', echoing his earlier work on 'the museum of accidents' (Virilio 1989), in which he argues that every new technology brings with it new accidents: electricity brings the electric shock, cars bring the car crash. What scares Virilio about the current age of networked communications, therefore, is the spectre of a *distributed* accident – a potential accident of global proportions. He borrows the notion of the 'information bomb' here: 'a bomb in which interactivity in real time would be to information what radioactivity is to energy' (Virilio 1995: 3). The stock market crash of 1989 is therefore prophetic of this 'accident of accidents' (see also Tenner

1996, on technology's 'revenge effects'). Echoing Porter's (2000) arguments about computers as both problem and solution, Virilio suggests that new technologies of deterrence will develop to ward off the great accident – but through an escalating militarization of information.

Like Baudrillard, Virilio has discussed the 1991 Gulf War as an exemplar of his ideas, as an information war, though his take on it differs from Baudrillard's. For Virilio, the key thing about the Gulf War was that the US military had been simulating and modelling the conflict well in advance of it happening, hence the brutal efficiency of their war machine. Moreover,

> The enemy in this instance occupied effectively a different historical period to the US, fighting for a territory in which they still believed, and in which they had a stake. For the information warrior, territory . . . has no meaning whatsoever. It has been assimilated into the data-streams of battle computers, and has become immaterial.
>
> (Cubitt 1999b: 131)

As Cubitt says, war has undergone a process of acceleration in Virilio's eyes, and has transformed into 'a thoroughly mediated struggle for absolute surveillance' (134). Now, it is important to remember that Virilio suggests that the organization of human societies is intimately connected to war – so his reading of the Gulf War has broad-reaching implications beyond the 'theatre of war'. Cities, governments, media – these, too, are ruled by the same logic.

In terms of theorizing the media, Virilio has developed a series of ideas about cinematic representation and perception, and the notion of 'substitution' – a formulation of the role of representation that bears similarities with Baudrillard's simulation (Armitage 1999b). However, his work on the media has been criticized for positing an out-moded model of unidirectional communication rather than recognizing mediation as a productive process, failing to address the transformations in media culture brought about by multimedia and infotainment. Moreover, his take on the negative effects of technology 'depends on the invocation of a human existing prior to and unmediated by technological devices' (Crawford 1999: 171) – a nostalgic, idealized notion. And, as Cubitt (1999b: 132–3) writes, Virilio understands mediation as a threat to subjectivity, when in fact 'what is being lost in the acceleration of communications media is only a historically specific mode of subjectivity, not subjectivity itself'. Picking up this theme, Douglas Kellner argues that

> Virilio's project is essentially conservative, wishing to preserve the human body and natural life against what he sees as a demonic technology which he regards as having a highly destructive impact on nature, human beings and socio-political life.
>
> (Kellner 1999: 103)

Surveying the contemporary technoscientific and cybercultural scene, then, Virilio fixes his sights on a number of recent developments that for him offer further evidence of technology's infection of society. He refers, for example, to the collapse of the distinction between human and machine – which he calls the 'transplant revolution' (biogenetics, nanotechnology, etc.) – as a war on the human body. This is part of his thesis on 'endo-colonization', described by Armitage (1999b: 12) as 'what takes place when a political power like the state turns against its own people, or as in the case of technoscience, the human body'. His critique of this process includes assaults on the performance artist Stelarc, on cyberfeminism and on cybersex – examples of what Virilio refers to as 'technological fundamentalism' (Virilio 1997; Zurbrugg 1999). Additionally, he stresses the disorienting and desta-bilizing effects of cyberspace in negative terms, aligning disembodiment with a loss of 'anchorage in one's body, nature and social community' (Kellner 1999: 111).

In line with his link between technology and militarization, cyberfemi-nists are classed by Virilio as '"collaborators" with the "Occupation" forces of multimedia "generals" such as Microsoft's CEO, Bill Gates' (Armitage 1999b: 13). In his condemnation of Stelarc, moreover, he counters the artist's posthuman prophecy of 'postevolutionary strategies' (Stelarc CR) with the put-down 'I believe that man is finished!' (quoted in Zurbrugg 1999: 179). Of course, Stelarc believes that 'man' is finished, too – but for very different reasons. Here we glimpse Virilio's Catholicism, with 'man' as God's last miracle; against this, Stelarc sees 'man' as finished in terms of evolution, urging us to move beyond the confines of the 'natural' body through the incorporation of new technologies. And while Stelarc enthuses over the possi-bilities for space travel, Virilio writes instead that we must 'stop speculating' about 'realms beyond the world, beyond Earth or beyond mankind' (quoted in Zurbrugg 1999: 186). In short, Virilio is a humanist in contrast to Stelarc's posthumanism. Interestingly, however, Stelarc confesses that Virilio is one of his favourite writers, and Zurbrugg (1999) plots points of convergence as well as divergence in their methods and projects.

So, while his proclamations mark him as a technophobe, Virilio argues that a dose of technophobia is a necessary counter to the over-enthusiastic embrace of cybertechnology – hence his critique of Stelarc. In this respect, at least, his work is of importance here. Even those critical of his position, such as Cubitt and Kellner, concede that his work provokes us to consider (or reconsider) key aspects of contemporary societies: 'clearly, speed and the instantaneity and simultaneity of information are more important to the new economy and military than ever before, so Virilio's reflections on speed, technology, politics and culture are extremely relevant' (Kellner 1999: 120).

## Summary

The aim of this chapter has been to explore ways of thinking about *cyber-culture as culture*. In order to move in some of the right directions, I have focused on different theoretical approaches to science and technology, including those emanating from science and technology studies, social construction of technology and actor-network theory approaches. These perspectives remind us, to reiterate a neat phrase from J. Macgregor Wise (1997: 189), that 'there are never technology questions that can only ever be answered by technology answers'. Finding ways to think about relations between humans and machines in cyberculture means remembering this. It also means, as John Armitage (1999a) says, being open-minded about the theories we use and the ways we use them. However, as my detour through the Sokal affair showed, not everyone agrees with this kind of intellectual promiscuity.

What I have tried to think about here, then, is what a cultural study of cyberspace might be like – prompted by Jonanthan Sterne's (1999) essay. It's not been my aim to provide a programmatic definition, however; I'm more interested in suggesting possibilities than proclaiming certainties. With that in mind, I have scouted around, and patched together in this chapter some fragments for cultural studies in cyberspace. I took a close look at Sterne's essay, as I think it has a lot of useful insights in it, then I attempted to summarize a small number of cultural theorists whose work can be (and has been) used to theorize cyberculture. I'm aware that this list is very short, and made up entirely of Frenchmen. But I hope I have been clear that the list is suggestive and illustrative rather than canonical. As I hope is clear by now, my take on theory is that multiplicity and contingency should guide us: we need *really useful theory*, and that can come from any number of sources. Just because, for example, Foucault can help us understand how rec.games.chess facilitates the fashioning of identities for participants doesn't mean we have to make a Foucauldian reading of every aspect of cyberculture. Using theory contingently means spotting the places where it helps, trying things out – as when Michele Willson (CR) gets assistance from Jean-Luc Nancy in her work on virtual community, or Thomas Foster (CR) uses Judith Butler's ideas about performativity to help him think about the body in cyberpunk.

There are, therefore, many more theories and theorists out there that we could have looked at – and which have been useful to particular projects. For example, we have not looked at psychoanalysis (one of Turkle's (1999) 'French lessons' comes from Lacan), as when Jerry Aline Fleiger (1997) asks 'Is Oedipus on-line?'. We could also have gone to the French feminists, such as Luce Irigaray, as Plant (1997) does in her writing on cyberfeminism. James Slevin (2000), meanwhile, theorizes the Internet with the help of Giddens and Bauman; media theorist Marshall McLuhan is highlighted by Levinson (1999) as a 'guide to the information millennium'; and Kevin Porter (2000) uses Barthes' work on mythologies (as well as Foucault) to think about cyberspace. The list could keep going – everyone has their favourite theories and theorists. We shall meet some more of these elsewhere in this book, in recognition of my own pick-'n'-mix approach – an approach that I think is one of the great merits of cultural studies.

In addition, we have not looked at theorists whose work has been *centrally* concerned with cyberculture – people such as Donna Haraway or Sherry Turkle. That's because their ideas appear throughout this book, and are explained and explored at multiple sites here. Cyberfeminism, cyborg theory, and other brands of 'cybertheory' have, of course, profoundly impacted upon the ways we think about science, technology, computers and cyberspace as cultural practices and artefacts. Not focusing on them here is, perhaps paradoxically, an indicator of how important their ideas are. To understand them, it is best to observe them *in situ*, to see them working in specific contexts – as we shall elsewhere in this book.

## Hot links

### Chapters from The Cybercultures Reader

Gareth Branwyn, 'Compu-sex: erotica for cybernauts' (Chapter 24: 396–402).

Thomas Foster, '"Trapped by the body": telepresence technologies and transgendered performance in feminist and lesbian rewritings of cyberpunk fiction' (Chapter 28: 439–59).

Donna Haraway, 'A cyborg manifesto: science, technology and socialist-feminism in the late twentieth century' (Chapter 18: 291–324).

Andrew Ross, 'Hacking away at the counter-culture' (Chapter 16: 254–67).

Stelarc, 'From psycho-body to cyber-systems: images as post-human entities' (Chapter 35: 560–76).

Michele Willson, 'Community in the abstract: a political and ethical dilemma?' (Chapter 42: 658–75).

### Further reading

Andrew Herman and Thomas Swiss (eds) (2000) *The World Wide Web and Contemporary Cultural Theory*, London: Routledge.

Donald MacKenzie and Judy Wajcman (eds) *The Social Shaping of Technology* (second edition), Buckingham: Open University Press.

Constance Penley and Andrew Ross (eds) (1991) *Technoculture*, Minneapolis: University of Minnesota Press.

Roddy Reid and Sharon Traweek (eds) (2000) *Doing Science + Culture: how cultural and interdisciplinary studies are changing the way we look at science and medicine*, London: Routledge.

## Websites

http://www.theory.org.uk
David Gauntlett's guide to contemporary culture: snappy and snazzy – the trading cards have already acquired cult status!

http://www.ctheory.com/ctheory.html
The Krokers' CTheory site – cutting-edge cybertheory, interviews and reviews.

http://www.otal.umd.edu/~rccs/
Resource Center for Cyberculture Studies, hosted by David Silver – reviews, links, news and promotion of cyberculture studies.

http://virtualsociety.sbs.ox.ac.uk/
Home page for the Virtual Society? Research programme, sponsored by the UK's Economic and Social Research Council – long list of projects, key findings, links.

# Chapter 5

# COMMUNITY AND CYBERCULTURE

Words on a screen are quite capable of . . . creating a community from a collection of strangers.

*Howard Rheingold*

ONE OF THE MOST PROMINENT and controversial aspects of emerging cybercultures is the question of community. In this chapter, I want to trace the debates about online or virtual communities, and look at research that attempts to shed light on the kinds of communities seen to be forming in cyberspace. The debate is controversial in that it highlights the tensions between different standpoints on the promises and limitations of cyberculture. It is also controversial because it has at its heart an argument about the relationship between online life and off-line 'real life' (RL). Finally, it is controversial because it involves making arguments about the status of RL communities as well as online communities. In each of these areas there has been considerable debate.

Getting a sense of perspective on the issues and questions surrounding online or virtual communities thus requires that we simultaneously look at arguments about off-line or RL communities. What are their contemporary characteristics? Have broader social, political, economic and cultural transformations altered our sense of membership and belonging in communities? These questions mean that we have to think about the changes brought about by processes such as detraditionalization, globalization and postmodernization – and then think about how these relate to arguments about RL and online community. We'll begin by looking at the broad terms of this debate.

## Arguments about community

Barry Wellman and Milena Gulia (1999) comment that much of the debate on virtual community has been polemical, split between those who argue that cyberspace re-enchants community (perceived as eroded in 'real life') on the one hand, and on the other those who argue that online community is damaging RL community, by encouraging a withdrawal from 'real life'. As they put it, the terms of this debate are problematic, in that they are 'Manichean, presentist, unscholarly, and parochial' (Wellman and Gulia 1999: 167). This means that, in their opinion, the debate is polarized into two totally opposing viewpoints (it is Manichean), lacks a sense of the history of community (it is presentist), depends largely on anecdote and 'travellers' tales' (it is unscholarly) and forces a separation between online life and RL (it is parochial). The two camps, which Wellman and Gulia refer to as 'duelling dualists', have thus established a partisan, antagonistic argument. While this is true to some extent – and it is certainly easy to find clear examples of both 'pro-' and 'anti-' arguments, as we shall see later – the debate has also generated considerable research, and a fuller picture of the overall 'terrain' of contemporary communities, both online and off, is emerging. It is that terrain that I want to explore here. So, while there are enthusiastic proponents of the social benefits of online community set in opposition to hostile critics of the phenomenon, it is possible to navigate a path somewhere between these camps, and to think about online community a bit more rigorously; and that's my aim in this chapter.

As I've already said, in order to get to grips with arguments about online community, we need to understand *arguments about community* as a whole – as James Slevin (2000: 91) writes, studies of online community need to be set in the broader context of 'a critical approach to the concept of "community" in late modernity'. So, we need to begin by thinking about what 'community' means today. And right from the start we begin to get a sense of the complexities of a term that is also very commonsensical and commonplace. Trying to summarize this in an earlier project with a very different focus – the food we eat – I once tried to elaborate on this:

> 'Community'. It's a word we all use, in many different ways, to talk about . . . what? About belonging and exclusion, about 'us' and 'them'. It's a common-sense thing, used in daily discussions, in countless associations, from 'care in the community' to the Community Hall; from 'community spirit' to the 'business community'. . . . Many of us would lay claim to belonging to at least one community, whether it is the 'lesbian and gay community' or just the 'local community' where we live. . . . [T]he term community is not only descriptive, but also normative and ideological: it carries a lot of baggage with it.
>
> (Bell and Valentine 1997: 93)

93

The study of community (and communities) has been a sustained effort to think through this complex; to think about what makes a community, and what its members get from belonging to that community (see Wilbur CR). In a lot of cases, the way this is approached is framed around something that is perceived to be a 'threat' to community – usually one or more of the transformations brought about by modernization (and subsequently post-modernization, as we shall see). Among the best-known examples of this kind of community-thinking comes from urban sociology – from the work and legacy of people like Ferdinand Tönnies and Louis Wirth from a century ago. Both argued that mass urbanization was transforming community – and transforming it for the worse (see Jary and Jary 1991).

Tönnies' (1955) *Community and Association*, originally published in 1887, outlined two types of 'community', named *Gemeinschaft* and *Gesellschaft*. The former is characterized as a 'total community': as fully integrated vertically and horizontally, as stable and long-lasting, as comprised of a dense web of social interaction supported by commonality and mutuality, manifest in shared rituals and symbols – as a local social contract embedded in place and made durable by face-to-face interactions. This is the 'traditional' community, where everyone knows everyone, everyone helps everyone, and the bonds between people are tight and multiple (someone's neighbour is also their workmate *and* the person they go drinking with *and* their relative, etc.). Set against this, and ushered in by urbanization, is the social arrangement Tönnies names *Gesellschaft* ('association' or 'society'). City folk, the argument goes, are removed from *Gemeinschaft*-like situations, and thrown together in the dense heterogeneity of the city. Their long-established bonds and norms are lost, and the social fabric is radically transformed. People's relationships become shallow and instrumental – because the city is so huge, *Gemeinschaft*-like communities can never grow; people are too busy, always on the move. This disembedding impoverishes communities, even as it broadens the social sphere: we might meet more people, but our relationships with them are partial and transitory. As Kollock and Smith (1999: 16) lament, 'there is a great deal of loneliness in the lives of many city dwellers'. The 'problems' of urbanization identified in Tönnies' formulation have, many would argue, been deepened by transformations brought about by post-modernization, which has radically reshaped the contemporary cityscape (Davis 1990).

The *ideal* of community enshrined in *Gemeinschaft* has an enduring legacy in the popular imagination, then, always (it seems) tinged with nostalgia. It might be argued, in fact, that community has become overwritten by nostalgia, in that the way it is talked about so often focuses on its perceived loss, or decline, or erosion. In party-political rhetoric, for example, community is seen as the stable bulwark of society, imagined in distinctly romantic, *Gemeinschaft*-like ways (epitomized in the UK by village life and in the US by small-town life). Contemporary social, political, economic and cultural transformations are today implicated in the 'death' of this kind of community. We need, therefore, to look at insights into the contemporary meanings of community, and their contestation.

We'll start with a discussion of one particular form of community, since the insights it offers will benefit our discussion. The type of community is the nation, and the insight comes from Benedict Anderson (1983), who famously suggested that nations are *imagined communities*. What this means is that the work of making a nation as a community depends on the use of symbolic resources and devices: because we can never know or interact with all those others with whom we share national identification, we need 'things' to coalesce a shared sense of identity around – a flag, a national anthem, a set of customs and rituals (sometimes referred to as 'invented traditions'). These kinds of communities, moreover, only exist because their members *believe* in them, and maintain them through shared cultural practices (Edensor 2001). We can make productive use of Anderson's insight at scales other than the nation, to consider the extent to which *all* communities are imagined and held together by shared cultural practice (rather than just face-to-face interaction). When we come to explore online communities in detail, this will be an important thing to remember.

Aside from the idea of imagined communities, what I want to do here is look at some of the processes that, like urbanization for Tönnies, are frequently signalled as in some way or another *threatening* community (though it might be less scare-mongering for us to say that they are *transforming* community). A lot of these are conceived as symbolic or symptomatic of late-modern (or post-modern) societies (Giddens 1991). I've already listed a couple of these, so let's return to them and flesh them out a bit. The first concept is *detraditionaliza-tion*, or the shift towards a 'post-traditional' society. The erosion of tradition is itself associated with another key transformation, *disembedding* – in turn linked with a third process, *globalization*. We need to discuss these together, as they are centrally implicated in changes to ideas of community.

*Globalization* can be thought of as the sum of a series of processes that have forged a sense of increasing connectedness between people and places dispersed around the world. It is defined quite neatly by Malcolm Waters (1995: 3) as 'a social process in which the constraints of geography on social and cultural arrangements recede and in which people become increasingly aware that they are receding'. Innovations in transport and communication have effectively shrunk the world – a process sometimes called 'time–space compression' (Harvey 1989). All kinds of things now move speedily around the world, criss-crossing it in complex, disjunctive ways: people, ideas, images, commodities, technologies, money (Appadurai 1996). All of these things, and our experience of them, are thus *disembedded* – no longer rooted in place, but characterized as global *flows*.

As Waters' definition makes clear, an important aspect of globalization is our *experience* or perception of this reshaping and shrinking of the world. Late-modernity, it has been argued, is marked by heightened *reflexivity* (Giddens 1991) – by a kind of self-scrutiny and self-consciousness, by which we rework our sense of who we are in the face of the global flows we come into contact with. Part of this reflexivity involves making choices about our identities and our politics; since we are *disembedded*, and able to access global flows of ideas and information, we can choose who we want to be (within certain structural limitations, of course!). And this disembeddedness and reflexivity enables us to question and transform the taken-for-granted, leading to *detraditionalization* (Heelas *et al.* 1996) – a chance to make over the social fabric anew and, in terms of our focus here, to *imagine* new forms of community.

Now, while all this sounds quite exhilarating, some critics argue that it has severe negative impacts for us all, for example by making us 'schizo-phrenic', and giving us a 'depthless' existence (Jameson 1991). Moreover, these processes may have transformed the forms and functions of commu-nity, but they have not led to an erosion of the *ideal* of community – in fact, many commentators have argued that the '*uncertainization*' of late-modern societies actually strengthens our need to 'belong' (Slevin 2000). As we shall see, in many such accounts there emerges a problematic *essentializing* of this need, which theorizes community as a 'natural' manifestation of an 'innate' human desire for association and identification – and this motif resurfaces in discussions of online communities, too.

Added to these concerns about late-modern or postmodern life are analyses of the intensification of the 'problems' of urban living under late modernity. As cities sprawl and fracture, and become the battleground for forms of social, economic and political struggle, so they become increasingly characterized as landscapes of alienation and foreboding. Ziauddin Sardar (CR: 743) writes that cities have come to be seen as 'little more than alien perpendicular tangles', adding that 'inner cities resemble bomb sites and fear and loathing stalk the streets'. 'White flight' and 'fortressing' – the paranoid emptying-out of cities as middle-class citizens retreat to gated suburban and exurban 'planned communities' – can thus be read as responses to this partic-ular city vision (Goldberg 2000). (Of course, the flipside to this formulation – as we shall see – is cities as spectacular sites of difference and cosmopolitan syncretism; see Young 2000.)

All of this, it should now be clear, has tremendous implications for how we think about community, and is useful for our discussion of online commu-nity. The notion of imagined community means that we can rethink how we conceptualize (and create) communities – and the Internet is an imaginative space to do this. Globalization can be argued to open up the whole world as a potential source of community – and the Internet has been seen as key to this. Disembedding allows us to choose our communities – and the Internet gives us a vast reservoir of choices. Reflexivity allows us to think about who we are and who we want to be – and the Internet is the ideal site to 'play' with our identities. Detraditionalization frees us from old obligations, and lets us give community a postmodern make-over – and again the Internet offers possibilities to substantially re-imagine the very notion of community. Cities have become too big, too fractured, too scary – and the Internet offers a safe space to build new communities in. In sum, in the face of all this disembedding, detraditionalizing, globalizing uncertainty, we need to find new way to belong – and the Internet is on hand to provide exactly that.

There is, however, an important paradox to be recognized here, summed up by this question: *is the Internet the solution or part of the problem?* As Heather Bromberg puts it:

> It does seem clear that people make use of this technology to combat the symptoms that are characteristic of . . . the 'postmodern condition'. The technologies themselves are highly characteristic of the postmodern by virtue of their fluidity and malleability. Ironically, however, it is their fluid and malleable nature which leads them to be used to combat that 'condition'.

> (Bromberg 1996: 147)

As we shall see, there are different perspectives on this matter. What should now be apparent, then, is that cyberspace is certainly seen to be *intensifying* the transformations in late-modern (or postmodern) conceptions and uses of community. It is not unique – as Wellman and Gulia (1999) remind us – but its role cannot be denied, and shouldn't be downplayed. Ultimately, however, we return to the central questions fought over by those 'duelling dualists' of online community: *Are these transformations in community a good thing or a bad thing? Are virtual communities ameliorating or exacerbating these transformations in the forms and meanings of community?* We need to turn our attention to those questions now.

## Arguments about online community

> Cyberspace is already the home of thousands of groups of people who meet to share information, discuss mutual interests, play games, and carry out business. Some of these groups are both large and well developed, but critics argue that these groups do not constitute *real* communities. Something is missing, they argue, that makes these online communities pale substitutes for more traditional face-to-face communities. Other respond that not only are online communities real

communities, but also that they have the potential to support face-to-face communities and help hold local communities together.

(Kollock and Smith 1999: 16)

In order to get a fix on arguments around online community, I want to begin by looking at the writings of Howard Rheingold, often cited as among the most enthusiastic proponents of the individual and social benefits of online community life. I will draw on the ideas he presents in an essay called 'A slice of life in my virtual community', first published in 1992 (Rheingold 1999) – ideas that recur in his book-length argument *for* online community, *Virtual Community: homesteading on the electronic frontier* (Rheingold 1993). Already, the title of that book might give us a hint at Rheingold's position – something which as also been seized upon by those who criticize his vision, as we shall see. The use of the terms 'homesteading' and 'frontier' give us a particular imagining of community, typical of what Wellman and Gulia (1999) identify as a nostalgic, pastoralist 'myth' of community. Rheingold is unapologetic about this, describing virtual community as 'a bit like a neighborhood pub or coffee shop' (422) and comparing its spirit of mutuality with 'barn-raising' (425). So, what is his version of online community like? He describes it thus:

In cyberspace, we chat and argue, engage in intellectual intercourse, perform acts of commerce, exchange knowledge, share emotional support, make plans, brainstorm, gossip, feud, fall in love, find friends and lose them, play games and metagames, flirt, create a little high art and a lot of idle talk. We do everything people do when they get together, but we do it with words on computer screens, leaving our bodies behind. Millions of us have already built communities where our identities commingle and interact electronically, independent of local time or location.

(Rheingold 1999: 414)

This process is, for Rheingold, simultaneously surprising and inevitable. It's inevitable for two reasons. First, it's inevitable because folks 'are going to do what people always do with a new communication technology: use it in ways never intended or foreseen by its inventors, to turn old social codes inside out and make new kinds of communities possible' (415). Second, it's inevitable because virtual communities are a natural response to 'the hunger for community that has followed the disintegration of traditional communities around the world' (418). In the place of these communities, we are left with the 'automobile-centric, suburban, highrise, fast food, shopping mall way of life' (421), which is lonely, isolated, empty. There's the logic of this kind of thesis on online communities: 'traditional communities' have disintegrated (an interesting choice of word, implying they have fallen apart and *dis-integrated*, i.e. become too heterogeneous), and human ingenuity, combined with a 'hunger' for community, can rewire CMC to rebuild those 'lost' communities in cyberspace – which is itself presented as virgin terrain, as a new 'frontier' ripe for barn-raising and communo-genesis.

Online communities are therefore thought of here as growing 'organically' to fill the space left by the demise of 'traditional' communities; at its simplest, online community-formation occurs 'when enough people bump into each other often enough in cyberspace' (413). *Virtual Community* expands this organic metaphor:

> In terms of the way the whole system is propagating and evolving, think of cyberspace as a social petri dish, the Net the agar medium, and *virtual communities, in all their diversity, as colonies of microorganisms that grow in petri dishes*. . . . Whenever CMC technology becomes available to people anywhere, they *inevitably* build virtual communites with it, just as microorganisms inevitably create colonies.
>
> (Rheingold 1993: 6; my emphasis)

There's a lot to think about in this formulation of cyberspace-as-petri-dish (as a kind of 'growth medium') and online communities as microorganisms that *inevitably* grow in the medium. It's troublesome in its essentializing of community-formation, for one thing; it also conjures particular images of communities as mould- or germ-like.

Rheingold fleshes out online community life by walking us through his 'virtual neighborhood' on the WELL – the Whole Earth 'Lectronic Link, a pioneering Bay Area based virtual community that grew out of the productive intersection in San Francisco of 1960s *Whole Earth* counterculture, computer hackers and hobbyists, and 'deadheads' (Grateful Dead fans) (on the 'secret history' of this melding, see Davis 1998). In the increasingly complex and heterogeneous world of the WELL, Rheingold indentifies those 'places' he most often visits as his 'customized neighborhood' (431); added together, these 'places' make a mosaic of his interests, intersecting with the interests of fellow WELLers. That the community condenses out of individuals' interests is made clear by Rheingold himself, in a passage where he compares the possibilities for finding likeminds in cyberspace with the difficulties of doing that through other media:

> You can't simply pick up a phone and ask to be connected with someone who wants to talk about Islamic art or California wine, or someone with a three year old daughter or a 30 year old Hudson; you can, however, join a computer conference on any of those topics, then open a public or private correspondence with the previously-unknown people you find in that conference.
>
> (Rheingold 1999: 423)

So, the possibility of community arises from shared interests – these then catalyse the social bonds that extend beyond the narrow focus of those interests. But how does a sense of community develop from that? Rheingold answers this question by discussing shared social codes ('netiquette') and reciprocity ('knowledge-potlatching') as social cement to bind those interest-groups as communities. In *Virtual Community*, he adds longevity, critical mass and 'sufficient human feeling' as the bonding material that turns association into community (Rheingold 1993: 5).

Now, I was mulling this over last night, as I drove home from work, and an analogy came to me. It was prompted by Steve Jones' (1995) comparison of the building of highways across America and the construction of the information superhighway, and by Rhiengold's mention of his '30 year old Hudson', and by a discussion by Wellman and Gulia (1999) about a BMW aficionados' online discussion group – and by sitting in my car. As a bridge between virtual community (above) and its discontents (below), then, I'd like to think this through. The analogy is this: I drive a car. *To what extent could I argue that I belong to a 'community of car drivers'?* Let's work it up. Part of my identity is as a 'car driver' – institutionalized by things like my driving licence (which gives me certain privileges, and functions as a broader 'badge' of my identity, to prove who I am). In that, I share part of my identity with other car drivers – it is something we have in common. This can itself be formalized or deepened (by joining an owner's club for my model of car, for example). Also, I might talk to another car driver about cars or driving, and through that build up a broader 'friendship' with them. I have a set of knowledges that all car drivers have to varying degrees: knowledge about driving, and about cars (though this has its limits – like my knowledge about computers – and I sometimes have to turn to 'experts' for help). Moreover, the 'community of car drivers' has a set of social conventions, some of them formalized (the Highway Code), some of them tacit (driving etiquette, like letting someone pull out in front of me at a junction). There's a broad reciprocity to this: if I let someone pull out in front of me, she or he might do the same favour for another driver. Likewise, if I break down at the side of the road, I hope that a passing driver might stop to help me out, just as I would assist a stranded fellow traveller. The community informally polices the transgression of this social code – by honking the horn, for example (and at its most extreme, by road rage). And my car also facilitates my membership of 'off-road' communities: when I drive to visit my family, or car-share with a colleague, or give a neighbour a ride home, or pick up a hitch-hiker. So, I return to my question: *does that make me part of a car driving community?* Whether the answer is 'Yes' or 'No' has, I think, implications for the question of online community. I think for now, however, my best answer is an unemphatic 'Maybe'. In order to transpose this conundrum to cyberspace, I'd like now to map out the ways in which online communities are 'made'.

## What makes an online community?

Let me start here by sharing another of my conundrums: I have been worrying about the distinction between a 'community' and a 'subculture' — especially since some of the groups I discuss as cybersubcultures in Chapter 8 have been named as communities by other researchers. For example, Nancy Baym (1998) discusses online soap opera fans as a 'community', and Nessim Watson (1997) describes fans of 'jam rock' band Phish as a virtual community, even as he debates the usefulness of the very term 'online community'. On the other hand, right at the start of *Virtual Community*, Howard Rheingold (1993: 2) calls the WELL a 'full-scale sub-culture', and Catherine Bassett (1997: 538) describes LambdaMOO as composed of 'subcultural spaces'. Clearly, in some instances, there's merely a slippage between the two words, both taken to mean the same thing — Baym's own work has used both to describe the same group of online soap fans, for example. But I think that the two words have very different *connotations*, so I started to wonder where the boundary between terms like these lies. I thought that maybe researchers looking at online social formations might more readily describe their study groups as communities than those who look at offline groups. Ziauddin Sardar expresses his exasperation at the misuses of 'community' in cyberspace:

> Belonging and posting to a Usenet group, or logging on to a bulletin board community, confirms no more an identity than belonging to a stamp collecting club or a Morris dancing society. . . . On this logic, the accountants of the world will instantly be transformed into a community the moment they start a newsgroup: *alt.accountants* (with *alt.accountants.spreadsheets* constituting a sub-community).
>
> (Sardar CR: 743)

I think we can guess from this that Sardar wouldn't see car drivers as a community, then! But his point is a valid one; some online groups aren't communities, and neither do they self-identify as communities. They may be too 'task-oriented' (and therefore not 'social' enough), or might not stimulate sufficient interaction to develop 'group-specific meanings', or they might be too divided and divisive to coalesce (Baym 1998). Shawn Wilbur (CR: 55) raises this question, too, when he asks if we can tell the difference between 'a community and a market segment, or a culture of compatible consumption?' I'd like to add my own question to his: why is it that commentators are so keen to see *communities* (rather than market segments or cultures of compatible consumption) in cyberspace?

Could it be that the technology effectively turns a subculture into a community? Bruno Latour (1991) once wrote that 'technology is society made durable', which we could maybe see as a way of thinking about how computers might make a subculture into a community. Or, does the technology merely give us a silicon-induced *illusion* of community? The 'aura' of cybertechnology – which we'll pick up on again later – might in fact be the cement that binds these communities together, just as earlier 'communications communities' were seen to form around the telegraph, the radio and the television (Stone CR). Paradoxically, of course, technologies such as the car are seen as moving us in the opposite direction – atomizing individuals in their 'metal cocoons' (Lupton 1999). Some technologies are seen as collectivizing, others as individuating, therefore. Computers presently sit uneasily in this formulation, potentially able to go either way, or pulling both ways simultaneously. Which direction you prioritize, it seems, depends on your perspective on and experience of computers and communities.

Baym (1998) gets round this issue by arguing that an online community is a community if participants *imagine* themselves as a community. And given the positively-invested rhetoric of community, it's understandable why there might indeed be a 'will-to-community'. In that sense, car drivers *might* imagine themselves as a community – for example when their 'right' or 'freedom' to enact their identities is threatened (by car tax or fuel prices), but in that kind of context community is a *defensive* concept, bringing people together only when they feel under collective threat. Maybe the 'ambient fear' of the death of community is the threat that prompts defensive communo-genesis in cyberspace, then? I doubt we can resolve this question here, but it's worth keeping in mind as we move now to look the 'stuff' of virtual communities.

Latour's aphorism about technology being society made durable refers to technology in its broadest sense, to the material traces left by social interaction (texts, tools, etc.) that 'carry' the society beyond the face-to-face. In the immaterial world of cyberculture, there are material traces, too – the texts that constitute the shared space of community: '[s]table patterns of social meanings, manifested through a group's on-going discourse, . . . enable participants to *imagine themselves part of a community*' (Baym 1998: 62; my emphasis). Analysing these discursive patterns has been a central strategy for getting inside online communities, and 'talk-and-text' type readings of online interactions are commonplace in the literature (see Watson 1997; Baym 1998, for examples discussed in this chapter).

The discursive patterns that most interest me are the social codes developed within online communities; the ways in which members of communities establish group norms and find ways to put these in place. These are interesting stories for a number of reasons. They reveal the implicit assumptions about what makes a community (what things are needed: money? laws? guns?), and they reveal the *limits* of the community. In order to explore these issues, I want to begin by looking at work on the kinds of social contracts drawn up in MUDs, and then move over to a virtual 'city', Lucasfilm's Habitat.

Kollock and Smith (1999) provide a summary of forms of social control in MUDs. It should be remembered that MUDs are particular kinds of online communities, with their origins in the fantasy role-playing world of Dungeons and Dragons. There has been a branching into two distinct types, 'social MUDs' and 'adventure MUDs', with the latter retaining most prominently the 'sword and sorcery' motifs (although this can still be traced in 'social MUDs' like LambdaMOO). The social codes therefore reflect the virtual world created – a world of magic and mayhem, where characters might kill or be killed, or use 'voodoo' to 'rape' each other (Dibbell 1999). Even when behaviour isn't that dramatic, the 'disinhibition' experienced online allows participants to behave in ways they wouldn't dream of doing IRL (Slevin 2000).

The list of modes of social control in MUDs picked out by Kollock and Smith includes eliminating specific commands in the software (such as the 'shout' command, to stop rowdiness); instituting 'gag' commands to silence miscreants; restricting the 'rights' of troublesome participants; public shaming; banishment; introducing admission policies (to vet potential participants); registering participants' identities (to increase accountability and prohibit anonymity); forming regulatory committees; establishing frameworks for mediation; and vigilante action. The less 'extreme' end of this spectrum includes elements of 'netiquette', which covers minor transgressions such as shouting, cross-posting, lurking and flaming. However, Elizabeth Reid's (1999) work on adventure MUDs refers to the prominence of public displays of punishment there as a return to 'Medieval' forms of social control, reversing Foucault's (1986) famous discussion of the historical move from punishment to discipline – an analysis at odds with the supposed 'freedom' on offer in cyberspace.

In his widely-known discussion of online 'rape', Julian Dibbell (1999) shows how the crisis brought about by Mr Bungle's use of 'voodoo' in LambdaMOO galvanized the community into a heated debate about appropriate modes of intervention and sanction. The fall-out from that singular event radically transformed the structure of LambdaMOO, ushering in universal suffrage, an arbitration system, and the facility to eject troublesome visitors (the '@boot' command). As for Mr Bungle, perpetrator of the virtual 'rape', he was 'killed' by one of the MUD's wizards (though he soon returned under a new name, Dr Jest). For Dibbell, this incident 'turned a database into a society'. Against this, Kolko and Reid read instances like this as moments of 'breakdown', in which 'the inability of the community to collaborate effectively interrupted daily routines' (Kolko and Reid 1998: 225) – the 'consensual hallucination' of cyberspace has to be matched by 'consensual discourse' if communities are going to be sustainable. Importantly, Kolko and Reid stress the problem for communo-genesis posed by the multiplicity of on-line identities – or, more accurately, from the way that multiplicity is re-singularized online. As people fracture their sense of self into multiple online selves, they paradoxically produce a portfolio of singularities, rather than recognizing that multiplicity dwells within an individual self. As they write, 'it has been all too easy for virtual communities to encourage multiplicity but not coherence, with each individual persona having a limited, undiversified social range' (227). This compartmentalization stands in the way of community-building in that it produces rigid online identities, making conflict-resolution and accommodation difficult. As we shall see later in this chapter, this issue is linked to the problematic of online community's dealings with otherness.

My second story of online social contract comes from Lucasfilm's Habitat, an early experiment in virtual cityscaping (see Ostwald and Stone CR). The evolution of a 'community' or 'society' in Habitat – different from LambdaMOO in that it is a graphical computer environment complete with buildings and avatars (cartoon-like depictions of Habitat's inhabitants, who can move around, and 'talk' to each other in speech-bubbles) – gives us another interesting set of insights into online community. Ostwald (CR) plots the story of Habitat, which also has part of its ancestry in role-play gaming, describing how inhabitants made a virtual community come to life on screen. As with Dibbell's reading of LambdaMOO, the first incidents to turn this software environment into a society were crimes, though in this case they were robberies. The 'Gods' who programmed Habitat refused to intervene, leaving the residents to sort the problem out – the crime-wave was meantime escalating, as the robbers now had guns (weapons were already in place in Habitat, as part of its gaming ancestry). Murders were committed, and gangs went on killing sprees (although avatars would rise from the dead next day). A meeting was called, a sheriff appointed, and some basic laws were hastily drawn up. Once these bedrocks had been established, Habitat grew in a recognizable way – like a town from the Old West. A church and a newspaper were established; the economic system stabilized and some folks got rich; formalized forms of government, with elections, were put in place. Before it was closed down (due largely to external factors), Habitat had become a simulation of smalltown America – showing us, I think, that self-organized communities in cyberspace can indeed perform a Rheingold-like act of homesteading. Of course, that they *needed* to perform homesteading is equally revealing – that a settled political, legal and economic system had to emerge to stem the tide of anarchy and lawlessness. We might say that the Habitat social experiment therefore failed, in that it produced a conservative virtual community. That's one prominent criticism levelled at online communities, and I want now to turn to this and other arguments *against* online community.

## Arguments against online community

To begin with – and I know this might seem unfair, or biased – I want to look specifically at arguments against Howard Rheingold. In his essay 'Cyberspace and the world we live in', Kevin Robins (in Bell and Kennedy 2000) gives Rheingold's virtual community thesis a thorough working over. Robins begins his critique by reminding us that any thinking we might do about cybercommunities has to be located in 'the world we live in': 'virtual communities do not exist in a different world. They must be situated in the context of [the] . . . new cultural and political geographies' of our time, he writes (CR: 86). What particularly concerns Robins, in fact, is the way in which the relationship between online life and RL is framed by writers like Rheingold. As he puts it, we can see in arguments for virtual community 'the sense of virtual reality as an alternative reality in a *world gone wrong*. Techno-sociality is seen as the basis for developing new and *compensatory* forms of community and conviviality' (87; my emphasis). In this 'world gone wrong', community has become a 'lost object', nostalgized and looked-for (or longed-for) in cyberspace. In particular, Robins argues, the sense of 'community' mobilized in accounts like Rheingold's 'freezes' history, and turns away from broader questions of society and politics: 'what we have is the preservation through simulation of old forms of solidarity and community. In the end, not an alternative society, but an alternative to society' (89). And, in its desire for a kind of smalltown, *Gemeinschaft*-like community, Rheingold's vision neutralizes difference, producing a virtual version of the American 'fortress communities' that Mike Davis (1990) describes. For all their proponents' chatter about inclusion and heterogeneity, the space of online community is, rather, a 'domain of order, refuge, withdrawal' (Robins CR: 91). As he writes in another essay, 'virtual culture is a culture of retreat from the world' (Robins 1999: 166). Arthur and Marilouise Kroker describe the withdrawal into VR as 'bunkering in':

> bunkering in is about something really simple: being sick of others and trying to shelter the beleaguered self in a techno-bubble. . . . Digital reality is perfect. It provides the bunker self with immediate, universal access to a global community *without people*: electronic communication without social contact, being digital without being human, going on-line without leaving the safety of the electronic bunker.
>
> (Kroker and Kroker CR: 96–7)

Being 'sick of others' reminds us that membership of online communities is elective and selective, as is withdrawal: 'cyberspace community is self-selecting; . . . it is contingent and transitory, depending on a shared interest of those with the attention-span of a thirty-second soundbite' (Sardar

105

CR: 744). Moreover, 'bunkering in' means cocooning oneself from the 'contamination of pluralism' found in the RL city (*Ibid*): being 'sick of others' thus also implies being sick of *otherness* – a point we shall return to later. Ultimately, Robins reads virtual life as regressive, infantile and Edenic (the second VR life-strategy the Krokers highlight is 'dumbing down'), and its will-to-community as manifesting a 'familial communitarianism' (Robins CR: 92; see also Robins 1999). (This should also remind us that in RL, too, similar sentiments are expressed in communitarian rhetoric seen, for example, in New Labour; see Driver and Martell 1997.)

Steve Jones also does some deconstructive work on visions of virtual community, and his comments are equally insightful and useful to us here. For example, he argues that:

> The situation in which we find computer-mediated communities at present is that their very definition as communities is perceived as a 'good thing', creating a solipsistic and self-fulfilling community that pays little attention to political action outside of that which secures its own maintenance. Community and power do not necessarily intersect, but such solipsism is a form of power, wielded by those who occupy the community.
>
> (Jones 1995: 25)

Moreover, Jones questions the entire 'community ideal', asking why we continue to hold up face-to-face interaction (or interface-to-interface interaction in cyberspace) as the best way to relate to one another and as the building-block of community. However, he argues that we always experience something lacking in the online simulacra of face-to-face interaction – and it might be that this 'gap' or 'lack' itself feeds the yearning for community: we're looking for that 'lost object', and will it into being on our screens.

Jones' point about the fetish of community is interesting, in that we need to contest the notion of community as a 'good thing'. Whenever I've talked with students about *Gemeinschaft*-like communities, the tales they tell of their experiences are equally ambivalent: the strong ties matched with small minds, community spirit matched with oppressive regulation, safety matched with surveillance. *The place where everybody knows your name is also the place where everyone knows your business.* Small, tight-knit communities are fine if you fit in, but are incredibly exclusive and uncomfortable places if you don't – witness the mass migrations of 'outcasts' such as sexual minorities from the country to the city (Bell and Binnie 2000). However, as Wellman and Gulia (1999) write, most RL communities are no longer like that – so why are online communitarians trying to reclaim a virtual *Gemeinschaft*? Are there no other ways of thinking about online sociality?

## Beyond online community?

In his book on new social movements, *Expressions of Identity*, Kevin Hetherington (1998) revisits Tönnies' work in the context of 'neo-tribes', also drawing on the notion of the *Bund*, or communion – partly because it offers a better way to think through the kinds of groups he's interested in. As he says, '[t]he term community is far too vague and its association with the organic, traditional and ascriptive ideas of a past way of life is too inaccurate when trying to account for . . . elective identifications and groupings' (Hetherington 1998: 83). Gordon Graham (1999: 131) also highlights the increasing conceptual meaninglessness of the term, arguing that 'it seems that we cannot fail to be members of some community or other'. Given the inaptitude of community as a term to describe online groupings, as noted by both Hetherington and Graham, might Hetherington's revival of the *Bund* offer us a new way of thinking about what people do together in cyberspace?

A now-neglected sociological concept, *Bund* was partly conceived (by Herman Schmalenbach, in the 1920s) as a 'third term' to add to Tönnies' dichotomy – and Hetherington reintroduces it in a way that, I think, is incredibly useful for thinking about online sociality. (Hetherington never turns his attention to online life, though he ponders in a footnote the possibility of exploring *Bünde* in cyberspace.) It might be, even, that talking of the 'virtual *Bund*' can lead us out of the impasse of arguments for or against virtual community.

Hetherington quotes from Freund (1978), who was busy dismissing the term *Bund* as 'a place for the expression of enthusiasms, of ferment, of unusual doings' (quoted in Hetherington 1998: 88) – to me, that sounds a lot like descriptions found in texts like *Virtual Community*. A *Bund*, then, is an elective grouping, bonded by affective and emotional solidarity, sharing a strong sense of belonging. Schmalenbach also identified the presence of 'charismatic governance' in *Bünde* (as a corrective to Weber); while this might imply a charismatic leader, Hetherington argues than charisma can also be collective: '[t]erms like 'energy' and 'commitment', describing characteristics that all members are expected to exhibit, are the means by which this generalized charisma is likely to be expressed' (93). In terms of cyberspace, we might add a notion of 'techno-charisma' – the aura of new technologies that lends them a charismatic appeal (Davis 1998). What's useful about this notion, then, is it allows us to disentangle ourselves from the Manichean, presentist, unscholarly and parochial arguments about online community; by recognizing that the problem is at least in part the over-freighted term 'community' itself. Ananda Mitra (CR: 677) spots this, too – as the trouble with 'the way we have been naturalized to think of communities'.

Hetherington also fleetingly discusses ways of re-evaluating *Gesellschaft*-like sociality, drawing principally on Georg Simmel's work on the ways in which individuals manage the heterogeneity and ephemerality of urban life (see Simmel 1995; originally published 1903). As Hetherington describes, Simmel's writings show how 'the individual uses the alienating experiences of modern life to promote a more cosmopolitan form of individuality' (Hetherington 1998: 95). This expressive individual, who wears his or her identity on the surfaces of his or her body, performs a new mode of communication based on signs. A similar manoeuvre – to turn urban anomie into something productive – can be found in other accounts, too. In terms of online communities, for example, Wellman and Gulia (1999) describe online life as city life; or, more accurately, as living 'in the heart of densely populated, heterogeneous, *physically safe*, big cities' (172; my emphasis) – note the stress on 'virtual safety', which marks cyberspace as preferable to cityspace.

Simmel's emphasis on making individuality work on the stage of the city streets also reminds me of Henning Bech's (1997) up-beat account of gay men's urban lives: of cruising, the gaze, the endless passage of strangers, the brief encounters. Anonymity, heterogeneity and ephemerality are here celebrated, even fetishized. Now, while I have a lot of sympathy for Bech's thesis, the introduction of homosexuality also makes me mindful of the exclusions and prohibitions played out in urban space (and not just for 'sexual dissidents'). Cities of difference are also spaces of exclusion. This rejoinder ushers in the final question for this chapter.

## Whose online community?

> While Internet use may hold out the possibility of emancipation, we must at the same time be aware of how it might create new mechanisms of suppression.
>
> (Slevin 2000: 109)

In order to think about inclusion and exclusion in online communities, I need to remind readers of the issues of information inequality that have already been highlighted in Chapter 2. Joining an online community is, in many accounts, described as unproblematic or 'easy' – *all you need is a computer and a modem*. Considering the question of who can find a 'home' in cyberspace, Susan Leigh Star in fact listed these minimal requirements (CR): having sufficient money to buy the equipment, and living in a 'traditional home' with the telecommunications infrastructure needed for connection (or access to these facilities at work); having access to 'maintenance people' to help out and to facilitate getting 'plugged in'; possessing the requisite physical and educational abilities (being literate, being able to sit at a computer and type – or being aided in that process); and having the time, inclination and ability to build up a social network, to make and sustain membership of a 'community'. Stacked up like that, we can see the many obstacles that stand in a lot of people's way.

Even assuming those obstacles can be overcome, things needn't be plain sailing from here on in. All kinds of social and cultural barriers are also in place. Most online communities beyond the scale of the national are still usually run in English, for one thing. Then there are the ways in which 'appropriate' criteria for membership might put up blocks, or lead to expulsion. Stone (CR) discusses an early San Francisco-based BBS known as CommuniTree, which worked as a homogeneous online community until it became too widely accessible (when Apple began giving computers to schools). The orderly community became rapidly 'choked to death' by the volume of postings, mainly from adolescent schoolkids. The 'Gods' who operated the system hadn't factored this kind of material into their vision of CommuniTree. In the end, as Stone writes, 'unlimited access to all conferences did not work in the context of increasing availability of terminals to young men who did not necessarily share the Tree gods' ideas of what counted as community. As one Tree veteran put it, "The barbarian hordes mowed us down" (Stone CR: 511). What this example shows us is one particular limit of one BBS – that it couldn't cope with the 'barbarian hordes', the undesirable others. As in Rheingold's writing of online community, the ideal-type is a friendly neighbourhood or coffee bar, where difference is contained.

Moreover, the broader question of difference online needs to be added to this mix. As discussed in Chapter 6, the possibilities for 'identity-play' in cyberspace have complex implications for how otherness is produced and consumed online. MUDs like LambdaMOO, which allow participants to construct fantastical new identities, tend towards forms of self-presentation that suppress RL axes of difference in favour of mystical hybrids and shape-shifters. Where RL identities are mobilized – notably gender identities – these tend to be stereotypical 'hyper-genderings' (Bassett 1997). So, some kinds of difference are fetishized, while others are invisibilized. Online disembodiment (or re-embodiment), held as liberatory, therefore raises intensely problematic questions about otherness in cybercommunities. As Sardar (CR: 744) laments, 'the totalizing on-line character of cyberspace ensures that the marginalized stay marginalized'.

Michele Willson's 'Community in the abstract' (CR) is insightful in this regard, especially in its discussion of online community membership as essentially self-serving: the benefits of membership are often described in terms of the individual member's quality of life, rather than in the quality of *relations between subjects*. Drawing on Jean-Luc Nancy's philosophical ponderings on community, Willson asks that we pay more attention to the sharing of the relationship between beings as constitutive of community. Insights from Emmanuel Levinas, provided by Tony Gorman's work on cities, similarly provide us with a rewriting of community, in this case as 'reciprocal alterity', or as 'a freely constituted ethical association founded on the indirect absolute recognition of all by each' (Gorman 2000: 225). Squaring these kinds of formulations with the evidence from online communities brings the question of otherness (alterity) in cyberspace into stark relief.

Dealing with difference online is partly a matter of boundary-drawing. As we've already seen, compartmentalizing the heterogeneity of cyberspace into 'neighbourhoods' of shared interests has become one important way in which communities are coalesced. Cohesion within the community is therefore sustained by bounding-out other communities (as well as individuals) – although there are overlaps between communities embodied in the mosaic of groups any member belongs to. Cross-posting between the communities someone belongs to can bring different communities into textual contact with one another. While this can be a productive cross-fertilization process, it can sometimes have antagonistic outcomes, as Ananda Mitra shows in his work on soc.culture.indian (CR).

What these few examples have in common, then, is that they serve as a reminder of the problematic relationship between community and exclusion. Finding ways to enlarge community (as a concept) and communities (as practised), as Willson and Gorman both propose, is one way to deal with this problem. Jettisoning the whole concept, and replacing it with something more suitable – *Bund*, maybe – is another strategy. I don't think we can resolve the question here; but we will need to keep a close eye on cybercommunities *and* our ways of understanding them, as both evolve symbiotically. Being mindful of the ways communities deal with difference, rather than merely celebrating their inclusivity, must be high on the agenda of everyone involved in thinking about communities in cyberspace.

## Summary

This chapter has outlined some key arguments about online communities, setting these in the context of transformations in the forms and meanings of community brought about by broader social, economic, political and cultural processes. Cyberspace is located at the heart of these processes. However, some people argue that cyberspace is the solution to the 'problem' of community (where real-life communities are seen to by 'dying'), while others suggest that cyberspace is in fact making thing worse (by encouraging further withdrawal from 'real-life'). In order to explore both sides of this debate, I worked through Howard Rheingold's writing, which seeks to promote online community-formation, and then looked at a number of critical responses to online community. In order to narrow the focus, the chapter discussed the 'social contracts' that bind members of particular online communities together, and related this to issues of exclusion and otherness in online groups. I also considered whether alternative ways of thinking about virtual social relations might offer a way out of the gridlock of the arguments about online community, and drew on Kevin Hetherington's discussion of the *Bund* as a different way of conceptualizing how CMC-based social groups work. Taken together, I hope that these aspects of the online community debate have assisted in thinking and rethinking the reasons why there has been so much interest in, and argument about, communities in cyberspace.

# Hot links

## *Chapters from* **The Cybercultures Reader**

Arthur Kroker and Marilouise Kroker, 'Code warriors: bunkering in and dumbing down' (Chapter 5: 96–103).

Ananda Mitra, 'Virtual commonality: looking for India on the Internet' (Chapter 44: 676–94).

Michael Ostwald, 'Virtual urban futures' (Chapter 43: 658–75).

Kevin Robins, 'Cyberspace and the world we live in' (Chapter 4: 77–95).

Ziauddin Sardar, 'alt.civilizations.faq: cyberspace as the darker side of the West' (Chapter 48: 732–52).

Susan Leigh Star, 'From Hestia to home page: feminism and the concept of home in cyberspace' (Chapter 41: 632–43).

Allucquere Rosanne Stone, 'Will the real body please stand up? Boundary stories about virtual cultures' (Chapter 32: 504–28).

Shawn Wilbur, 'An archaeology of cyberspaces: virtuality, community, identity' (Chapter 2: 45–55).

Michele Willson, 'Community in the abstract: a political and ethical dilemma?' (Chapter 42: 644–57).

## *Further reading*

Peter Ludlow (ed.) (1999) *High Noon on the Electronic Frontier: conceptual issues in cyberspace*, Cambridge MA: MIT Press (section V: self and community online)

Howard Rheingold (1993) *Virtual Community: homesteading on the electronic frontier*, Reading MA: Addison Wesley.

Marc Smith and Peter Kollock (eds) (1999) *Communities in Cyberspace*, London: Routledge.

### Websites

http://www.well.com
The WELL's homepage, with lots of info, links, instructions on how to join, etc.

http:///www.rheingold.com
Howard Rhiengold's homepage, with articles, archives, links.

http://www.moo.mud.org
General homepage for MOOs, with lots of links and ways to start MOOing.

http://www.fortunecity.com/bally/skull/100/lambdamooers.html
Rusty's LambdaMOO web index, listing all Lambdans, and linking to sites and information on LambdaMOO.

# Chapter 6

# IDENTITIES IN CYBERCULTURE

Cyberspace has come to be widely understood as a practical decon-struction of essentialism. Out there, bodies and identities alike may lose their connection to terrestrial limits, extending through a new range of possibilities, and in the process may reflect back upon the supposed naturalness, givenness, reification or territorialization of real life bodies and identities.

*Don Slater*

IN THIS CHAPTER, I WANT TO EXPLORE the implications of cyberspace and cyberculture for the ways we think about who we are: for our identities. In particular, I want to highlight arguments about partic-ular aspects or 'axes' of identity – those key sociological and cultural markers, race, class, gender and sexuality. The logic of this focus is that exploring questions of 'social' or 'cultural' identity through the lenses of race, class, gender and sexuality usefully illustrates the issues raised in the context of cyberspace. Moreover, these facets of identity have a long track-record of social and cultural inquiry attached to them (for an overview, see Zack 1998), and are subject of similar focus in cybercultural studies. They are all contested and complex terms, made even more so by their intersection with computer-mediated communications technologies.

It should be remarked at the outset that this chapter exists in tandem with – but also in tension with – the next chapter, on the body in cyber-culture. There are many related issues to consider, so there will be many potential overlaps (which I shall try to signal along the way). Chapter 7 will consider questions of disembodiment and re-embodiment in cyberspace, and will explore the figures of the cyborg and the posthuman – although we shall need to at least be aware of these things here. What I recommend, then, is a kind of primitive hypertext-like reading between these two chapters.

## Identity in question

To start this chapter off, we need to lay out the central questions and theories that constellate around the notion of identity today. This will necessarily be brief and partial, but I hope it will give sufficient background to contextualize the rest of the discussion. I'll begin by looking at a question posed by Stuart Hall (2000): *who needs 'identity'?* To think about this, Hall walks us through the terrain I'm interested in here; so let's walk with him. His essay begins by noting the 'explosion' of work on questions of identity from a range of intellectual perspectives, much of it unified by a concern to 'unpack' or 'deconstruct' the enduring notion of 'integral, originary and unified identity' — a conception of identity known as essentialism (Hall 2000: 15). This kind of identity, inherited from the Enlightenment's figuring of the 'Cartesian' subject, has indeed been enduring in western thought for hundreds of years, and still has a lot of common-sense currency — the idea that we are born the way we are, that there is a 'real me', that our identities are fixed and stable, and so on, are all manifestations of Cartesianism, and can all be described as forms of essentialism. In the academy, insights from a whole host of different scholars have led to a progressive eroding of this stable, unified, essential view of the self — it has, to use another of Hall's terms, become 'decentred':

> The question of 'identity' is being vigorously debated in social theory. In essence, the argument is that the old identities which stabilized the social world for so long are in decline, giving rise to new identities and fragmenting the modern individual as a unified subject. This so-called 'crisis of identity' is seen as part of a wider process of change which is dislocating the central structures and processes of modern societies and undermining the frameworks which gave individuals stable anchorage in the social world.
>
> (Hall 1995: 596)

In his later essay, Hall (2000) refines this point to argue that it is the ways we 'think with' concepts of identity that have been most radically transformed. Indeed, there is an endurance to the practical (and political) deployment of 'old identities', but new ways of conceptualizing those 'old identities' — away from unity, origin stories, stability and so on — have emerged. In particular, theoretical moves associated with postmodernism and poststructuralism have been signalled as reshaping the ways we think about who we are. A social constructionist view of identity, *contra* essentialism, stresses the temporal and spatial locatedness of identity, as well as identity as a process. Hall recognizes this, arguing for a shift from the term 'identity', which he sees as too loaded with those 'old' totalizations, to using the notion of 'identification' instead — which signals process, multiplicity, construction: our identifications are made, are mobile, are multiplex.

A number of key theoretical insights have done the work of unpacking and unpicking the unified, stable subject (Hall 1995). Collectively, as Jeffrey Weeks (1995) provocatively says, these decentrings suggest the need to consider identities as 'necessary fictions'. I think this is an interesting and useful term, though it needs careful handling — I have myself seen Weeks getting grilled by queer activists, angry that the site of their political struggle was being named a 'fiction'. The central decentring that leads to this formulation concerns taking apart the universality of identity and revealing it as constructed rather than essential. In particular, since Weeks' focus is sexual identities, Michel Foucault's work on the 'invention of homosexuality' (and more generally on the relationship between discourse, power/knowledge and identity) figures prominently. Through a 'genealogical' reading of the history of homosexuality, Foucault (1981) famously suggested that the identity 'homosexual' came into being at a particular time (and place), as a consequence of a particular set of discourses: 'homosexuality' was 'talked' into being by doctors, lawyers, clergymen, psychiatrists and so on — through this discourse, a set of sexual practices were organized into a sexual *identity* that worked (and still works) as a 'label' for a group of people. The function of discourse here is not just to describe but also to *define* the identities of particular individuals and groups — Foucault also looked at madness and criminality in this way. That accounts for the 'fiction' in Weeks' formulation; the politics of such a decentring makes this 'necessary':

> Such a view of identity does two things. First of all it offers a critical view of all identities, demonstrating their historicity and arbitrariness. It denaturalizes them, revealing the coils of power that entangle them. It returns identities to the world of human beings, revealing their openness and contingency. Second, because of this, it makes human agency not only possible, but also essential. For if . . . identities are made in history, and in relations of power, they can also be remade. Identities then can be seen as sites of contestation.
>
> (Weeks 1995: 98–9)

In my view, however, this overplays the potential for transformation at the same time that it underplays the endurance of essentialist views of identity. And, as Azzedine Haddour (2000) argues in a critique of poststructuralist takes on identity, such a radical view of identity is not open to everyone to make use of. However, with that *caveat* noted (and it is a powerful *caveat*, that we shall see again and again in this chapter), let's get back to Hall, and to identification. Summarizing his position, Hall writes that identification, as a 'strategic and positional' view of identity, is useful in that

> [i]t accepts that identities are never unified and, in late modern times,
> [are] increasingly fragmented and fractured; never singular but multiply
> constructed across different, often intersecting and antagonistic, dis-
> courses, practices and positions. They are subject to a radical histori-
> cization, and are constantly in the process of change and transformation.
>
> (Hall 2000: 17)

In sum, Hall writes that he views identification as 'points of temporary attach-
ment to the subject positions which discursive practices construct for us' (19)
– those 'discursive practices' construct the possible modes of identity that
are legible in culture (and these are contingent, located, specific). And, rather
than a once-in-a-lifetime subscription to identity, Hall suggests a looser affil-
iation (though this shouldn't be taken as implying 'free choice' – as it often
is in work on identity in cyberculture, as we shall see).

In line with this facet of contemporary thinking about identity is Anthony
Giddens' (1991) work on the late-modern self, in particular his discussion
of reflexivity and the 'project of the self'. Conceiving of identity as a 'project'
to be worked on has echoes of Weeks' 'necessary fiction' argument; Giddens
argues that the structural transformations of the contemporary period – globalization, disembedding, detraditionalization – have unshackled the subject,
enabling a reconstruction of individual and collective life-stories and identities. The fluid, fragmented late-modern or postmodern self has a new capacity
to make itself over, to reshape and restyle elements of identity – or at least
to make choices about which aspects of its self to privilege at any point.
Again, this might be taken to imply freedom of choice; and it does, but it
is *constrained* choice: those discursive practices highlighted by Hall set out the
*limits* within which elements of choice can only ever operate. This point has
been hotly debated in the context of the use of ideas of 'performance' and
'performativity' in theorizations of identity, the linking the 'project' of the
self with the 'projection' of the self (issues that we shall return to later).

In the context of online life, these questions are paramount, since the
(mainly) text-based mode of communication means that participants do have
reflexivity and choice in terms of their self-presentations (Slater 1998). Indeed,
this has been one of the core issues discussed in the context of cyberculture,
jokingly referenced in the famous cartoon 'In cyberspace, no-one knows
you're a dog'. If we type ourselves into being in cyberspace, the argument
goes, we can make and remake who we are endlessly, liberated from the 'meat'
of our RL bodies and all the identity-markers they carry. Obviously, the relationships between representation and identity need to be considered here, as
do the implications for rendering the self in text-only media (though Gauntlett
(2000) notes that websites are supplanting text-only forums as the prime location of identity expression in cyberspace). In the terms of one of Hall's (1973)
earlier discussions, for example, what are the relationships between encoding

(writing) and decoding (reading) identity-in-text (see Rheingold 1999)? Like the problematic figure of the decentred, poststructuralist subject, the disembodied, online subject asks that we raise a number of important questions about the contexts in which identities are mobilized (Poster 1995). These questions are at the heart of this chapter.

Absolutely central to Hall's argument about identification is the role of difference in constituting identity – all identities depend on exclusion, on 'otherness'. *Who we are is defined by who we are not*, and the practices of exclusion that define identity have to be recognized – an issue we have already witnessed in the context of online communities. The problematic of 'dealing with difference' that this idea ushers in – the so-called 'violence of the hierarchy' established between the included and the excluded – overshadows the project of identity. It certainly structures the ways in which identities 'work' in cyberspace – for some critics, cyberspace abolishes the hierarchy, invisibilizing difference, while for others it restates difference even as it fetishizes it, as we shall see as this chapter proceeds. However we understand who we are, it is clear that questions of identity demand that we think about the other.

## Self-identity in cyberculture

Having rather hurriedly sketched some of the issues at stake in the question of identity, I'd like to move into cyberspace now. As an opening, I want to consider the 'projection' or 'presentation' of the self that is reflexively enacted through the construction of one particular cybercultural artefact: the personal homepage. Charles Cheung (2000) discusses the production of the self via the homepage, and rehearses the arguments about the late-modern subject in order to contextualize this, as well as discussing Goffman's (1959) useful 'dramaturgical' account of the presentation of self. Goffman produced a way of thinking about the 'stages', 'props', 'scripts' and 'cues' that we use in our daily lives, and the 'parts' we play to each other (though Goffman problematically retains a 'back-stage' self, more 'authentic' than the 'front-stage' selves we act out). Defining the personal homepage as 'a website produced by an individual (or couple, or family) which is centred around the personality and identity of its author(s)' (Cheung 2000: 44), Cheung explores how these homepages encourage a reflexive presentation and narrativization of the self – albeit one defined by the medium and the imagined audience. (For a fascinating discussion of websites as aesthetic 'traps' aiming to capture an audience, see Miller 2000; on the 'explosion of narrativity' in cyberspace, see Poster 1995.)

Marshalling the identity-marking resources the web confers, personal homepages present the self through a number of devices: biography, links, photographs, up-datable 'news' or 'diary' pages, and so on. Proficiency with programming ('machine skill', as Haraway (CR) calls it) is displayed in the quality of the site, and a hits-counter quantifies popularity. Total control over the production of the site (within the structural confines of the medium) equates with total control over the production of the self, therefore – although that cannot secure the ways it is read, of course. Cheung also argues that personal websites offer their creators the chance to 'reveal' previously-hidden aspects of their identities; in this way, homepage authors suggest that it is the 'real me' that it is presented on a site (even though many admit to self-censoring, and to 'tailoring' the presented self).

Personal homepages operate at a variety of levels, of course: they may be intended for consumption primarily by family or close friends, or may be wanting to present one's self (or selves) to the whole online world – witness the phenomenon of Mahir Cagri's 'I kiss you!!!!' homepage (http://members.xoom.com/primall/mahir), which has propelled its author into cult celebrity status. As a self-conscious articulation of self-identity, then, homepages make a useful starting-point for opening up the question of identity in cyberculture, bringing with them issues such as author and audience, truth and deception, fluidity and authenticity. We shall see these terms recur in the rest of this chapter, which will consider particular aspects or axes of identity online, beginning with race.

## Race in cyberculture

From the outset, in discussing race in cyberspace, we encounter something of the complexity of identity – such is the complexity of the word itself, that some writers prefer to encase it in quotation marks, 'race', in order to immediately signal its problems. The first 'problem' is the essentializing tendency of a word like 'race', that assumes a homogeneous, unified set of characteristics and experiences can be mapped on to people with a shared heritage. Some writers prefer the term 'ethnicity', but this has itself become overloaded and problematic, with its links to contested terms like 'ethnic minority' and so on. Working definitions of both words can be unpacked and problematized – something we don't have space for here. What we need to establish is a way of thinking about 'race' or 'ethnicity' that we can then utilize to explore racial configurations in cyberspace; one that is constructionist rather than essentialist, one that recognizes 'race' as cultural, and as contested. Like Donald and Rattansi (1992: 1), my approach is pragmatic, concerned with exploring 'how the category ["race"] operates in practice' – in this case, in the practices of identity-work in cyberspace.

Kolko *et al.* (2000: 5) note that 'academic work on cyberspace has been surprisingly silent around questions of race and racism', offering their edited collection *Race in Cyberspace* as a way to 'put questions of race more squarely on the table when it comes to the study of cyberspace' (11). Set in the context of general debates on identity and embodiment/disembodiment in cyberculture, the question of race presented by Kolko *et al.* includes examining the figuring of race in representations of and in cyberspace (films, adverts, computer games, MUDs, avatars), the use of cybertechnology to construct spaces where 'ethnic and racial identity are examined, worked through, and reinforced' (9), issues of language in online interaction, and the implications of notions such as the cyborg for the formation of new 'cyberethnicities'. The key questions the editors identify are summarized thus:

> Does race 'disappear' in cyberspace? How is race visually represented in popular film and advertisements about cyberspace? Do narratives that depict racial and ethnic minorities in cyberspace simply recapitulate the old racist stereotypes, do they challenge them, do they use the medium to sketch out new virtual realities of race?
>
> (Kolko *et al.* 2000: 11)

I'd like to explore some of the answers to these questions suggested by authors in *Race in Cyberspace* here, drawing on other important work in the area along the way.

Jennifer Gonzalez's (2000) essay focuses on two artist-created websites, both of which work with avatars problematically dealing with issues of racial difference. The UNDINA site plays a virtual version of the Surrealist parlour-game 'exquisite corpse', shuffling body-parts to produce new combinations, while the Bodies[c] INC site invites participants to select body shape, surfacing ('skin'), gender and so on to build their own avatar. The avatars figured on the sites, Gonzalez argues, reduce race to a consumer-object, obscuring the histories of different representations and positions – by making race purely elective, they introduce a theme common to a number of writings on ethnicity in cyberculture: the fantasy of becoming the other (in the safety of cyberspace). While there are productive arguments made about emerging syncretic identities that 'mix' racial identifications (see, for example, Back 1996), Gonzalez is cautious about UNDINA and Bodies[c] INC, writing that both sites offer 'a new transcendental, universal, and, above all, consuming subject . . . as the model of future cyber-citizenship', adding that offering freedom to choose racialized 'appendages' in this way marks 'a new form of colonization . . . on the level of symbolic exchange' (Gonzalez 2000: 49).

This is, in fact, a central issue in work on race in cyberculture, and one that has parallels in discussions of gender and sexuality, too. The tension is between the liberatory possibilities of disembodied 'identity-play' on the one hand, and the symbolic violence that kind of appropriation does on the other. Nestled in this debate is, of course, the problem of authenticity – does arguing against these kinds of 'virtual ethnicity' (Poster 1998) reaffirm an authentic, *essential* racial identity outside of cyberspace? This kind of problematic depiction of racial identity is tracked in other essays in *Race in Cyberspace*, most notably in David Crane's (2000) exploration of the equation of black identity with resistive 'street' subcultures in cyberpunk movies. Here, blackness is made to signify authenticity, the real. The movies Crane discusses, including *Strange Days*, *Johnny Mnemonic* and *Jumpin' Jack Flash*, problematically figure the relationship between race and cybertechnology. As Crane (2000: 87) writes, 'blackness functions to authenticate – and envision – oppositional identities and ideologies associated with cyberspace', thus rendering black identities other to cyber-identities.

Fantasies of racial otherness in cyberspace also include the deployment of stereotypes in video games (Ow 2000) and in adverts by computer companies (Nakamura 2000) – in the former, Orientalist martial-arts experts mark racial difference again as an 'identity-choice' for gamers; in the latter, visions of 'pretechnological' cultures and landscapes are used as backdrops to set against images of high technology – Arabs on camels with lap-tops, for example. Both are manifestations of what Lisa Nakamura (CR) calls 'identity tourism' in cyberculture – a term used to encapsulate the manifold ways that racial and ethnic identities are appropriated, adopted and consumed. Her discussion of race in the multi-user domain LambdaMOO is particularly insightful here, in its description of 'racial passing': playing the 'fantasy other' in MUDs, like virtual cross-dressing, reaffirms stereotypes in a location where we might expect the proliferation of new identity formations instead. In her discussion of Asian identity in LambdaMOO, Nakamura depressingly concludes that Asianness is both domesticated and erased there (see also Tsang CR); although she also points towards other more productive or transgressive possibilities that might 'jam the ideology-machine' and question the essentializing of race (Nakamura CR: 719).

Such a 'jamming' project is described by Beth Kolko (2000), in the context of MOOScape – a MUD that foregrounds the marking of race by requiring an '@race' command from users as part of their 'desc' (online self-description). MOOScape thus works as an on-going social experiment about the impact of visibilizing race in MUD interactions. While this is still *elective*, offering participants the freedom to choose their racial descriptor (Kolko notes that these have included 'academic' and 'pastry' alongside white, Asian and American), it does remind users that race matters in cyberspace, that it is an issue that cannot go unremarked. It also visibilizes *whiteness* rather than leaving it as an unmarked category, in contrast to other MUDs, where users only elect to signify race if they want to fetishize it in their new online identities. It also forces the issue of racial passing into the open – an act which in itself can serve as a sobering corrective to those who celebrate other forms of online passing, especially around gender (Foster CR).

Two important areas that *Race in Cyberspace* doesn't address – which the editors acknowledge – are questions of global information inequality and the 'racial demographics of the cyber-workforce' (Kolko *et al.* 2000: 11). A materialist perspective on race in cyberculture needs to be set alongside the symbolic and experiential readings offered by that book. The issue of information inequality remains a pressing concern, and a necessary dampener to the most excessive claims of cyberspace's democratic potential, suggesting instead a reading of cyberspace as the latest manifestation of western (and especially American) cultural imperialism (Sardar and Stratton CR). The language of cyberspace shows this very clearly; as Mark Poster (1995: 28) writes, 'the dominant use of English on the Internet suggests the extension of American power, as does the fact that email addresses in the United States alone do not require a country code. The Internet normalizes American users.'

In terms of access to and impacts of technology among particular ethnic groups even *within* the United States, Bobby Dixon's (1997) essay 'Toting technology: taking it to the streets' raises some important questions in the context of African-American communities. Critiquing the notion of 'technological coolness' manifest in black American consumerism, Dixon notes that 'electronic redlining' exists in cyberspace just as it does in US cities – mapping who owns what, who works where, who's 'in' and who's 'out'. However, he does also see 'unusual opportunities' for black organization and protest, calling for black Americans to be 'intelligent consumers of information' rather than passive consumers of technological coolness (Dixon 1997: 147), and encouraging churches and schools to go online. The reappropriation of cybertechnology can rewire it, then, and disadvantaged communities can be empowered in/by cyberspace – if the structural impediments of the 'technology gap' can be overcome (and that's a big 'if'; see Mele 1999). Moreover, for globally-dispersed diasporic communities, the Internet can become a site of reterritorialization; a place to reconstruct collective identity and even build a imagined 'digital homeland' (Mitra CR).

But overcoming that technology gap is not an option everyone can enjoy: 'digital ghettos' that don't get wired emblematize the redlining of cyberspace, while on a global scale, maps of flows across the cyberscape similarly visibilize the spaces of information poverty (Dodge and Kitchin 2001). As many of the critics whose work we've been looking at here lament, cyberspace remains predominantly white, western space – though some emphasize those 'unusual opportunities' that might enable a recoding of the racial politics of cyberculture. Moreover, as we shall see in the next section, commentators have repeatedly stressed that cyberspace is also predominantly *male* space – though this, too, is open to forms of contestation and disruption.

## Gender in cyberculture

While academic work on cyberspace has been 'surprisingly silent' about race, the same cannot be said of gender; work on gender in cyberculture has, by contrast, been prolific and diverse. Finding a way to summarize the range of positions and arguments is a difficult task, and I'm sure that my reading here remains partial. Nevertheless, what I hope to do in this section is to pick out work from a variety of perspectives, all of which works to think through the promises and constraints embodied in the 'gender-technology matrix'. I think that a central question we need to keep in our minds here concerns the possibility that cyberspace has (or can, or could) create a 'new space' for rewiring the gender-technology relationship; indeed, this has been a key concern for many of the writers whose work I shall be referring to here. The long-running contextual 'back story', then, concerns women's access to, use of and relationship with technology (or, rather, *technologies*) – the problematic equation of technology with men, the male and the masculine, and the concomitant exclusion of women from what we might call the 'circuit of technoculture'. Feminist critiques of science and technology have explored this issue from a range of angles, and with a focus on different technologies, including most notably reproductive and domestic technologies (Wajcman 1991). Bringing this argument into the domain of cyberspace, some critics have suggested that computer technology represents yet another sphere of exclusion or domination for women, while other writers argue that CMC can become a 'new space for women' (Light 1995). At the same time, the possibilities of identity-play already signalled in this chapter mean for some theorists that gender will cease to carry its RL ideological loadings in cyberspace, or might cease to matter or even exist there. These are the arguments I shall focus on here, through an exploration of selected feminist responses to cyberculture. Revisiting my trope of 'storying cyberspace', I want to suggest that 'storying cyberfeminism' equally involves meshing the material, the symbolic and the experiential, and shall explore these three types of story here.

Materialist readings of the gender-technology matrix stress women's lack of access to computer technology and to 'machine skill', and highlight the persistent 'maling' of cyberspace at a number of levels. Margaret Morse (1997), for example, explores women's 'technological ineptitude', implanted by the education system's gendered assumptions, as inhibiting women's participation in cyberculture, noting also the stark issues of information inequality. The gendering of information inequality at the global scale is also a recurrent theme in the edited collection *Women@Internet* (Harcourt 1999) – though a number of the contributors urge feminists to resist the masculinization of cyberspace, and to develop new ways of using CMC. Lourdes Arizpe suggests four foundations for feminist interventions in the evolving cyberculture:

First, women must not be left behind in the gap between those that have access to the new information technologies and those that do not. . . . Second, women should be active agents in ensuring that the star-like potential of information technologies is directed towards enhancing human well-being rather than strengthening existing power monopolies. Third, the meanings of tomorrow must be created today and women, especially young women, now have greater freedom of spirit and of experience to be creative. . . . Fourth, the possibilities that new forms of communication and expression have placed in our hands . . . are awesome. It is up to us to navigate them for our place-based knowledge and action.

(Arizpe 1999: xv–xvi)

This represents a powerful call to action for women as 'active agents' in shaping cyberculture, and for seeding it with feminist politics rooted in RL. Set against this, however, is a 'deep sense of unease about the travellers women encounter in the corridors of cyberspace, the asymmetries of access to the cyberworld, and the sheer power of global technocapitalism' (Harcourt 1999: 21) – the question becomes, then, whether these issues pose insurmountable barriers to feminist engagements with cyberculture. While there are still those who argue that this is the case, an increasing volume of work suggests instead the fruitful possibilities for women that cyberspace offers.

Katie Ward (2000) separates out feminist engagements with cyberspace into two types, which she labels 'online feminism' and 'online cyberfeminism'; the former is concerned more centrally with using CMC as a way to further feminist politics generally (through global communication, consciousness-raising, and so on), while the latter engages more with the technology itself, seeking to rewire it for a new cyberfeminist politics. While I think there are some problems with this division, it is nevertheless useful in that it encourages a closer reading of the aims and methods of particular groups and individuals. The essays in *Women@Internet* can, I think, be largely characterized as examples of 'online feminism'. Nina Wakeford (CR) gestures towards this distinction, too, in her discussion of sites such as Cybergrrl, geekgrrl, Nerdgrrl and Homegrrrl, all of which work to recode cyberfeminism (or maybe, as Ward suggests, 'cyberpostfeminism') – a strategy summed up by one of the geek-grrrl site's creators, quoted by Wakeford (CR: 355): 'Grrrls enjoy their femininity and kick ass at the same time'. The use of the word 'grrrl' in these sites signals a particular take on cyberfeminism, which is partly about a distancing from what some participants label 'victim feminism', and the use of terms like 'nerd' or 'geek' similarly signals their embeddedness in computing culture. Sadie Plant (CR: 325) refers to this as the 'cyberfeminist virus', borrowing the imagery from VNS Matrix, who posted a cyberfeminist manifesto in the early

1990s. Flowing out from this virus, Plant's essay also writes cyberfeminism as 'an irresponsible feminism', using the image of the 'replicunt' as an embodiment of this move:

> The replicunts write programs, paint viral images, fabricate weapons systems, infiltrate the arts and the industry. They are hackers, perverting the codes, corrupting the transmissions, multiplying zeros, and teasing open new holes in the world. They are the edge of the new edge, unashamedly opportunist, entirely irresponsible, and committed only to the infiltration and corruption of a world which already rues the day they left home.
>
> (Plant CR: 336)

Like Andrew Ross' discussion of hacking (CR), then, replicunts and geek-grrrls become 'the enemy within' – contaminants who use their machine-skill to subvert and reclaim cyberculture.

For some critics, however, such a viral recoding of cyberspace is overly optimistic, and its postfeminist politics problematic. Judith Squires (CR), for example, signals a more cautious approach, and one which has an eye to the gendered representations found in cyberpunk as well as the theoretical stances of writers like Haraway and Plant. In the imagery of cyberpunk Squires finds a problematic restatement of gender, often through 'exaggeratedly masculine and feminine bodies' (Squires CR: 364; see also Cavallaro 2000). Squires' critique is powerfully echoed in a series of readings of gendered representations in and of cyberspace, which turn again and again on the regenderings of 'disembodied' subjects in cyberspace (see also Chapter 7). Claudia Springer's (1996) *Electronic Eros*, for example, scans popular cybercultures for manifestations of the 'techno-erotic body', finding all too often depictions that problematically reinstate powerfully stereotypical genderings. Against arguments that disembodiment in cyberspace promises a 'post-gender' future, analyses of images and experiences highlight this regendering, even in areas of cyberspace that have self-consciously attempted 'post-gendering', such as MUDs.

Probably the best-known (and certainly most-researched) multi-user domain is LambdaMOO. This site has attracted considerable attention from academics (and others) interested in gender in cyberspace, especially since it offers participants the choice of ten genders to use in their online interactions (users are required to post a 'desc' – a self-description that must include their gender). These ten genders are male, female, spivak (indeterminate), neuter, splat (a 'thing'), egotistical, royal, 2nd, either, and plural – which then determine the on-screen pronouns used by the program: *he* for male, *she* for female, *it* for neuter, *we* for royal, *they* for plural and so on (see Kendall 1996; Danet 1998; Kaloski 1999). The intention behind these many genders is to allow participants freedom from RL genderings, to experiment with 'virtual cross-dressing' – it also bears traces of MUDs' Dungeons and Dragons heritage, emphasizing fantasy and play (though not unproblematically).

Ann Kaloski (1999) reports her adventures in LambdaMOO, on the trail of the 'bisexual cyborg'. Excitedly donning alternate genders, and composing alluring fantastical descs, she soon found herself confronted by the limitations of Lambda, as she cruised the MOO's 'sex rooms' as a tall, down-covered spivak. After getting very little by the way of action, Kaloski received a telling message: 'If you want sex, change your gender to female'. Similar issues are recounted by Lori Kendall (1996), who also tracks performances of 'virtual drag' in MUDs, arguing that the medium of MUDding makes all participants 'drag up' – and that this in itself leads to stereotypical gender performances, since 'passing' calls for being believable, and being believable is easier the more stereotypical and 'conventional' the performance is. More problematically, gender identities become more rigidly defined, and RL genders most rigidly of all, as evidenced by examples Kendall cites of players feeling 'betrayed' when the RL gender of another participant is revealed as different from their MUD desc:

> Back when I viewed MUDS as a REAL reality, I fell in love with a female character. . . . But anyways turned out 'she' was a he. Since then my personal policy is to NEVER get involved with anyone on a mud in a deep personal way.
>
> (MUDder, quoted in Kendall 1996: 218)

Counter to this, Shannon McRae (1996) suggests that MUD regenderings can allow participants to explore new eroticisms, for example on so-called FurryMUDs or FurryMUCKs, where participants take on anthropomorphized animal identities – though Kendall also notes sites like these, spotting on them a similarly problematic 'hypergendering' (Bassett 1997). Kaloski (1999) uses this hypergendering to argue for the malleability of gender, reading it as a form of 'camp' that, deploying a version of Judith Butler's (1990) thesis on performativity, unravels the essentialism of gender; to show that in RL as online, *all* genders are masquerades or performances (see also Danet 1998).

However, I find Kendall's line of argument more persuasive, in its highlighting of the *lack* of spill-over between online gender-play and RL iden-tity – though this may be particularly an issue in MUDs, where fantasy and reality are often held apart by the screen – although the well-known case of 'virtual rape' in LambdaMOO shows how this distinction can be blurred (Dibbell 1999). Even in MUDs, in fact, gender-switching is only practised by a small number of participants, and is viewed by many players as 'dishonest' (Roberts and Parks 1999). In other online contexts, where 'fantasy' is not foregrounded, virtual cross-dressing has been seen to be even more problematic, as in the famous example of the 'cross-dressing psychiatrist', where issues of trust and deception come to the fore instead (Stone 1995). In this case, a male psychiatrist masqueraded on-line as a disabled woman, and built up a close circle of online friends. When his conscience got the better of him, he decided to 'kill off' his online persona, 'Julie', and then came clean about the whole incident. Those who had befriended 'Julie' felt bitterly betrayed by the deception.

Set against this is the work focused on the online experiences of people who self-identify as transgendered. Stephen Whittle (2001) argues that cyberspace has become a valuable resource for transgendered people, facilitating support networks and a political community, as well as offering 'safe' space to experiment with gender. Indeed, Stone (1995: 180) goes as far as arguing that 'in cyberspace the transgendered body is the natural body' – a notion also neatly captured in Susan Stryker's (CR) discussion of the transsexual body *as* technology (see Chapter 7). Whittle suggests that transgendered people already know all about 'consensual hallucination' through their RL identities, and have an 'in-built' expertise that makes them especially at home in cyberspace. In these discussions, then, we see gender-play as personally and politically productive – as enabling new bodies, identities and communities that extend beyond cyberspace.

Evidently, forms of gender-play are context-specific and open to different interpretations, then. One of the examples McRae (1996) focuses on, for example, is a 'virtual love story' from LambdaMOO, initially between an 'RL heterosexual man playing a female persona' (Jel) and an 'RL lesbian' playing a 'virtual version of herself' (Plastique). After their brief online affair ended, Plastique entered into a relationship with a male persona, who turned out to be Jel, too – and he assumed that the 'virtual woman' he was seducing was an 'RL man'. This complex story, McRae says, suggests that for some participants LambdaMOO offers a safe place to experiment with gender, sex and sexuality. It nicely brings out the themes of fantasy/reality and trust/deception – though with an outcome very different from Stone's 'cross-dressing psychiatrist' or Dibble's 'rape in cyberspace'. Virtual sex, MUD sex and its many online variants have, in fact, attracted a lot of academic and media attention, so I'd like to turn to some of that material now, en route to a broader discussion of sexual identities in cyberspace.

## Sexuality in cyberculture

For a time, the subject of 'virtual sex' was one of the hottest topics of discussion about cyberspace. Read as a response to the 'panic' surrounding HIV and Aids, forms of disembodied online sex – 'sex without secretions' –

received a lot of attention (Dery 1996). Scenarios for 'teledildonics' in virtual reality suggested a future for sexual interactions in cyberspace based on tele-presence, augmented by sensory body-suits and VR helmets, through which the simulation of sex could be realized (Rheingold 1991). The film *Lawnmower Man* plays out this scenario very vividly. For the moment, teledildonics remains a fantasy, however, and 'virtual sex' lags behind. Its most common manifestation today is jokingly referred to as 'one-handed typing' (Kaloski 1999) – as masturbation combined with varieties of online 'talking dirty' and fantasizing between participants. David Gauntlett describes this scenario:

> People of all sexual orientations have used the Internet for 'cybersex', which involves people telling each other what they are doing to each other (within their shared cyber-imagination) as they fumble their way towards sexual satisfaction.
>
> (Gauntlett 2000: 15)

Gareth Branwyn (CR: 398) similarly defines 'compu-sex' as 'a curious blend of phone sex, computer dating, and high-tech voyeurism'. To meet the apparently insatiable demand for forms of virtual sex, a whole online sex industry has evolved to provide every imaginable format of cybersex (or, at least, every format possible within the constraints of the medium) (di Filippo 2000). On top of these formalized 'industry' sites, of course, there are countless 'amateur' spaces – homepages, websites, BBSs and so on – though the boundary between 'amateur' and 'professional' is often blurred, as in the burgeoning webcam culture (Snyder 2000). A great many of the sites do not concern themselves directly with issues of sexual *identity*, other than perhaps to remove some of the stigma attached to practices like voyeurism, exhibitionism and the consumption (and production) of pornography. Even then, the cultivating of such a 'libertarian' ethos often does not equate with stretching the boundaries of sexual practice and identity in new and productive ways. Indeed, many of the sexual interactions online are 'hyperconventional', fail to 'produce new sexual configurations' and are 'more consumerist than deconstructive' (Slater 1998: 99–100). There are, however, important issues emerging for rewirings of sexual identities in the context of cyberculture. These will be the principal focus of this section.

To begin, let's return to Jel and Plastique, to LambdaMOO and gender-play. As we've already seen, the possibilities of gender-switching can be argued to open up new possibilities for sexual identities – though there are many occasions where such possibilities are also foreclosed. As Nina Wakeford writes:

> Men pretend to be women to attract the attention of 'real' women, who are in fact themselves other men pretending to be women. The

practice of such cross-dressing does nothing to unsettle the assumption and practice of cyberspace as a process of heterosexuality.

(Wakeford 1996: 99)

This double-coding of online identities and RL identities makes virtual interactions like those in LambdaMOO a complex parlour-game, with endless second-guessing and an overall climate of suspicion. Even with the increasing use of visual media in cyberspace, photographs are assumed to be electronically enhanced ('Photo-shopped') or just plain counterfeit, and webcam downloads are viewed as suspiciously self-conscious (and therefore 'fake') performances (Snyder 2000). But the important point to reiterate here is that none of this does very much to unsettle either the assumed authenticity of RL bodies and identities (and the *links between* bodies and identities) or the dominant heterosexual scripting of the majority of online sexual interactions (Slater 1998). As Wakeford continues, '[n]ot surprisingly, non-heterosexual performances are at the margins of cyberspace' (*Ibid*). Nevertheless, in a later essay, she is able not only to locate, but also to theorize from, what she labels 'cyberqueer spaces', listing and exploring newsgroups, BBSs, mailing lists, chat rooms and websites made by and/or for lesbians, gay men, bisexual and transgendered people, and queers (Wakeford CR).

In 'Cyberqueer', Wakeford signals the problematic coming-together of queer theory and cyber-theory; in particular, this cross-fertilization is embodied in discussions of the de-essentializing of identities and an emphasis on performance and performativity instead. The disembodiment offered in cyberspace facilitates the kinds of identity fictions that queer theory is associated with. David Gauntlett (2000) points to this resonance, too, but like Wakeford seems weary of its uncritical reiteration in utopian readings of cyberspace. Part of the dampening of that utopianism, for Wakeford, comes from remembering the socio-economic and institutional frameworks that construct barriers to free and universal participation online. Issues such as censorship and harassment are also important, and frequently serve to reinforce the 'straightness' of cyberspace. The commodification of cyberspace is further signalled as problematic, in turning potential spaces of resistance into objects of consumer choice and capital accumulation, while the 'new edge' cyberculture is seen as 'post-political' – both charges that have been levelled against queers (Bell and Binnie 2000). Donald Morton (1999: 306), indeed, reads both cyberspace and queer theory as problematic manifestations of late capitalism: 'postgay queerity and postleft political cyberpunk are the latest forms of bourgeois individualism'.

In the face of these limitations and criticisms, however, Wakeford still finds evidence of forms of activism, sociality and identity-work in her cyberqueer survey. One of the most frequently-cited positive features of cyberqueer spaces is safety – or at least comparative safety. The anonymity

offered makes cyberqueer spaces important sites for coming-out, while
retaining the protective shell of the RL closet (Woodland CR). Wakeford
keenly stresses the need to think contextually, about particular cyberqueer
spaces, in order to get a better grasp on the promises and limitations extant
there. Such a contextual reading of different cyberqueer spaces is undertaken
by Randall Woodland (CR), who explores a number of North American sites
aimed at gay men. The frameworks the different sites establish for modes of
participation show the range of cyberqueer spaces that Wakeford is mindful
of – from commercially-run sites like those hosted by America Online to
queer-coded spaces in LambdaMOO.

On America Online, Woodland finds lesbian and gay topics listed alongside more than sixty 'Clubs and Interests', a feature of the system that he
reads ambivalently:

> Gay and lesbian concerns take their place among forums devoted to
> such interests as woodworking, backpacking, genealogy, pet care,
> quilting, and *Star Trek*. . . . Though it might be a public relations
> triumph for gays and lesbians to be no more controversial than Trekkers
> or woodworkers, there is also the risk of trivializing the concerns of
> queer folks by labelling them a 'club' or (special?) 'interest'. The rele-
> vance of this to queer identity is two-fold: being queer is almost as
> socially acceptable as being a Trekker, but no more important. Such a
> minimizing of the distinctiveness of gay identity has its drawbacks:
> constructing homosexuality as this kind of 'lifestyle choice' is a common
> tactic of the religious right.
>
> (Woodland CR: 428)

Such a 'normalizing' of homosexuality is not unique to cyberspace, of course,
but has been a tactic of 'assimilationist' rights groups in the US and elsewhere, where making homosexuals equatable with Trekkers might indeed be
seen as desirable (Bell and Binnie 2000). The other sites Woodland
visits have, for him, more interesting ways of locating queer identities in
cyberspace – though these also have their problems. A private, LA-based
BBS called ModemBoy, for example, imagines queer space in a simulated
high school; its participants become 'horny, sexually compulsive adolescent
boys' (419), potentially limiting further exploration of identity beyond the
fantasy scenario of the school. Weaveworld (part of LambdaMOO), by
contrast, codes its queerness more obliquely, via Clive Barker's novel of the
same name.

It's obvious from his writing that Woodland is much more 'at home'
here than walking the halls of Modem Boy High, though Weaveworld's imagining of a pagan-inflected heterotopia might be equally off-putting and
excluding. Dan Tsang (CR) picks out one way that such exclusions work in

queer cyberspaces, through his focus on 'queer 'n' Asian virtual sex'. Returning to themes visited earlier in this chapter, Tsang highlights the fetishizing of Asian-American identities online, setting this in the context of the *whiteness* of US gay culture off-line and on. In the face of this, however, he nonetheless signals some productive outcomes for queer Asians and Pacific Islanders in cyberspace, rehearsing arguments about safe space, coming out, and community- and identity-work facilitated (albeit in a circumscribed form) on some of the sites he discusses.

Tsang and Woodland both make clear the point that, as with gender identities, there are particular modalities of 'queerness' more readily mobilized online – a kind of 'hyperqueering' analogous to Bassett's (1997) notion of 'hypergendering' in MUDs. Modem Boy shows this, with its high school locker room scenarios; Thomas Foster (CR: 449) spots this, too, writing that 'cyberspace permits [only] a kind of spectacularized gayness' – the textual performance of sexuality has to trade in stereotypes just as much as the performance of gender. This issue reminds me of RL questions of exclusion in the context of 'queer space' – the codes and looks that permit (or prohibit) entry to bars and clubs, for example (Bell and Binnie 2000). Central to this dynamic of inclusion and exclusion is class; and I want to turn my attention to class identities in cyberspace now.

## Class in cyberculture

> *Are you on the network?* could become as big a social and economic differentiator in the late 1990s as *Are you employed?* ha[d] been in the early 1990s; indeed, the answer to either question might now well depend on your access to the other.
>
> (Haywood 1998: 25)

Academic work on the subject of class in CMC has largely been materialist – by which I mean that it has focused on issues of information inequality, the reordering of socio-economic structures in the information society, and questions of social exclusion from cyberculture. This line of enquiry essentially follows on from broader debates about the shifting forms and meanings of class in postindustrial and globalized societies, which have explored the move from production to consumption as the basis of class identities, questions of class mobility, and issues of 'new' class formations in the information, knowledge and symbolic economies (Castells 1996). Less attention has been paid to issues of class-based identities mobilized in cyberspace, other than to note the middle-class habitus of the majority of cyberspace's inhabitants. There do seem to be similar (and similarly important) questions to consider, however: are there issues of class fetishism and class-passing also to be tracked in cyberculture? How is class performed in textual interactions? Does class 'disappear' in cyberspace?

To begin with, I want to sketch out some of the arguments about new class formations in the digital economy. Alessandro Aurigi and Stephen Graham (1998) provide a useful and fairly representative typologization of what they call the 'social architecture of cyberspace' (63). They identify three key groups:

- The 'information users': an elite of transnational service workers, who have the skills and knowledges to achieve positions of dominance in the digital economy (the digital elite).
- The 'information used': less affluent and less mobile workers, whose main connection with the digital economy is as home-telematics consumers (the digital shoppers).
- The 'off-line': marginalized underemployed/unemployed and 'technologically intimidated' groups who lack the financial resources to participate at all in cyberculture (the digital underclass).

This kind of social polarization is especially connected with the Internet's morphing into an 'information superhighway', which is seen by many critics as reducing the democratic, participatory ideals of many-to-many communication in favour of corporate production and niche consumption – this particularly effects the 'information used', who do have access to the technology but who find themselves recast as passive consumers by the new 'information infrastructures' (Aurigi and Graham 1998: 65).

The formation of new digital elites comprising footloose knowledge workers, and the realignment of the other class groups in line with access to technology, is vividly described by Kroker and Weinstein as the creation of 'virtual class' and 'data trash'. Here's their definition of the former:

> The social strata in contemporary pan-capitalism that has material and ideological interest in speeding-up and intensifying the process of virtualization and heightening the will to virtuality. The elite components of this class include technotopians who explicitly advance the cause of virtualization through offering a utopia of juvenile power (virtual reality flight simulators in all the entertainment complexes), and cynical capitalists who exploit virtuality for profit.
>
> (Kroker and Weinstein 1994: 163)

This definition brings together two groups, then: capitalists wanting to exploit the new markets cyberspace opens up, and 'technotopians' who are driven by the fetish of technological advance. These two are brought together in the guise of the 'new edge' cyberculture, which combines techno-savvy with a marketized and individualized work ethic (Terranova 2000). The 'new edge' version of the digital elite, however, is only representative of one version of the virtual class. Aurigi and Graham focus their attention more squarely on the transnational corporate class – a group that has already attracted considerable attention in view of its centrality to forms of globalization (Hannerz 1996). This 'executive elite' holds the key jobs in multinational corporations, and has been rendered increasingly 'footloose' by advances in information and communication infrastructures. Moreover, these corporations have themselves 'gone digital'.

Those corporations are also the same ones who are interested in selling to the 'information used' – the social class that is the primary target market for the new digital products and services. This 'pay-per' consumer class is subject to what Oscar Gandy (1995) calls 'the panoptic sort' – the systems of information-gathering and market research that have proliferated with the virtualization of the life-world. The increasing reliance on non-human 'expert systems' to make decisions about, for example, credit-worthiness, is based upon the gathering, sorting and selling of vast amounts of data, gleaned from all manner of automated transactions. At its most benign this can mean being targeted by direct mail companies who have built up a 'profile' of your shopping habits. But it can also mean being denied access to credit by a machine that scans your financial biography. In this new information economy, class becomes a marketing concept – a further indication of what Gandy refers to as the 'viral contamination' of the Internet by commercial forces (Gandy 1995: 47).

However, the 'information used' is at least online, if only as consumers and marketing avatars. The digital underclass is invisible, except where its movements are tracked by surveillance systems aimed at keeping people in their 'electronic ghettoes'. If, as has been argued, the digital elites are both the main beneficiaries and the main drivers of time–space compression, then the digital underclass lives where 'the space of flows comes to a full stop [and where] . . . time–space compression means having time to spare and the space to go nowhere at all' (Thrift 1995: 31).

Aurigi and Graham note that social policy efforts to grant access to cyberspace for this group have a lot of obstacles to get over (and, conversely, members of that group might have very significant barriers to overcome, and getting access to the Internet might be a pretty low priority). As they note, it is important not to lose sight of the issues of social exclusion when reading (and writing) about the global digital revolution:

> All too often academics who participate in such debates, who receive high-quality Internet access for free, fail to appreciate the enormous structural inequalities in access to communications and computing infrastructures that are deeply woven into urban social geographies.
>
> (Aurigi and Graham 1998: 61)

According to some recent statistics, for example, less than 5 per cent of people in the lowest 40 per cent income group were online in the UK in 2000.

Of course, these inequalities are inscribed at a number of spatial scales, from within the home to across the globe. In the book *Cyberspace Divide*, Trevor Haywood (1998) signals a now-familiar note of caution (reminding us that the computer can too easily screen off such differentials), and Mike Holderness maps global information inequality, concluding that 'the sharpest, most clearly enumerable divides in cyberspace are those based on where one lives and how much money one has' (Holderness 1998: 37). Added to this is the question of the impact that information inequality has on other forms of inequality – Holderness reminds us of the link between 'bits' and 'atoms' which means that the digital and the material are conjoined. Think about, for example, the rise of online shopping and its impacts on offline outlets unable to compete for customers or give big discounts – exactly those that might service 'marginal' populations. Lastly, we must be mindful of the relationship between access and use: maps solely of Internet access and use are too simplistic, in that they fail to account for kinds of access and types of use. 'Simple access to networks does not necessarily imply that use develops, that this use has any meaning, or that it necessarily brings power and advantage to users', write Aurigi and Graham (1998: 63), reminding us that alienated forms of labour exist in digital sweatshops, too (see also Terranova 2000), and also that the commodified 'pay-per' access to the Internet made available to the 'information used' represents something very different from the digital elite's access to and use of cyberspace.

A critical reading of these new virtual classes is provided by Frank Webster and Kevin Robins (1998), who urge us to see continuity rather than change when it comes to thinking about digital elites. Their analysis suggests that members of the transational corporate class are still wielding the same economic, social and cultural capital that marked pre-digital business elites – they have merely added cyber-capital to their portfolios (we'll come back to these forms of capital in a minute). As the press coverage of 'dot.com millionaires' can be read to show, the nerds and geeks still need socially-skilled networkers (in the business rather than electronic sense) to get their deals. The system (capitalism) remains intact, and in fact becomes 'turbo-capitalism' – more rational, more calculating and more alienating. The result is, for Webster and Robins, starkly pessimistic: 'a cultural apartheid between the mobile elite and the immobile residue of the "unproductive masses"' (Webster and Robins 1998: 39). Such a scenario is depicted by Kroker and Weinstein (1994) as 'virtual class war' – a war between 'cyborg masters' and 'robot slaves' (Webster and Robins 1998: 40).

Thus far, then, we have considered new class formations in cyberculture, and set these in the context of information inequality and the system that Kroker and Weinstein name 'virtual capitalism'. But, as I said at the start of this section, there are other questions that need asking in thinking about class and cyberculture. To begin, I want to return to a notion mentioned in the last paragraph: the idea of 'cyber-capital'. What I mean by this is an extension of Pierre Bourdieu's famous formulation, in *Distinction* (1984), of cultural capital – of the symbolic resources used by social classes to mark themselves as different from (better than) other classes. To think this through in relation to cyberculture means we need to think about the symbolic meanings of forms of cyber-capital, including hardware and what Haraway (CR) calls 'machine skill'. As discussed in the context of home pages earlier in this chapter, machine skill can be utilized to mark distinction by showing technological proficiency – by making an alluring site.

Materializing knowledge and skill by crafting a good site is, therefore, one way in which cyber-capital works. At other levels, we might read the fetish for new hardware products as ways of marking distinction – something that some computer manufacturers have capitalized on, transforming computers from dull grey functional boxes to aesthetic objects (the iMac and its relatives are good examples; see McIntyre 1999).

However, other forms of machine skill and other kinds of hardware get coded very differently. Being good at computer games might be read as evidence of time-wasting slackness, just as having a satellite dish (in the UK, at least) codes the owner as a 'couch potato' rather than someone actively and discerningly consuming globalized TV products (Brunsden 1997). At present, too, the 'meaning' of mobile phones might be read as ambivalent – WAP phones are being marketed for their connectivity, but mobile phone use can become loaded with negative connotations, many of which have a class-based inflection to them (arguments about 'noise pollution', for example – too much chattering is seen as common). Indeed, the iconic practice of cyberculture – surfing the web – can itself be recast as idling, or as potentially deviant, as can the over-enthusiastic embrace of technotopianism. So, the notion of the 'digital underclass' as 'technologically intimidated' needs a little complexifying – the question might better be shaped around a class-based notion of what constitutes 'responsible' or 'respectable' uses for technology.

My point in discussing 'cyber-capital' is to draw attention to the manifold ways that social class and cyberculture are inter-related, and to usher in symbolic dimensions alongside the more fully-explored material aspects. While there has been little work to date on the mobilization of particular class identities in cyberspace, I want to suggest that the endurance of class in the digital age can only be fully understood when more broad-ranging analyses have been undertaken. Insights from socio-linguistics, for example, could pick out the ways in which 'classed' writings and readings of textual interactions in cyberspace impact on the way communication works between participants. Other research agendas might focus on the symbolic as well as material blocks that limit access to virtual worlds for different classes, the extent to which (and the forms in which) class 'appears' or 'disappears' online, and so on.

## Summary

This chapter has attempted to think about certain aspects of individual and collective identity – race, gender, sexuality and class – in the context of cyberculture. Drawing on debates about social identity in contemporary societies more broadly, I hope to have located cybercultural identities in the context of the so-called 'decentring of the self'. A brief look at personal homepages led us into the issues, by showing how self-identity is self-consciously crafted in cyberspace, and how websites are by turn used to project an image of the self. Focusing in on particular aspects of identity has then allowed us to build up a picture of the key issues and questions – some of these are common across identity-categories, others are more centrally located within one of the axes of identity discussed. Common themes include the visibility or invisibility of identity online, the modes of self-presentation used by participants, issues of 'otherness' and 'passing', and questions of the *politics* of particular online identity-strategies. Grounded work on particular sites gives useful contextual insights into these issues – though interpretations of modes of identification online vary quite markedly, as the discussion of gender-play in LambdaMOO highlighted. Ultimately, what we might conclude from the material presented in this chapter is that identities do matter online; but that their relationship to RL identities is complex, variable and contested.

## Hot links

### *Chapters from* The Cybercultures Reader

Gareth Branwyn, 'Compu-sex: erotica for cybernauts' (Chapter 24: 396–402).

Thomas Foster, '"Trapped by the body": telepresence technologies and trans-gendered performance in feminist and lesbian rewritings of cyberpunk fiction' (Chapter 28: 439–59).

Ananda Mitra, 'Virtual commonality: looking for India on the Internet' (Chapter 44: 676–94).

Lisa Nakamura, 'Race in/for cyberspace: identity tourism and racial passing on the Internet' (Chapter 46: 712–20).

Sadie Plant, 'On the matrix: cyberfeminist simulations' (Chapter 19: 325–36).

Ziauddin Sardar, 'alt.civilizations.faq: cyberspace as the darker side of the West' (Chapter 48: 732–52).

Judith Squires, 'Fabulous feminist futures and the lure of cyberculture' (Chapter 22: 360–73).

Jon Stratton, 'Cyberspace and the globalization of culture' (Chapter 47: 721–31).

Susan Stryker, 'Transsexuality: the body and/as technology' (Chapter 37: 588–97).

Daniel Tsang, 'Notes on queer 'n' Asian virtual sex' (Chapter 27: 432–38).

Nina Wakeford, 'Cyberqueer' (Chapter 25: 403–15).

Nina Wakeford, 'Networking women and grrrls with information/communication technology: surfing tales of the world wide web' (Chapter 21: 350–9).

Randal Woodland, 'Queer spaces, modem boys and pagan statues: gay/lesbian identity and the construction of cyberspace' (Chapter 26: 416–31).

## Further reading

Wendy Harcourt (ed.) (1999) *Women@Internet: creating new cultures in cyberspace*, London: Zed Books.

Beth Kolko, Lisa Nakamura and Gilbert Rodman (eds) (2000) *Race in Cyberspace*, London: Routledge.

Brian Loader (ed.) (1998) *Cyberspace Divide: equality, agency and policy in the information society*, London: Routledge.

Jenny Wolmark (ed.) (1999) *Cybersexualities: a reader on feminist theory, cyborgs and cyberspace*, Edinburgh: Edinburgh University Press.

## Websites

http://www.arts.ucsb.edu/bodiesinc
Bodies$^c$ INCorporated avatar site – discussed by Jennifer Gonzalez (2000).

http://www.dux.ru/virtual/digibody/undina/!undina.htm
UNDINA avatar site – discussed by Jennifer Gonzalez (2000).

http://webcamworld.com
Lots of information about webcams and webcamming, plus web ring and links.

www.planetout.com
Commercial lesbigaytrans site, offering a worldwide community, links and resources.

http://www.cybergrrl.com/
One of the best-known sites, with its motto 'A woman's place is online'; also includes chat, BBS and internal email system.

# BODIES IN CYBERCULTURE

> We are less and less creatures of flesh, bone, and blood pushing boulders uphill; we are more and more creatures of mind-zapping bits and bytes moving around at the speed of light.
>
> *R. U. Sirius*

IN THIS CHAPTER I WANT TO EXPLORE one of the most hotly-debated terrains of contemporary culture – the question of embodiment. To do this, I will begin by sketching some of the general arguments in social and cultural theory about the body, and then move into cyberspace via a discussion of debates about disembodiment – about the possibilities of transcending the physical body in cyberspace, often referred to as the experience (or dream) of 'leaving the meat behind'. The chapter will then focus in on three cyber-bodies, in order to flesh out (so to speak) these arguments and questions: the posthuman, the cyborg, and the Visible Human. Drawing on the extensive literatures discussing these three instances of cybercultural (dis)embodiment, my aim will be to present a range of perspectives on the 'place' of the body in cyberculture and in cybercultural theory. To begin, then, a few comments on the body's place in social and cultural theory more broadly.

## The body in theory

Barbara Brook (1999) asks a simple question at the start of her book *Feminist Perspectives on the Body*; a simple question, that is, that rapidly becomes more and more complicated. Her discussion is a useful place to start, because it points towards some of the key questions that have vexed social and cultural theorists trying to think about 'the body':

> What about the body? Try reading that . . . with different emphases! *What* about the body? What *about* the body? What about the *body*? Think too about that strange collective single entity that is thus named . . . ['T]he body' is not the way you would immediately designate yourself, nor is it possible to come up with a picture of what 'the body' is, since that single term strives to encompass all the multiple ways human material is formed and arranged not only within space but also through time.
>
> (Brook 1999: 1)

As Brook goes on to note (with some irony), sociology has witnessed a 'discovery' of the body over the last decade; in fact, there has been something of an *explosion* of bodies across the humanities and social sciences. After its disappearance in the wake of the Cartesian privileging of the mind, and its removal from theory (where it got in the way of thinking), 'the body' has re-emerged as a central concern across a range of disciplines, including history, philosophy, geography, sociology and cultural studies. The huge body of work produced has focused in on particular bodies, things bodies do, things done to bodies, what bodies mean, and so on. Theory has unsettled 'the body' as a taken-for-granted and natural thing, locating it instead in webs of signification and power: bodies are produced in complex ways and located in historical, geographical and cultural contexts. The 'body in theory' has become, in fact, a multitude of bodies, read in a multitude of ways.

Such an intense focus on bodies has had a paradoxical effect, as Williams and Bendelow (1998) note:

> As a consequence of these developments, the body is both everywhere and nowhere in social theory today. This is perhaps most graphically illustrated in recent post-structuralist thought where bodies are radically reconfigured as fluid, multiple, fragmented and dispersed. In this respect, a central paradox emerges, namely that, along with a range of other social and technological developments at the turn of the century, the recent upsurge of interest in body matters undermines still further our sense of what, precisely, the body *is*, and perhaps more troublingly, what it may *become*.
>
> (Williams and Bendelow 1998: 1–2)

Part of this paradox arises from the proliferation of perspectives on embodiment, which seemingly compete more than they connect with each other. Moreover, theorizing about the body has been critiqued for being over-abstract, never getting into the materiality of bodies (Holliday and Hassard 2001). All the work on the body has served, in some ways, to make it less clear – and it is equally difficult to recognize oneself in much of this work as it is in the phrase 'the body' itself. As we shall see, this feature of 'the body in theory' has spilled over into considerations of embodiment and disem-bodiment in cyberculture.

As one way of addressing this paradox, some researchers have turned towards the empirical and experiential exploration of embodiment; instead of abstractly theorizing about 'the body', they have talked to people about their bodies, and thereby brought theory back into the realm of the 'lived body' (Williams and Bendelow 1998). This trajectory is an important one to consider in the context of cyberculture, where experiences need to be set alongside fantasies of dis/embodiment (Lupton CR; Bell 2001) — something we shall return to in a while.

This materialist reading of corporeality should not be seen as a rejection of theory, of course. There have been, as already signalled, incredibly impor-tant theoretical insights made about 'the body'. Most of these have been concerned with what we might call 'de-naturalizing' the body — unpacking the processes by which bodies are made in culture (and not just by nature). As Anthony Synnott (1993: 3–4) says, '[t]he body, therefore, with all its organs, attributes, functions, states and senses, is not so much a biological given as a social creation of immense complexity, and almost limitless vari-ability, richness and power'. How we think about our bodies and body-parts, the uses to which they are put, the shapes we make them take (or are *made to make them take*) — these are all instances where culture (and history, geog-raphy, society . . .) intersect with the bones and guts and goo. Insights from post-structuralists, feminists, phenomenologists, ethnomethodologists and countless other theoreticians have fleshed out the body in productive and insightful ways — even if, at the end of the day, we have proliferated bodies of work at the same time as proliferating bodies. We still might not be able to agree on what the body *is*, but we certainly have an expanding collection of resources to *think the body with*.

Brook and Synnott both remind us that talking about 'the body' is a nonsense; instead, we need to talk about *bodies* in all their multiplicity and variability. Thinking about bodies in the plural reminds us, too, of the rela-tionships between bodies, their overlaps — as well as the gaps between bodies, their differences. For bodies do a lot of the 'identity-work' that goes on in culture and society — we deploy our bodies (or aspects of our bodies) as, if you like, embodiments of our *self* (Synnott 1993). One domain where this has been explored is in terms of the 'fit' between bodies and selves, and the ways in which bodies can be actively reshaped to make them correspond to an individual's sense of who they are (or who they want to become). And this is one place where technology in its broadest sense can also intersect with bodies — especially the technologies of dieting, exercise and cosmetic surgery that reshape bodies to 'fit' with cultural norms (issues that have been extensively discussed in feminist research; see, for example, Bordo 1993; Davis 1995).

Feminist research on the body has, in fact, increasingly been concerned with thinking about body–technology interfaces; for example, work on reproductive technologies from The Pill to donor insemination has explored the impact of these technologies on the experiences of and discourses surrounding embodiment (Oudshoorn 1994; Farquhar 1996). Increasingly, as we shall see, this kind of commingling of bodies and technologies has come to be theorized as 'prostheticization' or 'cyborgization'. Other important areas of research concerning bodies and technologies include work on medical technologies more broadly, other forms of body modification (such as tattooing and piercing), and what we might call 'technologies of representation' – how discourses shape bodies, and how that shaping is mediated by the ways in which bodies are shown to us (Tasker 1993; Balsamo 1996; Featherstone 2000; Marchessault and Sawchuk 2000). All of these research agendas are important for considering embodiment in cyberculture, as we shall see in the next section, which focuses on the idea that cyberspace offers us the chance to escape our bodies and become, as *Mondo 2000* editor R. U. Sirius put it, 'creatures of mind-zapping bits and bytes moving around at the speed of light' (quoted in Terranova CR: 271).

## Leaving the meat behind

'I'm trapped in this worthless lump of matter called flesh!'

(BBSer, quoted in Dery 1996: 248)

The motif of the body as 'meat' – and the prospect of leaving it behind – is a recurrent theme in cyberculture. Related to our earlier discussion of identities in cyberspace, this theme also picks up on the 'freedom' CMC offers users to jettison their RL bodies (and identities) and remake themselves in the non-material realm of bits and bytes. The origins of this 'dream' lie at least in part in the literature of cyberpunk, and particularly in those 'functionally modified' hybrid figures that populate the landscapes of the genre's fictions (Tomas CR). The notion of 'jacking in' to cyberspace found, for example, in William Gibson's work, most potently symbolizes this mind–body split, with the 'meat' discarded and the unconstrained consciousness flowing free in (and as) data:

'Jacking in' is the instantaneous rite of passage that separates body from consciousness. That disembodied human consciousness is then able to simultaneously traverse the vast cyberpsychic spaces of [the] global information matrix. Access therefore promotes a purely sensorial relocation.

(Tomas CR: 183)

As we have seen repeatedly already, the kinds of images produced by cyberpunk have had important effects in shaping how participants in cyber-culture perceive themselves. This 'uploading of consciousness' is often held as the ultimate limit-experience of cyberspace; as Lupton (CR: 479) says, '[t]he dream of cyberculture is to leave the meat behind and to become distilled in a clean, pure, uncontaminated relationship with computer tech-nology' – though some feminist critics argue that this is essentially a 'boy's dream' (Brook 1999).

Translating this dream into practice, moreover, appears to require a working version of Gibson's 'consensual hallucination', not just because the direct interfacing of mind and machine has yet to become a reality, but also because the 'meat' is not that readily discarded – it's the meat that sits at the screen, typing and reading. This leads Anne Balsamo (CR: 490) to recast the 'dream' of disembodiment in terms of repression: '[t]he phenomenolog-ical experience of cyberspace depends upon and in fact requires the wilful repression of the material body'. We have to find a way to forget our body, therefore. However, as many commentators remind us, this is an impossible task; the meat can never be fully left behind:

> Cyberspace developers foresee a time when they will be able to forget about the body. But it is important to remember that virtual commu-nity originates in, and must return to, the physical. . . . Even in the age of the technosocial subject, *life is lived through bodies*.
>
> (Stone CR: 525; my emphasis)

In the end, it seems, however much we might wish the body would dis-appear, there's more meat than we can repress or dream away or forget, and we remain embodied – albeit in new ways. As I've written elsewhere, what we find in cyberculture are *techno-bodies*, rather than *tech-nobodies* (Bell 2001). (However, it should be noted that some commentators argue that the 'direct' interfacing of bodies-as-text in cyberspace *can* effectively make the screen [and the body] disappear – just as our immersion in a movie or tv programme can let us forget that we're sitting in front of a projection; see Dyson 1998.)

One of the best essays to discuss this whole question is Deborah Lupton's 'The embodied computer/user' (CR). Lupton's central focus is on *experiences* of/in cyberspace, rather than the imaginings of cyberpunk. Against the image of the disembodied computer user, then, she keeps the meat in keen focus, for example by reminding us that '[w]hile an individual may successfully pre-tend to be a different gender or age on the Internet, she or he will always have to return to the embodied reality of the empty stomach, stiff neck, aching hands, sore back and gritty eyes caused by many hours in front of a computer terminal' (Lupton CR: 480) – an issue neatly summed up by Margaret Morse's (1994) question, 'What do cyborgs eat?':

> Travellers on the virtual highways of an information society have . . .
> at least one body too many – the one now largely sedentary carbon-
> based body at the control console that suffers hunger, corpulency,
> illness, old age, and ultimately death. The other body, a silicon-based
> surrogate jacked into immaterial realms of data, has superpowers, albeit
> virtually, and is immortal – or, rather, the chosen body, an electronic
> avatar 'decoupled' from the physical body, is a program capable of
> enduring endless deaths.
>
> (Morse 1994: 157)

Barbara Brook (1999) also discusses this question, via Susan Wendell's (1996) work on the 'disabled body', noting that the disembodiment of cyberspace cannot 'free' the consciousness from the subjective experience of pain (see also Gromala CR). Moreover, as Lupton elaborates (CR), we might actually want to actively resist *total* absorption into cyberspace, not least because of our lingering fears about what this might mean for us (we shall return to this dilemma in the context of the cyborg, too). Getting a fuller picture of how we think about our relationships with computers – by talking to users – has, in fact, become an important strand of cybercultural work, as we shall see in Chapter 9 (see also Lupton and Noble 1997; Turkle 1999).

Nevertheless, in some circuits of cyberculture at least, the dream of a meat-free future endures – especially, perhaps, in high-tech subcultures (Terranova CR) and in the work of those researching robotics and artificial intelligence (see, for example, Moravec 1998). But the freeing of the mind from the burden of the body is only one way of imagining the body–technology relationship brought about in cyberspace. Other theories stress the conjoining or mixing of carbon and silicon, the 'wetware' of the flesh with the hardware and software of our machines. One way of signalling this new union is through the notion of posthumanism – signalling the 'end of the human' as we know it, and its morphing into new hybrid forms.

## The posthuman

> As you gaze at the flickering signifiers scrolling down the computer
> screen, no matter what identifications you assign to the embodied enti-
> ties that you cannot see, you have already become posthuman.
>
> (Hayles 1999a: xiv)

As N. Katherine Hayles (1999a: 283) writes, 'the prospect of becoming posthuman both evokes terror and excites pleasure' – and I think this partly depends on which version of posthumanism you're looking at. While some are apocalyptic and antihuman, as Hayles says, other formulations of human–machine interfacing are conjured that have potentially productive outcomes. Importantly, posthumanism is not (always) about jettisoning the body; rather, technological augmentation – prostheticization – offers in place of the disappearance of the meat its transmutation into new formations:

> This vision is a potent antidote to the view that parses virtuality as a division between an inert body that is left behind and a disembodied subjectivity that inhabits a virtual realm, the construction of virtuality performed by Case in William Gibson's *Neuromancer* when he delights in the 'bodiless exultation of cyberspace' and fears, above all, dropping back into the 'meat' of the body. By contrast . . . [in the posthuman model], human functionality expands because the parameters of the cognitive system it inhabits expand. *In this model, it is not a question of leaving the meat behind but rather of extending embodied awareness in highly specific, local, and material ways that would be impossible without electronic prosthesis.*
>
> (Hayles 1999a: 290–1; my emphasis)

The notion of 'extending embodied awareness' is one that has excited interest across the research fields of cybernetics, artificial intelligence (AI), robotics, artificial life (A-Life or AL) and virtual reality (VR). In some of the more fanciful future-facing scenarios, distributed systems are imagined, in which the human body is integrated with a variety of artificial and virtual prostheses; in some cases, indeed, the body continues to be rendered as 'meat' to be progressively replaced by machines:

> Picture a 'brain in a vat', sustained by life-support machinery, connected by wonderful electronic links to a series of artificial rent-a-bodies in remote locations, and to simulated bodies in virtual realities.
>
> (Moravec 1998: 92)

The Australian performance artist Stelarc, whose work draws on and makes use of new technologies, has famously declared that 'the human body is obsolete' (Stelarc CR: 562). In this version of posthumanism, evolution through natural selection is over – the 'natural' body cannot get any better on its own, so the next evolutionary step is to meld carbon and silicon. As robotics researcher Hans Moravec puts it:

> Our minds were evolved to store the skills and memories of a stone-age life, not the enormous complexity that has developed in the last 10,000 years. . . . The portion of absolutely essential human activity that takes place outside of human bodies and minds has been

steadily increasing. Hard-working intelligent machines may complete this trend.

(Moravec 1999: 116)

Welcoming technology into and on to the body can thus extend our capabilities, first by replacing worn-out organic elements and then by enhancing our 'natural' capabilities (technology evolves exponentially, so our posthuman bodies can be improved infinitely). In this kind of scenario, where human life is at an evolutionary dead-end, we have no choice but to get with these 'post-evolutionary strategies' (Stelarc CR: 562). Moravec prophesizes: 'as intelligent robots design successive generations of successors, technical evolution will go into overdrive. Biological humans can either adopt the fabulous mechanisms of robots, thus becoming robots themselves, or they can retire into obscurity' (Moravec 1998: 87), adding in another essay that 'meek humans would inherit the earth, but rapidly evolving machines would expand into the rest of the universe' (Moravec 1999: 121). The convergence of A-Life, AI, robotics and VR ushers in, some writers suggest, a new 'post-biological age'.

Stelarc himself calls for a post-biological hardening, hollowing and dehydrating of the organic body, to make it more durable and functionally adaptable. The hollow body then becomes a container for a variety of cyber-technological implants and devices, partly so it can survive in outer space – an idea that links back to the 'origin story' of cyborgs in space research. This strategy produces what Stelarc calls the 'cyberbody' in place of the organic 'psychobody':

> THE PSYCHOBODY is neither robust nor realiable. Its genetic code produces a body that malfunctions often and fatigues quickly, allowing only slim survival parameters and limiting its longevity. Its carbon chemistry GENERATES OUTMODED EMOTIONS. *The Psychobody is schizophrenic.* THE CYBERBODY is not a subject, but an object – not an object of envy but an object for engineering. The Cyberbody bristles with electrodes and antennae, amplifying its capabilities and projecting its presence to remote locations and into virtual spaces. The Cyberbody becomes an extended system – not merely to sustain a self, but to enhance operation and initiate alternate intelligent systems.
>
> (Stelarc CR: 571)

As we can see, part of the hollowing out of the body means, for Stelarc, getting rid of all the primitive bad programming – emotions, subjectivity, humanness. This has been seen as problematic, not least for critics who want to hang on to what makes us human, rather than accepting the prognosis of the 'Post-human Manifesto' that 'all technological progress of human society is geared towards the redundancy of the human species as we currently know it' (Pepperell 1995: 180). Moreover, the posthuman future pushes panic buttons in its side-stepping of questions of power, of who gets to play the posthuman and who will be left behind, discarded as 'data trash' or harvested for bio-tech uses (Kroker and Weinstein 1994; Dery CR). Sympathetic readings of this posthuman forecast could see an end to hunger, pain and illness and the opening-up of new ways and forms of life (Hayles 1999a). Antagonistic readings, however, see instead the formation of new and increasingly powerful elites, and a tragic loss of the rich patterning of human life lived as mortal, fallible and imperfect. Moreover, as Catherine Waldby notes, there are likely to be unforeseen side-effects produced in this melding of bodies and machines, as borne out in biomedicine's current attempts at poshumanizing:

> Prosthetic transformations – surgery pharmaceuticals, artificial organs and limbs – involve the provocation of often unpredictable instabilities and losses, as well as therapeutic gains. Such transformations may involve a whole redistribution of the embodied subject's qualities, capacities, orientations and positioning in the world which do not necessarily produce a predictable outcome.
>
> (Waldby 2000b: 113)

In line with this, Diana Gromala (CR) discusses 'sim-sickness' experienced in VR, when the body and mind are incapable of resolving the contradictory information coming from virtual and real stimuli simultaneously. The push to overcome this and other side-effects both reveals the desire to shed the reluctant meat, and signals its recalcitrance.

Of course, the kinds of scenarios depicted in Stelarc's or Moravec's work remain highly speculative, though there have been significant developments in the fields of AI, A-Life, robotics and VR technologies (see, for example, a number of essays in Druckrey 1999). In terms of current versions of posthumanism, many writers point towards medical prostheses as a first evolutionary step, citing heart pacemakers, cochlear implants, contact lenses, 'bionic' limbs and immunizations as our first moves towards posthumanity. Moreover, on the fringes of cyberculture, Gareth Branwyn (1998) tracks a 'neurohacking' subculture willing to experiment with posthuman possibilities drawn more from sci-fi's repertoire. Witness this email received by Branwyn: 'I am interested in becoming a guinea pig (if you will) for any cyberpunkish experiment from a true medicine/military/cyber/neuro place. New limbs, sight/hearing improvements, bio-monitors, etc. Or even things as simple as under the skin time pieces' (Branwyn 1998: 323). Tiziana Terranova (CR) discusses similar high-tech subcultures, finding manifestations of posthumanism in, for example, those folk associated with California's Extropy Institute. Echoing Stelarc and Moravec, the Extropians' FAQ file defines the posthuman thus:

> Post-humans will be persons of unprecedented physical, intellectual, and psychological ability, self-programming and self-defining, potentially immortal, unlimited individuals. Post-humans have overcome the biological, neurological, and psychological constraints evolved into humans. . . . Post-humans may be partly or mostly biological in form, but will likely be partly or wholly postbiological – our personalities having been transferred 'into' more durable, modifiable, and faster, and more powerful bodies and thinking hardware.
>
> (quoted in Terranova CR: 273)

Note the phrasing of the statement about constraints '*evolved into* humans', which reads as if we have a kind of built-in obsolescence, hidden away in our DNA. Pushing this argument further, in *Evolution from Space*, the astronomers Fred Hoyle and Chandra Wickramasinghe (1983) suggest that humans may even have been engineered extra-terrestrially, to evolve as interim 'hosts' for a future silicon-based lifeform (which is, as yet, still 'parasitic' on humans). For them, the whole trajectory of life on Earth is pre-programmed for us to develop new creatures (intelligent machines) that will come to usurp and dominate us (exactly the narrative played out in films such as *The Matrix*, of course). As Peter Weibel (1999: 211) says, in time these parasites will leave their hosts: 'the intelligent robot will construct and improve on itself, without us and without the genes that are our make-up. In evolutionary competition DNA will have lost out'.

Populating the planet with this new techno-biodiversity is already under way, some writers argue, with the 'creation of avatars, intelligent search agents and other smart machines: "life" in cyberspace is positively bursting forth in all directions – a silicon facilitated Cambrian explosion of genus and species limited only by the human imagination' (Wertheim 1998: 57). Again, there are different ways of reading this. Indeed, Hayles concludes her survey of posthumanism by calling for a version 'conducive to the long-range survival of humans and of other life-forms, biological and artificial, with whom we share the planet and ourselves' (Hayles 1999: 291) – rather than the vision of *The Matrix*, with machines taking over, she imagines a benevolent kinship in which we all live long and prosper. The jury is, it seems still out on the final verdict for our posthuman future. As A-Life expert Christopher Langton asks:

> We are literally at the beginning of a new epoch of life on Earth, an epoch that will be dominated by life-forms that we have had a significant

role in shaping. *Will they sustain and nurture us, and us them? Or will they destroy and replace us, or we them?*

(Langton 1999: 268; my emphasis)

As already noted, it is in the field of medical prosthesis that our first steps towards posthumanism can be witnessed. So, while the 'basement neurohackers' Branwyn discusses are pushing the posthuman agenda in one direction, the group of people currently evolving into posthumans, it might be argued, is the elderly. Mark Dery (1996: 231) quotes Thomas Hine (1991): 'Today's old are already in one technological vanguard', since their bodies have become welcoming hosts to new body parts and pharmacological enhancements, defying the built-in obsolescence of the ageing process. Mike Featherstone (CR) explores the implications of virtual reality and prosthetics for the elderly, an idea also discussed by Hans Moravec (1998: 92): 'aging users of remote bodies may opt to bypass atrophied muscles and dimmed senses, and connect sensory and motor nerves directly to electronic interfaces'. There are, of course, broad-reaching ramifications for these kinds of scenarios. While Featherstone considers a Haraway-like reading of the interface between the ageing body and the machine, which opens up the possibility of an emancipatory version of the posthuman (matched in Hayles' call for an 'inclusive' posthumanism), other critics are wary that overcoming the ageing process points towards the desire for immortality. In this light, Claudia Springer (1998) tracks the quest for immortality in cyberpunk, and in the wildest imaginings of VR, A-Life and AI research. She quotes one of Moravac's many predictions, this time on future possibilities for reviving the dead: 'Superintelligent archaeologists with wonder instruments . . . should be able to carry this process to a point where long-dead people can be reconstructed in near-perfect detail at any stage of their life' (Moravec 1988, quoted in Springer 1998: 70). As we shall see later in this chapter, the Visible Human Project represents an attempt to achieve such a revivification, though this centres on reassembling the body, rather than the mind – the exact opposite of the scenarios imagined by Moravec and played out in cyberpunk, where the 'brain in a vat' lives on through remote or virtual bodies.

Posthumanism, then, raises numerous questions about what makes us human: our minds, our bodies, our mind-bodies? This is, for many writers, the real potency of posthumanism. Catherine Waldby (2000b: 48) suggests that the best way to view the posthuman is as a 'particular kind of critical moment', adding that:

The possibility of the posthuman is not to do with the transcendence of the human, its replacement, but rather with the recognition and exposure of the networks of production which constitute human techno-genesis.

(Waldby 2000b: 49)

This recognition is often literalized in cyberpunk and sci-fi, in films such as *Blade Runner* or *Total Recall* that blur the boundaries between human and machine, raising issues about the status of memory in making us human (Landsberg CR). Once these questions hit home, uploading the immortal consciousness and jettisoning the withering body starts to sound like a nightmare, a 'never ending row of tomorrows . . . Just more of the same emptiness' (Starlin and Graziunas 1992, quoted in Springer 1998: 70). As both Springer and Robert Rawdon Wilson (1995: 253) note, this is part of the posthuman's dilemma: 'the sense of being an improved artifact and of having been once a fully human person' — experiencing what Wilson refers to as prosthetic consciousness, defined as a 'reflexive awareness of supplementation' (242). Our awareness of being posthuman might give us feelings of omnipotence, or of impotence (*Robocop* plays this out vividly). However, there's another side to prosthetic consciousness: what happens when our prostheses become conscious? In many sci-fi scenarios, from *2001* through *The Terminator* to *The Matrix*, the moment at which machines become sentient marks the moment of their turning against us. Weibel (1999: 222) poses another apocalyptic question here: 'Will virtual machines become the main protagonists in a global process that reduces the human to a mere spectator and parasite?' — like the humans as batteries in *The Matrix*, kept happy through a simulated virtual life. Against this kind of scenario (though less prevalent in popular culture), pro-posthuman futurologists express excitement at the possibilities this new joint kinship offers; a kinship in which 'machines become as complex as us, and we will be proud to see them proclaim themselves as our descendants' (Weibel 1999: 211).

Of course, to repeat a point made earlier, these issues and paradoxes are a feature of the different ways we think about posthumanism. Hayles' call to rethink the posthuman away from either helplessly apocalyptic and hopelessly Edenic scenarios, and to reimagine our future kinship with machines, asks that we take the opportunity to actively shape the future that lies before us. This has many echoes with Donna Haraway's work on cyborgs, in its attempt to redirect the ways we imagine human–machine relations. And it is to Haraway and her cyborgs that we shall now, in fact, turn our attention.

## The cyborg

A cyborg is a cybernetic organism, a hybrid of machine and organism, a creature of social reality as well as a creature of fiction. . . . By the late twentieth century, our time, mythic time, we are all chimeras, theorized and fabricated hybrids of machine and organism. In short, we are all cyborgs. The cyborg is our ontology; it gives us our politics.

(Haraway CR: 291–2)

The first cyborg to be named as such, as Donna Haraway (1995) reminds us, was a white rat in a US laboratory, implanted with an osmotic pump, in the late 1950s. At this time, in a prefiguring of Stelarc's posthuman extra-terrestrialism, early cyborg research was directed towards producing a human–machine 'hybrid' that could survive in space (Clynes and Kline 1995) – though the 'humanness' of the subject would remain intact: 'their bodies (like machines) would be modified so that their minds (which would remain unchanged) could continue the work of rational technoscience and space exploration, still human, still gendered' (Kirkup 2000: 8). The image of the prostheticized rodent or the spaceman, of course, is not the usual popular representation we associate with cyborgs: more often, we think of the Terminator, or Robocop, or The Six-Million-Dollar Man, or any of their cinematic and televisual progeny. As we have already seen with the figure of the posthuman (which we might see as one variant of the cyborg), the fusing of the biological and the technological can have a variety of motives, and produce a diversity of 'types':

> Cyborg technologies can be *restorative*, in that they restore lost func-
> tions and replace lost organs and limbs; they can be *normalizing*, in that
> they restore some creature to indistinguishable normality; they can be
> ambiguously *reconfiguring*, creating posthuman creatures equal to but
> different from humans, like what one is now when interacting with
> other creatures in cyberspace or, in the future, the type of modifica-
> tions proto-humans will undergo to live in space or under the sea having
> given up the comforts of terrestrial existence; and they can be *enhancing*,
> the aim of most military and industrial research, and what those with
> cyborg envy or even cyborg-philia fantasize.
>
> (Gray *et al*. 1995: 3)

Versions and variants of all these cyborgs currently inhabit the Earth, and many more inhabit our collective imagination; while there has been consider-able dispute about who might in fact have been the 'original' cyborg (Frankenstein's monster? Christ crucified? The first human tool-maker?), there is broader agreement about the current proliferation of cyborgs (and the pro-liferation of *ways of thinking about cyborgs*). To get a handle on these, the best place to start is *The Cyborg Handbook* (Gray 1995); and in terms of under-standing the current academic interest in the figure of the cyborg, Haraway's 'A cyborg manifesto' (CR) remains the pivotal essay. So, in this section, I'll try to give some shape to the cyborg as a particular form of cyber-body; one to be found in theories, representations and practices of cyberculture.

Against the meatless dream of jacking in, the cyborg 'reminds us that we are always embodied, but that the ways we are embodied aren't simple' (Gray *et al*. 1995: 7). This is important; thinking about human–machine

149

relations through the figure of the cyborg keeps the body in view, while also raising vital questions about the boundaries of the body, about nature, culture and technology, and about much more besides. Cyborgs ask us about 'much more besides', in fact, due to their status as 'boundary figures' whose hybridity unsettles the neatly-ordered worldviews that we have inherited. As Barbara Brook (1999: 139) writes, this *use* of the cyborg 'is considered to have potential for changing basic patterns of thought in modern western society because it throws into confusion conventional points of reference'. The cyborg, then, can be heroized or romanticized as a liminal, troubling metaphor for instability, fluidity and hybridity. As Branwyn notes, 'the romantic allure of the "cyborg" seems to captivate the fringes of digital culture' (Branwyn 1998: 324) – and its mainstream, too, we might argue (though in different forms and with different meanings, maybe).

Let me begin with the contention that today, *everyone is a cyborg*. This statement depends, I think, on how the cyborg is conceived. While the 'classical' notion of the cyborg figures an intimate connection between the organic and the technological – most obviously in terms of implants and prostheses – we can broaden this out by thinking about the ways our lives are *touched by technologies* in significant ways. It's not too much of a stretch to see car-driving, for example, as an instance of 'cyborgization' (Lupton 1999). The car enhances the human body's mobility and load-carrying capacity; moreover, there is a kind of symbiosis at work, which brings the car and driver together as a complex system (Dery 1997; Kennedy CR). And in the context of cyberculture, our increasing reliance on computers (to remember things, to help us write, to communicate with each other) marks another cyborgizing moment. As Tony Fitzpatrick (1999: 97) writes, this cyborg is 'the product of the daily interaction of perception/cognition with the screen, where the body melts into the electronic images that it receives, reflects and transmits'. Moreover, as David Hess (1995) persuasively argues, we can think of most members of urban societies today as at least 'low-tech cyborgs', since our existences are shaped and sustained by computers as well as phones, cars, televisions. If we extrapolate a bit, and think about the ways that transnational computational systems such as the stock market map out across the globe, and can certainly have impacts even for 'off line' communities, then it is possible to argue that everyone is a cyborg in this sense.

This line of argument, however, side-steps questions of *experience* and of *power*. In terms of the former, we can frame a question: How important is it that we realize that we are cyborgs, or understand ourselves as cyborgs? Again, this can be manifest in more or less spectacular ways – how our lives have to change if we haven't got a car, or can't find the network for our mobile phone, or have to take drugs to stay healthy. Or how we would feel if our computer got a virus, or crashed, or was stolen. This self-consciousness about cyborgization is an important consideration, also played out in key moments of films like *Robocop* and *The Net*. Factoring it into arguments about who is a cyborg can be useful, in further complicating the equation. If we do see ourselves as cyborgs, how do we feel about this? Do we dream of a posthuman future, or hate our over-reliance on machines? To some extent, of course, the answers to these questions are entirely contextual – some technologies and uses of technologies are more welcome than others. Shaping the forms, meanings and images that cyborgs take (or might take) can be seen, in fact, as a powerful response to these issues. It is part of the project Donna Haraway embarks on in 'A cyborg manifesto', and which she also spots in a slogan: 'Cyborgs for Earthly Survival!' (Haraway 1995: xix). Issues of power and agency are thus central to her reading and writing of the cyborg.

It's not an understatement to say that, since its first publication in the mid-1980s, the Cyborg Manifesto has had a profound and wide-reaching impact on the ways we now think about the cyborg, as well as on (cyber)cultural and (cyber)feminist theory more broadly. Although the essay has been critiqued at a number of levels, it has at its core a way of thinking about the cyborg as metaphor which is creative, ironic, and political. For Haraway, the task is to rethink what cyborgs are about, whilst always being mindful of their implication in webs of science and technology, and in the military–industrial–entertainment complex – as she puts it, '[t]he main trouble with cyborgs . . . is that they are the illegitimate offspring of militarism and patriarchal capitalism, not to mention state socialism' (Haraway CR: 293). However, the cyborg also dwells in the imagination; it is 'a creature of social reality as well as a creature of fiction' (291). It is ambivalent and complex, offering possibilities for both domination and freedom:

> From one perspective, a cyborg world is about the final imposition of a grid of control on the planet, about the final abstraction embodied in a Star Wars apocalypse waged in the name of defence, about the final appropriation of women's bodies in a masculinist orgy of war. . . . From another perspective, a cyborg world might be about lived social and bodily realities in which people are not afraid of their joint kinship with animals and machines, not afraid of permanently partial identities and contradictory standpoints.
>
> (Haraway CR: 295)

Moreover, the cyborg's boundary-blurring status – as *neither/both* human and machine – is suggestive of ways of resisting other reductive binaries, too: nature/culture, self/other, inside/outside. In one of her most famous

151

cyborg aphorisms, Haraway writes that the cyborg is 'resolutely commited to partiality, irony, intimacy, and perversity. It is oppositional, utopian, and completely without innocence' (292).

Identifying three key 'boundary breakdowns' as setting the stage for the cyborg – the human/animal, organic/machinic and physical/non-physical – Haraway expands her 'cyborg myth' into a tale of 'transgressed boundaries, potent fusions and dangerous possiblities which progressive people might explore as one part of needed political work' (295). This is the cyborg for Earthly survival – a way of recasting our relationship with technology – and crucially, for Haraway, a way of recasting gender, race, class and sexuality. To reimagine the cyborg, Haraway assembles numerous resources, including feminist theory (especially what Sandoval (CR) names US Third World feminism; see below) and feminist science fiction, in order to find new ways of seeing and thinking cyborgs. Ultimately, alongside and through these cyborgs, Haraway writes a potent ironic political and theoretical 'myth':

> Cyborg imagery can suggest a way out of the maze of dualisms in which we have explained our bodies and our tools to ourselves. This is a dream not of a common language, but of a powerful infidel heteroglossia. . . . It means both building and destroying machines, identities, categories, relationships, space stories.
>
> (Haraway CR: 316)

Jenny Wolmark (1999: 6) comments that it is the cyborg's 'propensity to disrupt boundaries and explore differently embodied subjectivities . . . [that can] be regarded as its most valuable characteristic' – though for some critics the hybridity and indeterminacy of the cyborg is allied with 'postmodern' theories, seen as inherently problematic in their avoidance of 'RL' bodies, issues and politics (Brook 1999). As Gill Kirkup (2000: 5) says, the cyborg's 'usefulness for cultural deconstruction of gender has become apparent, but its usefulness as a tool for material change is yet to be proved'. Judith Squires (CR: 369) similarly notes that 'the cyborg myth has a certain seductive imaginative power, but it is a myth . . . that can swing both ways', an observation which leads her to call for 'both a vision of cyborgs that may help to heighten our awareness of the potentiality for new technologies, and *the political pursuit of the practical manifestation of an appropriate technology*' (371; my emphasis).

Extensions, rewirings and critiques of Haraway's cyborgs have used her work as a point of departure in many directions (for a discussion of the 'celebrity' of the cyborg brought about by the Manifesto, see Haraway 2000). For example, Jennifer Gonzalez looks for images of cyborgs across history, from eighteenth-century automata to figurings in contemporary art, cinema and advertising. By tracking images and representations of cyborgs, Gonzalez aims to link the emergence of particular ways of thinking about the human/nonhuman boundary (as well as the gendered and racialized boundaries of bodies) with particular moments in human history:

> The image of the cyborg has historically recurred at moments of radical social and cultural change. . . . [W]hen the current ontological model of human being does not fit a new paradigm, a hybrid model of existence is required to encompass a new, complex and contradictory lived experience. *The cyborg body thus becomes the historical record of changes in human perception.*
>
> (Gonzalez CR: 542–3; my emphasis)

Importantly, she sees in these images problematic renderings of race and gender – problems which lead her to witness limitations in Haraway's formulation of the cyborg (though she simultaneously acknowledges her debt to it). Echoing Kirkup's criticism, Gonzalez ends her essay by writing that cyborg bodies do not yet 'function as radical alternatives. It may be that the cyborg is now in a new and progressive phase, but its 'racial' body politics have a long way to go' (Gonzalez CR: 550) – the cyborg is a useful metaphor for reading shifts in the human condition, but is that enough?

Francisco Javier Tirado (1999: 202) makes a similar point when he argues that 'although the cyborg brings transgression and is a notion which speaks of hybridization and crossbreeding rather than purity, we have hardly started to follow through the implications of this', to more fully locate the cyborg in the realm of everyday life. For Tirado, the cyborg-as-metaphor limits our analysis to the realm of representation, and he urges instead a Deleuzian approach to the cyborg as becoming or as event, and a Foucauldian archaeology of the cyborg form:

> Human subjects and conceptual or material objects among those living can now no longer be conceived in singularities isolated from the dynamic, correlative, multipartite systems within which they appear. . . . Becoming cyborg continually removes order in so far as it transgresses all limits or unceasingly reconstitutes them. Order in its own dynamics is unrelentingly removed into this becoming. We need a different logic to that of frontiers to try to approach an everyday existence populated by becoming cyborg. This search is itself a political action. . . . It forces us, therefore, to confront the multiple and the varied, the fragmentary and the unfinished, the nomadic and the hybrid.
>
> (Tirado 1999: 210, 215)

In another reading of Haraway with a different (yet related) focus, Chela Sandoval (CR) tracks the correspondences between cyborg feminism and what she calls US Third World feminism, and notes Haraway's indebtedness to US Third World feminist work, such as Gloria Anzaldua's (1987) theorizing of *la mestiza*, the borderlands. As Sandoval says, there are clear resonances between Haraway's Manifesto and other ways of theorizing 'oppositional consciousness'. As she sees it, 'colonized peoples of the Americas have already developed the cyborg skills required for survival' – 'cyborg consciousness' has a long lineage sited in forms of opposition to domination. Picking up Haraway's talk of 'joint kinship with animals and machines', Sandoval sets this alongside US Third World feminist work on affinity, which brings people together without the necessity of denying difference: 'such lines of affinity occur through attraction, combination and relation carved out of and in spite of difference' (Sandoval CR: 379). The methodology of the oppressed which Sandoval outlines, through practices such as semiotics and deconstruction, similarly chimes with the cyborg metaphor, since both represent forms of differential or oppositional consciousness, and both suggest new ways of thinking, acting and living together. Moreover, at the opening of her essay, Sandoval remembers the labourers of the New World Order, reminding us of the racialized and gendered 'cyborg politics' of employment in Silicon Valley:

> These workers know the pain of the union of machine and bodily tissue, the robotic conditions, and in the late twentieth century, the cyborg conditions under which the notion of human agency must take on new meanings. . . . Cyborg life: life as a worker who flips burgers, who speaks the cyborg speech of McDonalds, is a life that the workers of the future must prepare themselves for in small, everyday ways.
>
> (Sandoval CR: 374–5)

For Sandoval, therefore, there are important political resonances here, which can serve to open up the cyborg metaphor as a much broader sign of oppositional consciousness in the way that Tirado also asks for – through an embedding of the cyborg in 'small, everyday' things.

The final engagement with Haraway that I want to focus on here is Nina Lykke's (2000) essay, 'Between monsters, goddesses and cyborgs'. Its title evokes Haraway's closing (and best-known) aphorism in her Manifesto: 'I would rather be a cyborg than a goddess' (Haraway CR: 316), as well as her talk of the 'promises of monsters' (Haraway 1992). Lykke uses these three metaphorical figures as ways to explore feminist studies of science, which in itself is used to think about the 'great divides' of our times: human/non-human, science/non-science, and so on. Things that transgress the human/non-human boundary, like Frankenstein's monster, reveal the drive to keep those two domains forcefully separated. Drawing on Bruno Latour's (1993) conception of 'the work of purification' (producing dichotomies, such as nature/culture) and 'the work of translation' (producing hybrids and networks of 'nature–culture') as modern paradoxes (we want to keep things separate, but also facilitate boundary-crossing), Lykke locates the cyborg and the goddess within this monstrous realm – though each performs a very different version of monstrosity. And, in the space of the academy, she sees feminist science studies as equally monstrous – where monstrosity is a strength (a form of oppositional consciousness) rather than a weakness. (Tirado (1999: 215) makes a similar argument for his version of 'cyberpsychology' as 'a project that is always open, without doctrinal or methodological limits'.)

Tracking the goddess through ecofeminism, and the cyborg through feminist cyberpunk, Lykke teases out the similarities and differences between the metaphors. Both goddesses and cyborgs, for example, 'deconstruct the hegemonic position of the human subject of science vis-à-vis non-human objects and others . . . [and both] try to rethink the world as interaction between material-embodied and semiotic actors and subjects' (Lykke 2000: 85) – they are both powerful boundary figures, therefore. But there are differences in their 'boundary-ness':

> They blur the boundaries between human and non-human, between the material world and the semiotic world of signs and meanings, in different ways. The cyborg of virtual reality tends to absorb the material into the semiotic. The material is constructed as potentially changeable by semiotic, sign-producing acts, by programming and reprogramming. The goddess is different. When she represents a mythical reality to her adherents, we might say that she . . . tends to absorb the semiotic into the material. For adherents, the goddess is – not just a name, a semiotic device; she IS.
>
> (Lykke 2000: 85)

However, Lykke is wary of instating this difference, since it has too many echoes of the purifying divisions of science (such as the distinction between natural and artefactual). So, in the end, her call is to reject neither, but to further blur these boundaries: 'Why not instead talk much more of their monstrous sisterhood? Why not explore the potentials of cybergoddesses?' (Lykke 2000: 85).

As I hope has now become clear, Haraway's Manifesto has been an incredibly important catalyst to all kinds of cyborg theorizing since its publication. It enters the landscape of our imaginations, which is increasingly populated by boundary figures, from smart robots to avatars, and from *Blade Runner*'s replicants to cyberfeminism's replicunts. The cyborg embodies the desire and dread of cyberculture more powerfully, I think, than any other figure, meta-phorical or otherwise. As we increasingly live with, and as, cyborgs, we shall continue to witness the work of boundary creatures, including those that we cannot even as yet imagine. In the next section, I want to turn towards a very particular posthuman or cyborg figure, and one which raises a number of very important questions about embodiment in cyberculture: the 'Visible Human'.

## The Visible Human

If the [Visible Human Project] figures prefigure some new future for the human body, they imply the possibility of frightening, rather than consoling, transformations.

(Waldby 2000b: 6)

The US National Library of Medicine's Visible Human Project (VHP) repre-sents the coming together of biomedicine and cyberspace in a unique and extraordinary way. The project arose from the NLM's interest in producing a digital archive of the human body, to function as a biomedical resource for research and teaching, and as an aid in the development of telemedicine tech-niques (remote surgery, for example). The productions of the project, the Visible Man and Visible Woman, are complete, anatomically-detailed, three-dimensional virtual renderings of human corpses, constructed using an array of medical imaging and computational technologies. This digital 'Adam and Eve' (as they have become popularly known) stage the reverse of Lyyke's goddess: the goddess is the word made flesh, whereas the VHP figures are flesh made word (or, more accurately, *flesh made code*). They also reverse the dream of leaving the meat behind; in place of the uploaded consciousness imagined in cyberpunk, the VHP figures are *all meat* – even if it is digital meat. The stories these figures can tell us about posthumanism, biomedicine, and the body in cyberculture are therefore far-reaching and many-layered. Catherine Waldby (2000b: 50) concurs, writing that the VHP 'offers presen-timents of a possible future, a spectre which allows speculation about the multiple ramifications of the cybernetic turn'. In this section, therefore, I want to explore some of these ramifications, walking you through the uncanny corpses of the VHP.

The facts of the production of these Visible Humans are well known (and well detailed in Waldby 2000b), and have themselves been the focus of a lurid fascination that attends the entire project. The donated corpses (having been selected to represent 'typical' or 'normal' bodies) were MRI scanned, frozen in gelatin to $-85°C$, quartered, scanned again, sliced through (into thousands of slices between 0.3 and 1 mm thick) and photographed repeatedly, as each layer of their bodies was planed away, turning to dust. The digitized photographs thus produced can be reassembled and manipulated by computer programs, to produce a data-set that is infinitely manipulable. Animated 'fly-throughs', cross-sections at any chosen plane, pathological reconstructions, explorations of particular parts or systems within the body (the skeleton, the circulatory system) – all of these and countless more applications are possible. Accessible in cyberspace, the Visible Humans are eternally available for scientific and educational (not to mention recreational) scrutiny and use. They have been established to act as clinical benchmarks of normal human anatomy, and to be universally available – and amenable: 'As perfectly co-operative image-objects the VHP figures make their exhaustively visualised bodies available for all forms of display and optical penetration, without recalcitrance or resistance' (Waldby 2000b: 136).

Waldby picks out three key features of the VHP dataset that are important to note here: the VHP body is endlessly (i) replicatable, (ii) transmittable and (iii) subdividable. This means that it can be reproduced infinitely, without loss of quality, proliferating VH clones from a single, standard data-set – so researchers are all working on the same, standard databody. It circulates in cyberspace, enabling transcontinental research (which, in an interesting shift from one of the 'origin stories' of the Internet, replaces time-sharing of computers with *body-sharing*). It can be segmented, pulled apart and stripped away, allowing users to focus in on particular facets of the body – such as projects on the colon and the knee already using the VHP databody – without 'destroying' the integrity of the whole dataset (Waldby 2000a).

All of these features are premised on the VHP body operating as a biomedical norm or benchmark, as has already been noted. RL bodies can then be compared with this 'gold standard', in a virtual version of traditional anatomical medicine. This requires, of course, obfuscating all the differences between bodies, since these would work to obscure the comparison of live subjects with the VHP's biomedical norms:

> While the project programs in qualitative differences, these can never have the excessive effects of differences among and within embodied subjects; differences of resistance and idiosyncrasy, of the personal meaning of illness and its psychosomatic consequences, of the abjection and vulnerable mortality of fleshly bodies.
>
> (Waldby 2000a: 35)

Diana Gromala's work can usefully be reintroduced here, since her art project *Dancing with the Virtual Dervish* is concerned with using medical imaging technologies to explore the subjective experience on pain – exactly those aspects of embodiment that the VHP has deleted from its bodies. She has built an 'immersive, interactive virtual environment' constructed using numerous medical images of her own body assembled into a database, in order to elicit 'a reinhabitation of the body, one which conflates pain with pleasure and unknowable states of death' (Gromala CR: 607). Setting her *Virtual Dervish* alongside the VHP nicely brings out the ways in which biomedicine constructs a peculiarly *dead* body, stripped of feeling – no matter how much it is reanimated in cyberspace. By contrast, Gromala's work attempts to reintroduce subjectivity into clinical biomedical imagery.

In one very significant respect, the attempt of the VHP to procure 'standard' bodies has been short-circuited, by allowing the past life of 'digital Adam' to come to the surface. The facts of his life have, in some senses, come to overshadow the ways the project is read: the donated corpse is that of a murderer, Joseph Paul Jernigan, executed by lethal injection in Texas in 1993 (after twelve years spent on death row). This fixes the VHP into an older lineage of biomedical research, including anatomical investigation, where the subjects were often criminals, low-lifes and outcasts. Moreover, Jernigan's story brings into focus the status of the criminal subject, 'a subject whose status as a live ward of the state rendered him in death a subject stripped of his rights to certain privileges of citizenry – most notably, the right of bodily privacy' (Cartwright CR: 623). In this way, his use in the VHP eternalizes his status as prisoner; as Waldby puts it, he is condemned to 'an afterlife of arrest, incarceration and punishment' (Waldby 2000b: 154). Moreover, the manner of Jernigan's execution prefigures his unending 'prosthetic death'. He was administered a lethal injection through a catheter, which 'functioned as a kind of prosthetic disciplinary hand of the State of Texas, allowing prison officials chemically to reach into Jernigan's body and switch off the basic unconscious mechanism that regulated his breathing' (Cartwright CR: 621). Jernigan has, then, become an uncanny object of fascination, his virtual body forever inscribed with his life of crime. The fact that, in some visualizations, his tattoos are still visible only serves to reinstate his individualized embodiment (see, for example, Waldby 2000b: 2).

The Visible Woman, 'Eve', has not reaped the posthumous posthuman celebrity of Jernigan; she remains as an anonymous 59-year-old Maryland housewife who died of a heart attack. While at one level this represents an attempt to avoid the 'personalizing' of the VHP databodies that haunts Jernigan, it nevertheless brings its own ghost, in terms of the spectre of anonymity: unknown corpses may be more biomedically 'suitable', but their fate seems even more inhuman, as their identities are erased and they more fully become mere 'meat'. Anonymity thus brings home the callousness of anatomical science, concerned with the dead body rather than the living person. And in terms of the production and reproduction of these bodies, standardization is (at least potentially) achieved by turning 'away from the uncertainties and resistances of feminine sexuality and maternity and towards the reliable procedures of the laboratory' and the database (Waldby 2000a: 36). Virtual cloning ensures comparability, then, removing the complicating differences between RL cadavers. Inevitably, this aspect of the VHP has led to panics about scientists 'playing god' or 'meddling with nature', and has prompted what we might call Frankensteinian readings of the project as yet another attempt at parthenogenesis (male self-reproduction without women). Sarah Kember (1999), for example, offers this kind of analysis, bringing together medical imaging technologies and new reproductive technologies as instances of science's parthenogenic desire. Waldby, however, argues that this is too simplistic, preferring instead to think about invention rather than creation and standardized commodity production instead of masculine self-creation. In place of parthenogenesis, Waldby offers iatrogenesis (or, rather, 'IatroGenic desire'), which she defines as the desire to create 'kinds of bodies which are stable, self-identical entities rather than fields of perverse contingency', and as the desire for '*programmable matter*, for a capacity to order materiality according to the algorithmic efficiencies of the computer' (Waldby 2000b: 113, 114).

Of course, in the realm of popular culture, Frankensteinian fears are a commonplace reaction to science – and this virtual couple has attracted *immense* popular interest. Their arrival in cyberspace has, moreover, coincided with a slew of Hollywood 'cyberthrillers' addressing questions of virtual bodies and identities: *Strange Days, Johnny Mnemonic, Hackers, Virtuosity* and *The Net* (see Springer 1999). The VHP in fact 'seems to confer factual realization on what had been considered merely science fiction' (Waldby 2000b: 5). Indeed, the two have already physically crossed over, when VHP data were animated to simulate the building of a virtual humanoid in the movie *The Fifth Element*. Together, the Visible Humans and their Hollywood relatives form a fascinating and complex family, embodying as they do many of the hopes and fears of cyberculture, as well as asking other questions – questions about life and death most notably:

> As virtual apparitions of dead bodies, the VHP figures seem possessed of disconcerting presence and highly uncertain status. These corpses were dismembered, their flesh effectively destroyed in the process of imaging, yet they reappear as recomposed, intact and reanimated bodies in virtual space, 'copied' into the eternal medium of data. They are consequently difficult to locate within any proper distinction between the living and the dead.
>
> (Waldby 2000b: 6)

As Waldby says, the Visible Humans are 'kinds of still life' (140) – *but are they still kinds of life?* Or are they, as she suggests, the digital undead, virtual vampires or cyber-zombies – mournfully existing in the netherworlds between life, death and afterlife? In that fate they join a growing genus of life/death boundary figures that are profoundly unsettling:

> The vivification of information has changed the terms of the relationship between the living and the dead. Dead animals can be cloned and revived, dead humans can be cryogenically preserved or maintained on life support systems, tissue samples can be cultivated to produce immortal cell lines or to regenerate organs, computer code becomes artificially lively, and corpses can be reanimated as Visible Humans. Death has become increasingly uncertain, and its borders are constantly breached and reconfigured.
>
> (Waldby 2000b: 160)

In the sci-fi thriller *Virtuosity*, one of the movies that coincides and resonates with the VHP, the liveliness of databodies is played out in an interesting scenario. In the film, a composite serial killer has been put together in cyberspace for use in police training simulations. The construct, known as Sid 6.7, 'escapes' from cyberspace, enjoying living in the borderlands between states; as Springer (1999: 209) writes, 'he frolics through actual reality, overturning all norms and conventions and flaunting the freedom of "the new malleability"'. Reading *Virtuosity* alongside the VHP is, therefore, quite provocative: could the Texan murderer and Maryland housewife similarly cross back into RL, and if they did, what or who would they be? As with the futurological speculations about A-Life and posthumanism, we are as yet uncertain about the outcomes of these experiments in bringing life to cyberspace, and cyberspace to life.

## Summary

This chapter has considered the body in cyberculture, set in the general context of arguments about embodiment in social and cultural theory. In cyberspace, the RL body comes to occupy an *ambivalent* location, played out in a number of ways. The idea of leaving the meat behind – jettisoning the RL body and uploading the consciousness as data – was tracked in cyberpunk fiction and in areas of contemporary cyberculture; it was also set alongside the 'reality' of the embodied experiences of computer use. The chapter then moved on to focus in on three kinds of cyber-body: the posthuman, the cyborg and the Visible Human. Posthumanism raises a lot of interesting and troubling questions about what makes us human, and about whether we want to retain or transcend our humanness. Processes of prostheticization can be seen as enabling new posthuman entities to evolve past the Darwinian dead-end of our DNA. Alternatively, these processes can be read as surrendering ourselves over to mastery by machines. The discussion of posthumanism broadens out into the area of 'postbiology', raising questions about artificial life in cyberspace. Similar ambivalences circle around the cyborg – a figure brought to prominence in cybercultural theory thanks to Donna Haraway's Manifesto. Haraway weaves an 'ironic political myth' that works to rethink the cyborg as a disruptive boundary figure. Extensions and critiques of her Manifesto have shown the productive potential (but also the limitations) of this kind of cyborg-thinking. Finally, the databodies produced by the Visible Human Project were scrutinized, and revealed to similarly embody particular tensions and questions – for example around the blurring of the distinction between life and death. Although there are interesting overlaps between our three cyber-bodies, each raises its own issues, and asks that we look carefully at the bodies we populate cyber-space with.

## Hot links

### *Chapters from* The Cybercultures Reader

Anne Balsamo, 'The virtual body in cyberspace' (Chapter 31: 489–503).
Lisa Cartwright, 'The Visible Man: the male criminal subject as biomedical norm' (Chapter 40: 619–24).
Mark Dery, 'Ritual mechanics: cybernetic body art' (Chapter 36: 577–87).
Mike Featherstone, 'Post-bodies, aging and virtual reality' (Chapter 39: 609–18).
Jennifer Gonzalez, 'Envisioning cyborg bodies: notes from current research' (Chapter 34: 540–51).
Diana Gromala, 'Pain and subjectivity in virtual reality' (Chapter 38: 598–608).
Donna Haraway, 'A cyborg manifesto: science, technology and socialist-feminism in the late twentieth century' (Chapter 18: 291–324).
Barbara Kennedy, 'The "virtual machine" and new becomings in pre-millennial culture' (Introduction ii: 13–21).
Alison Landsberg, 'Prosthetic memory: *Total Recall* and *Blade Runner*' (Chapter 11: 190–201).
Deborah Lupton, 'The embodied computer/user' (Chapter 30: 477–88).
Chela Sandoval, 'New sciences: cyborg feminism and the methodology of the oppressed' (Chapter 23: 374–87).
Judith Squires, 'Fabulous feminist futures and the lure of cyberculture' (Chapter 22: 360–73).
Stelarc, 'From psycho-body to cyber-systems: images as post-human entities' (Chapter 35: 560–76).
Allucquere Rosanne Stone, 'Will the real body please stand up? Boundary stories about virtual cultures' (Chapter 32: 504–28).
Tiziana Terranova, 'Post-human unbounded: artificial evolution and high-tech subcultures' (Chapter 17: 268–79).
David Tomas, 'The technophilic body: on technicity in William Gibson's cyborg culture' (Chapter 10: 175–89).

## Further reading

Anne Balsamo (1996) *Technologies of the Gendered Body: reading cyborg women*, Durham NC: Duke.

Chris Hables Gray (ed.) (1995) *The Cyborg Handbook*, London: Routledge.

N. Katherine Hayles (1999) *How We Became Posthuman: virtual bodies in cybernetics, literature, and informatics*, Chicago: University of Chicago Press.

Gill Kirkup, Linda Janes, Kath Woodward and Fiona Hovenden (eds) (2000) *The Gendered Cyborg: a reader*, London: Routledge.

Catherine Waldby (2000) *The Visible Human Project: informatic bodies and posthuman medicine*, London: Routledge.

## Websites

http://www.stelarc.va.com.au/
Stelarc's homepage, with lots of info on his work and performances.

http://www.extropy.org/index.htm
Homepage for the Extropy Institute, leading players in posthumanism.

http://www.nlm.nih.gov/research/visible/
The Visible Human Project homepage, with links to numerous projects using the data, including some amazing animated fly-throughs, and commentaries, history of the Project, and so on.

http://www.frc.ri.cmu.edu/~hpm/
Hans Moravec's homepage, detailing his work on robotics.

http://www.internetv.com/dancin.htm
Video-stream of a performance of Diana Gromala's *Dancing with the Virtual Dervish*.

http://www.geocities.com/Athens/Agora/7256/
The Cyborg Syllabus: links to host of sites dealing with AI, A-Life, robotics, etc.

# Chapter 8

# CYBERSUBCULTURES

The street finds its own uses for things
*William Gibson*

**IN THIS CHAPTER I WANT TO EXPLORE** what we might call 'subcultural' or 'countercultural' uses of cyberspace. By this I mean ways of using computer technologies that subvert in some way dominant social norms or dominant formulations of what technology is for. These might be oppositional to the corporate political and economic structures increasingly dominating the shape of cyberspace, or they might be more broadly oppositional, signalling aspects of subcultural identity and politics. There's a lot of ground to cover, so I want to force cybersubcultures into an uneasy separation, into two groups: those that use cyberspace to advance their project, in the same way they might use other forms of communication; and those that signal an expressive relationship to the technology through subcultural activities. This split is uncomfortable in that there are many grey areas, where the technology might not be central to the group's identity, but where its defining characteristics have certainly reshaped the way the group works. I'll try to make this problem clear as we proceed. Ultimately, I want to argue that the nature of cyberspace itself might be said to encourage the proliferation of cybersubcultures, first by allowing us to collectivize our obsessions globally, and second by requiring that we prioritize aspects of ourselves in order to make sense of the infinite streams of information that circulate online. But before we get that far, I want to begin by making a few remarks about subcultures generally, and then move in to describe and explore selected cybersubcultures.

## Subcultural work

Cultural studies has a longstanding interest in subcultures, expanding on a substantial body of work in sociology and anthropology concerned with 'gangs' and 'delinquency' (see Gelder and Thornton 1997). Prominent work from Birmingham's Centre for Contemporary Cultural Studies – such as Dick Hebdige's work on punk – evidences that interest; and a focus on subcultural activities remains central to the intellectual project of the discipline, though the term subculture has faded a little, replaced by terms like 'counterculture' or the blander 'youth culture' (Epstein 1998). It might be wise to begin, then, by looking at the term 'subculture' itself, since it has been seen to be somewhat problematic. The problem with the term is the prefix 'sub-', which might suggest that subcultures are 'beneath' culture – and in some senses, we might argue, they are. But this shouldn't mean they are subsumed, or relegated; 'sub-' doesn't mean substandard, then. It might instead be taken to indicate, as Sarah Thornton (1997: 1) says, 'subordinate, subaltern or subterranean' – the excluded, the oppressed, the underground. It is, she says, a term used to describe 'groups of people who have something in common with each other . . . which distinguishes them in a significant way from other social groups'. Of course, there's more to it than that. Subcultures aren't just groups of people with common interests that stand in opposition to other groups; they must be doing some kind of *cultural work* with those interests and that opposition. In 'classic' subcultural theories, the identified group is working through its opposition – which is usually to the 'mainstream' or 'parent culture' – through a repertoire of expressive activities. As Hebdige's (1979) *Subculture: the meaning of style* shows, this is often codified through dress, 'attitude' and lifestyle, and circulated through the subculture's own 'micromedia' output: music, fanzines, flyers and so on.

The mainstream/subculture antipathy can be worked through in a multitude of ways. In the case of punk (which has come to be held up as *the* subculture *par excellence*), the mainstream is rejected, criticized and lampooned. Stylistic articulations of this come in the form of dress (second-hand clothes, safety pins, Nazi regalia, aimed at shocking mainstreamers), music (home-made, emphasizing lack of musical virtuosity – set against the pomposity of previous rock music), politics (anarchy and nihilism in opposition to party politics) and lifestyle (drug-taking, being on the dole, causing trouble, against conformity and respectability). Hebdige's discussion of *brico-lage* – the resignification of a patchwork of symbols, given new meanings in new contexts – remains important in showing us how subcultures adopt, transform and rework that which already exists – as William Gibson put it, 'the street finds its own uses for things'.

More recent subcultures similarly work to stress their non-mainstream credentials, as Thornton's (1995) work on dance music culture clearly illustrates. In the case of cybersubcultures, as we shall see, the target of oppositional cultural work is still often the mainstream – but the location of cyberspace in relation to the mainstream (especially corporate capitalism) makes for more complex processes of identification and rejection. (Of course, subcultures like punk have had to address this, too – for example the place of the music business in promoting punk rock.)

A second thread of subcultural work in cultural studies which we must be reminded of here is the problematic media coverage often given to spectacular displays of subcultural identification – most notably, in the past, in terms of rivalries between subcultures. Here Stanley Cohen's study of the media frenzy surrounding Bank Holiday battles between mods and rockers stands out as a definitive work. *Folk Devils and Moral Panics* (1972) stresses the role of the 'mainstream' media in consolidating subcultural identification by reporting it in particular ways: by picturing a 'war' between totally opposing factions – mods *versus* rockers – the British media effectively manufactured (or at least deepened) the subcultural allegiances within each group and their staunch hostility towards one another. Thornton, too, discusses media coverage of rave culture as ambivalently criticizing and promoting subcultural work. And, as we shall see, media reporting of cybersubcultures – particularly hackers – continues this trend, stereotyping groups but also spotlighting (and often inadvertently heroizing) their activities.

In part as a response to mainstream media misrepresentation, then, subcultures have long been engaged in their own media work. Of course, oppositional media output has a much longer history than that; as long as there have been means to reproduce and circulate standpoints and opinions, there have been 'micromedia' products – broadsides and rants, pornographies and incendiaries have been rolling off small presses for centuries, just as radio spawned pirate stations and cinema guerilla film-making. Slotting in cyberspace to the media platforms available has undoubtedly transformed the ways that countercultural publicity works, as we shall see, reshaping what McKay (1998) names 'DiY culture' by further blurring the distinction between author and audience, and by opening up new channels of resistance. Countercultural websites, bulletin boards and e-zines are proliferating in cyberspace, coming from a bewildering variety of angles, existing alongside other media forms. While in some cases these countercultural sites are little more than a translation of existing methods via new technology (Duncombe 1997), in other cases the form, content and aesthetic of new micromedia products signals a radical departure from other print or broadcast forms. Moreover, we might argue that the medium shapes the subculture, too, in many cases; as subcultures become more 'cyber-savvy', so they more effectively utilize the new tools at their disposal in line with their mission. Recent anti-capitalist actions in Seattle and Prague, for example, show how countercultural activity is itself becomes increasingly decentralized and web-like – a point we shall return to later.

Those anti-capitalist actions remind us that a further related topic should be brought in at this moment: new social movements. Another contested term — what is 'new' about them? — this is nonetheless a further focus of attention on activities similar to those of subcultures. Framed by a similarly long history of underground political agitation, new social movements have risen to prominence in the west since the 1960s and have reshaped the terrain of social and political protest. Associations with a wide range of movements, from hippie culture and green politics to post-materialism and New Age beliefs, are drawn together in a customized mixture of 'lifestyle politics' that rejects party politics in favour of flexible identifications across a range of concerns, calling for the 'democratization of everyday life' (Melucci 1989). New social movements have been quick to recognize the potential of cyberspace, especially in terms of forging global connectedness and transcending the parochialism of nation-based politics. Although conventionally set apart from subcultures, where emphasis has been placed more on elements of style, there are clear parallels and cross-overs between the work of new social movements and that of subcultures — both operate oppositionally, for one thing, and both groups make effective use of *bricolage*. In terms of what we're interested in here, both use a kind of *techno-bricolage* to reinvest technology with subversive meaning and intent, wrestling it out of the hands of those in power and reclaiming it for their own ends. However, as we shall see later, that act of wrestling is ideologically and materially difficult. Audre Lorde's (1984: 112) famous aphorism that 'the master's tools will never dismantle the master's house' means for some people that cyberspace can never be disinvested of its codings as one of the master's tools; the only option here is to reject those tools, too — a strategy mobilized by so-called Neo-Luddites, whose anti-technological stance must not be forgotten in our discussions.

As I wrote a few notes to guide myself through this chapter (in which, initially, I *had* forgotten the neo-Luddites!), I soon became overwhelmed by the variety of cybersubcultures and by the links between them. As I said earlier, I want to untidily separate them into two groups, in order to simplify my discussion. First, I shall turn my attention to those cybersubcultures that make use of new media to further their project, and then follow that with a look at cybersubcultures signalling an expressive relationship to the technology — and that's where neo-Luddites sit alongside hackers and cyberpunks. And, in order to show you what I mean by the untidiness of this act of separation, I want to begin by talking about something which in some ways isn't a cybersubculture, but in many other ways is: on-line fan culture.

## Fan cultures

Cultural critics have long had an interest in consumers of cultural products, and work on fan cultures has recast the producer–consumer relationship away from earlier ideas, like those embodied in the 'culture industry thesis', that people who listen to music or read books or watch tv or go to see films are mere passive 'dupes' subjected to the commercial and ideological impera- tives of the media industry. In place of this reductive reading of consumption, work such as Henry Jenkins' (1992) *Textual Poachers* has stressed fans' active engagement with and participation in the meaning-making processes of recep- tion and reading. Jenkins' work on television fans shows us how these processes are interrupted and rewired by groups of fans, who have evolved their own cultural work, manifest in conventions ('cons'), fanzines, 'slash' fiction and 'filk' songs (fan-composed songs, often performed at conven- tions). I suppose we should start, therefore, by asking if this means that fan groups constitute a subculture.

At one level of definition, the answer to that question has to be yes and no. Fan cultures are like subcultures in their lifestylization of an obsession, in their practices of *bricolage*, and in terms of the impact that being a fan of something can have on a person's identity and social relations. Punks, it must be remembered, were as much *fans* as anything else; yet the privileged status given to certain kinds of subculture in cultural studies sets them apart from a group of people who organize their lives around a shared love of *Blake's 7* or *The X-Files*. This is partly to do with a question of the kinds of cultural politics that subcultures are supposedly engaged in, and which fans are thought not to be engaged in (Pullen 2000). However, as we shall see, this dichotomy does something of a disservice to fan cultures. Alongside that, popular representations of fan culture tend towards a definite stereo- typing which lends fans less cultural credibility, making them perhaps less worthy of intellectual scrutiny. Again, I'd like to counter the assumptions embedded in such stereotyping. As Kirsten Pullen (2000: 54) writes, 'fans form an alternative community that rebels against mainstream norms and creates a space for . . . open communication' – which comes close to a defi- nition of fan culture as subculture (especially, as Pullen notes, with fans that follow 'marginal' or 'cult' tv).

Perhaps the most widely-circulating stereotype of fan culture is the 'Trekkie', the die-hard *Star Trek* fan whose interest in the show is obsessive. (*Star Trek* fans themselves prefer the term 'Trekker', maybe to distance them- selves from the connotations attached to the stereotype.) The 'Trekkie' is figured as someone whose (limited) social life revolves around *Star Trek* con- ventions, dressing as a Klingon, collecting overpriced *Star Trek* memorabilia and having a head full of mindless trivia about the show and its stars (Tulloch and Jenkins 1995). It's interesting to compare this image with some of those associated with cyberspace – with computer 'geeks' and 'nerds', for example, or with the media construction of hackers as immature and asocial. And although it is an over-written stereotype, we can pick out some features of our phantom 'Trekkie' here to explore in more detail in the context of cyberspace.

Caricaturing the 'Trekkie's' social life as revolving around his or her obsession can be re-read as testifying to the depth of involvement and investment in the show that fans articulate. The cons and the Klingon outfits are evidence of fans' self-organizing and self-producing cultural work. The memorabilia and the trivia are symbols of the show that circulate among fans, enabling them to build up what Thornton (1995) calls 'subcultural capital' – revealing fan culture as a dense social field, made durable by objects and knowledges. Add the work of *bricolage* in 'slash' fiction (homoerotic stories about male characters written by fans), 'filk' songs and re-edited sequences of shows made on video, and we are beginning to get a fuller sense of 'fan-cultural work' (Jenkins 1992). And now we have to add to that the role of the Internet in that work.

At its simplest, we could argue that cyberspace just extends fan culture's appropriation of media platforms. Just as the VCR made it possible for fans not only to record, rewatch and circulate their favourite shows but also to edit them into new, inventive scenarios, so cyberspace enables fan culture to carry on doing what it's always done, only more so. As Clerc (CR: 217) puts it, 'for many fans, Net groups are a continuation of off-line practice. . . because they have always engaged in the sort of long-distance communication we see on-line' – cyberspace has supplemented the circulation of zines, letters and so on. Cyberspace has thus given fans a new forum to meet, chat, create and disseminate. In this way it is a technology of *enlargement* – giving fans a global meeting-place and market-place. This point is picked out by Kirsten Pullen (2000: 55), who notes that 'the Web has opened up the boundaries of fandom, allowing more people to participate in fan culture, and designating more television programmes, celebrities and films as worthy of fan activity'. But that's not the end of the story. Cyberspace, it has been argued, has *transformed* the ways that fan culture works – though this might be either a good thing or a bad thing.

Susan Clerc's (1996; CR) work is very useful here, as is Pullen's on fans of *Xena: Warrior Princess*. Both offer insights into the workings of fan cultures on- and off-line. Both give us a picture of the diversity of activity around particular fan-objects (tv shows, films, bands) and show how cyberspace has impacted upon particular fractions of broader fan cultures. Clerc's essay in *The Cybercultures Reader* has at its heart a consideration of the ways in which gender relations in fan culture are reshaped in cyberspace. The 'maling' of cyberspace can mean that on-line fan sites are more male-dominated than off-line fan cultures, for example. 'Cyberfandom' therefore might be seen to reinstate gendered norms that off-line fan culture has already negotiated;

when Clerc (CR: 221) writes that 'to grossly generalize, men communicate for status, and women communicate to maintain relationships', she is pointing out that cyberspace has effectively reordered the genderings of fan culture. Female fans, of course, are not simply accepting this reordering, but are opening up (cyber)spaces for themselves in ways that are resistant to 'maling'. Often, in keeping with much of fan culture, these are heavily ironic – the Star Fleet Ladies Auxiliary and Embroidery/Baking Society is the name given to one small private mailing list for female *Star Trek* fans.

The stories of *Star Trek* fandom on-line take us back to a point Pullen made, about cyberspace broadening-out the kinds of shows and stars that fans now cluster around. Her discussion of fan culture as a subculture relied to an extent on particular kinds of programmes – and *Star Trek* is the classic example, as a marginal or non-mainstream show with a huge loyal fan-base (it was initially shunned by networks, and only slowly grew its 'cult' following) and with an open narrative (the 'metatext') that has plenty of space for fan interpretation and reworking. As Pullen notes, this kind of programme has dominated off-line fan cultures; the coming of cyberspace has, however, led to fan cultures developing around more and more types of tv show, including 'mainstream' ones:

> It seems as though the Web has mainstreamed fandom, allowing more viewers to participate in activities usually reserved for alternate communities interested in marginal texts; and fans' pervasive presence on the internet suggests that stereotypes of the fan as a fringe obsessive may give way to views of the fan as an average Web user. *On the internet, it seems as though everyone is a fan*, and nearly everything is worthy of fan adulation.
>
> (Pullen 2000: 56; my emphasis)

I've highlighted part of what Pullen says because it links in well with my argument about cyberspace encouraging subcultural (in this case fan-cultural) identification. The sheer amount of material in cyberspace asks that we make our own priorities, and that could be said to make us decide whether or not we're a fan of something (or *enough of a fan* of something to engage with other fans on-line). It also asks us to think about our fan practices in more detail; hence the proliferation of specialized sites dealing with different aspects of the show, different characters, and so on – Pullen estimates that there are more than 1,200 *Star Trek* websites out there, while the show she focuses on, *Xena: Warrior Princess*, has 200 dedicated sites (see also Clerc 1996; Jones 2000). On top of this, Pullen highlights the use of 'official' websites by tv companies, which blurs the boundary between fan activity and promotion, further contributing to the 'mainstreaming' of cyberfandom.

These forms of mainstreaming have, in some cases, provoked responses from within fan communities — some of which are hostile. Probably the most remarked upon is the treatment of newcomers to sites, derided as 'newbies' who clog up discussions with their FAQs. Established fans thus mobilize forms of subcultural capital to police membership. It should be remembered that this kind of policing occurs off-line, too — but the opening-out of fandom on-line makes the issue of membership more prominent (Clerc 1996).

But what is it that fans do on-line? Clerc says that they do what they do off-line, too: the principal fan activity, she argues, is discussion and analysis of storylines, character motivations, plots and so on. The open structure of the 'metatext' gives avid viewers space to think and interpret:

> Unresolved endings and hanging threads are both a source of pleasure and frustration for fans. . . . The frustration of not having all the threads tied together is also a source of pleasure, giving rise to analysis of the gaps in the narrative.
>
> (Clerc 1996: 38)

As Clerc's discussion of *X-Files* fandom shows, fans pore over episodes, tracing long-running narrative arcs, deploying the knowledge they have of the show in order to make sense of storylines, and sharing their thoughts with like-minds. *The X-Files*, of course, is ripe for this kind of fan-analysis (although Pullen considers it too mainstream to fit the 'classic' model of a fan-friendly show); the form of its metatext, it might be argued, mirrors its content, with a focus on complex conspiratories and countless gaps and threads (Bell and Bennion-Nixon 2001). Further, *X-Files* fandom, in line with the show's metatext, actively blurs the distinction between 'fact' and 'fiction' in its conspiratorial narrative, so fans draw not just on previous episodes of the show but also the broader conspiracy culture circulating in cyberspace — which I'd like to focus on next.

## Conspiracy cultures and fringe beliefs

In this section I want to begin by looking at so-called conspiracy cultures, and then broaden out the discussion to include forms of 'fringe' belief that we might align with conspiracies — things like ufology, for example. There has been growing interest in these kinds of topics, undoubtedly assisted by cyberspace. At its simplest, as with fan culture, cyberspace has enlarged the number of participants in conspiracy culture, broadened the range of topics read conspiratorially, accelerated the propagation of conspiracy theories, and facilitated the knitting of dense, web-like linkages between different, often seemingly disparate, theories. In fact, as several people have commented, the web lends itself to the propagation, proliferation and circulation of 'fringe' beliefs like conspiracy theories:

> The Web is by its nature a kind of conspiracy-machine, a mechanism that encourages an ever-broadening network of speculative leaps, synchronistic links, and curious juxtapositions. A 'subcultural search engine' called Disinformation even uses a Yahoo!-like system to filter the fringes of the Web for dark plots, kook cosmologies, revisionist histories, and the latest signs and portents.
>
> (Davis 1998: 245)

*The X-Files* has its part to play in this, too, by popularizing (or mainstreaming) conspiratorial thinking (Lavery *et al.* 1996). But prior to that popularizing, there have long been forms of conspiratorial knowledge circulating, again through the micromedia of small-press books and magazines, conferences and conventions, and so on (Fenster 1999). So, like fan culture, conspiracy culture has been both enlarged and reshaped by its encounter with cyberspace:

> The resemblance between the Web and conspiracy thinking is almost uncanny: each relies on odd, seemingly random, links that have always already resisted a reconciling closure or coherence. Each demonstrates a preoccupation with minutia, evidence, documentation. Each occupies and disrupts a popular, populist political field.
>
> (Dean 2000: 63)

We might take this to mean that *cyberspace turns us all into conspiracists* as well as fans – certainly the popularity of conspiracy and fringe sites on the web would indicate a wide-reaching fascination with esoterica, perhaps reflecting the anxieties of our millennial *zeitgeist*.

Davis' description of the Web as a 'conspiracy-machine' and Dean's comments on the overlapping concerns of both spheres are echoed in Richard Thieme's account of ufology on-line (CR). Thieme's intervention makes use of the notion of the 'meme' – a kind of contagious idea, that spreads across cyberspace. The UFO meme that Thieme tracks can be read as an accelerated form of urban folklore – hearsay and rumour which spreads through a locale or a culture, sedimenting as 'fact' through repetition (a notion played with in the horror-movie *Candyman*). Cyberspace has facilitated a speeding-up of this memetic contagion, as well as disembedding it from a particular place, thus rendering it global. Thieme's essay is great for highlighting the inner workings of on-line conspiracy culture, as he bounces from site to site in search of 'the truth'. Once something is documented in cyberspace, he notes, it is then quickly circulated (having been picked up, maybe, by the kind of subcultural search engine Davis mentions – though often that 'search engine' is a person trawling for 'evidence'), building up a protective coating of 'truth' by little more than dense cross-posting and citation. This process always reminds me of the virus warnings that arrive in my in-box with increasing frequency, transmitted memetically by cyberspace's 'worried well' (see Chapter 3).

The discussion of UFO memes provided by Thieme is useful for thinking about the status of knowledge in cyberspace more broadly, but it is particularly pertinent to thinking about so-called 'fringe beliefs' – the kinds of things that often don't get a lot of airtime in 'mainstream' culture. The vast marginals milieu in cyberspace covers just about every conceivable topic; while some of these are merely off-the-wall curios, others can be more sinister. In this context, the circulation of Far Right materials on the web has gathered considerable attention – equalled only, perhaps, by paedophile pornography as today's on-line 'moral panic'. The presence of such 'fringe' material raises difficult issues around censorship (Zickmund CR). For now, I'd like to look briefly at Far Right web-use as a kind of subcultural use of cyberspace (however problematic that might be – though there have been subcultural studies of politically troublesome youth groups, such as skinheads; see Moore 1994).

Far Right presence on-line replicates the arguments we have already witnessed about other kinds of subcultural work in cyberspace: material can be circulated more widely and freely, a multitude of perspectives can be developed, and the Far Right political project furthered by strategic uses of cyberspace. Issues of censorship and regulation figure very prominently, of course – and Far Right Internet use pushes those who argue against any on-line censorship, since the circulation of so-called 'hate' materials questions the democratic potential of cyberspace (Whine 1997, 2000).

Moreover, as Michael Whine notes, cyberspace has reconfigured Far Right activism. He writes that is can be argued

> that a new virtual racism has evolved through the medium of the Internet, that the interpenetration of various nationalist movements is amplified within cyberspace, and that it is possible for far right groups of markedly different types to establish common networks and ideological alliances, particularly around a shared common enemy.
>
> (Whine 2000: 235)

The use of media as a fringe propaganda tool predates the Internet, of course; but the unique features of computer-mediated communication lend themselves to 'fringe' political activities more readily, circumventing issues of access and censorship. Manuel Castells' (1997) discussion of the American Militia and Patriot movements similarly maps the network of groups whose only meeting-ground is cyberspace, echoing Whine's statement about the enthusiastic promotion of the Internet as a propaganda tool by extremists. The question raised in analyses such as Whine's is: what can be done about 'cyberhate'?

The most widely-cited response to Far Right presence in cyberspace is 'flaming' – sending hostile messages to newsgroups and mailing lists, often with the aim of jamming or crashing hosts by overloading them with incoming mail ('flaming out'). As Whine (1997) notes, flaming out extremists by bombarding them with messages contesting their world-view can, at least temporarily, restore the illusion of a democratic consensus in cyberspace. Susan Zickmund (CR) makes a similar argument, though her recommendation is not the use of flaming to clog up Far Right sites, but instead that the openness of cyberspace creates a communicative space that can be used for dialogue and argument – given that cyberspace might be the only place large numbers of people come into any kind of contact with Far Right activists, it might in fact be the best place to challenge their politics. This argument restates the role of cyberspace as a new public sphere – a notion open to considerable contestation. Here, it is argued, ideas and opinions can commingle, get discussed and challenged, and new forms of politics can thus be enacted.

Other political uses of cyberspace are treated as less problematic by critics, particularly if their project can be cast as in some way 'pro-democracy'. Tim Jordan (1999) cites emails coming from Russia, bypassing state censorship of other media channels, and the location of an anti-McDonald's website in the Netherlands where laws around libel are more relaxed. Of course, exactly the same strategies can be used to circulate 'cyberhate' – that might be the cost of keeping cyberspace open for public debate.

As I've already mentioned, and as Castells highlights in his work on the militia movement, cyberspace has transformed the way that new social movements organize and operate, both by globalizing them and by facilitating the decentralized, web-like structure of networks and groups. The demonstrations at World Trade Organization meetings in Seattle and Prague vividly showed this, with a loose collective of protesters from all over the world, linked through the Internet, coming together to contest a key symbol of multinational capital. On-going reportage of the protest was compiled and transmitted on the Internet, in part to counteract the perceived biases of mainstream mass media coverage. Further, and in common with other movements in, for example, environmental politics, protesters stressed the leaderless, non-hierarchical, decentralized structure of the collective. Almost mirroring the logic of ARPANET as a network resistant to strategic strike, these groups have no 'command centre' that can be attacked or infiltrated.

New social movements are, as has already been discussed, associated with 'lifestyle politics', embodied in the slogan 'The personal is political'.

Movements associated with lifestyle politics include those concerned with the environment, and with 'race', disability, gender and sexuality (Giddens 1991). All of these aspects of life politics have been transformed by cyber-space, in much the same way as the groups I've focused on. However, the transformations in politics and practice are less remarked than in the subcul-tural groups I am now going to turn my attention to: those whose very identity enunciates some kind of relationship to technology, particularly cybertechnology.

## Technological subcultures

One way to make a distinction between those subcultures I have looked at so far and those that I am now moving on to is in terms of their relation-ship to technology. The groups I am now turning my attention towards are, in a sense, *all about technology* – they are subcultures that have come into being because of cyberspace, rather than those above, which pre-existed it. However, as we shall see with my first example, so-called MUDders, these groups had their antecedents, too – but the effect of their contact with cyber-space has radically transformed their form and structure. As we move on to discuss 'hi-tech' subcultures such as hackers and cyberpunks, we'll see a clearer articulation of this. However, we'll start with MUDders, and try to work things out from there.

## MUDders

MUDs stands for multi-user domains, or multi-user dungeons. The latter hints at MUDs' origin as an adaptation of the role-playing subculture of Dungeons and Dragons – complex games in which players weave fantastic worlds and take on characters to interact with each other in elaborate and long-running fantasy scenarios, often drawing on Tolkien-esque imagery of goblins and wizards, castles and mazes (Curtis 1999). The first MUDs, which are essentially software programs, appeared in the 1980s as on-line platforms for these kinds of games (Ito 1997). MUDs quickly proliferated and special-ized to create a universe of text-based virtual worlds with players scattered around the on-line world. MUDs are thus interesting and particular on-line social systems, where issues of community, identity and sociality coalesce and are contested – they are also favoured sites for Internet researchers, because of what they embody and enact (Bromberg 1996).

Sherry Turkle (1997) identifies two types of MUD: the 'adventure' type, which most resembles the Dungeons and Dragons scenario, and the 'social' type, which she defines as 'relatively open spaces in which you can play at whatever captures your imagination', adding that 'the point is to interact with other players and, on some MUDs, to help build the virtual world by creating one's own objects and architecture' (on object-oriented MUDs, or MOOs) (Turkle 1997: 181). MUDding has interesting overlaps with fan culture; there are on-line fantasy games based around 'cult' tv programmes, such as the *Star Trek* MUD called TrekMUSE that Turkle reports in *Life on the Screen*. Like fan culture, an issue frequently discussed is the depth of MUDders' involvement in the subculture, and Turkle gives us some 'pen portraits' of MUDders to show this. These two factors tend to give MUDding the same stereotypical associations that we've already discussed in the context of fandom – because MUDs are 'fantasy' places, MUDders are seen as disconnected from real life (RL), preferring to play out parallel lives in parallel worlds. This stereotype does a disservice to MUDding as a site to negotiate social relations and technological relations, and as a space of creativity and community (Curtis 1999). However, Turkle notes a particular kind of sociality and community that has emerged on MUDs; the 'fantasy' world being built by them is a world of harmonious and homogeneous middle-class community (which these participants perceive to have been eroded in RL). Withdrawal from RL is, of course, a central problematic of cyberculture, as we saw in Chapter 5.

This transformation in the function some MUDs play in MUDders' lives also gives MUDding a 'therapeutic' edge – as a (safe) place to work through personal issues. This leads us into another central concern with MUDs: that the depth of engagement participants experience and the bond of trust between users can mean that events occurring in MUD-space spill over to effect the person in real life (IRL), as debates over on-line 'rape' testify (Dibbell 1999). Agreed codes of conduct within MUDs have evolved in order to iron out 'undesirable' behaviours among players – Pavel Curtis (1999: 368) lists the 'manners' of LambdaMOO, one of the largest and best-known MUDs. These include 'Be polite', 'Don't spoof', 'Don't shout' and 'Don't hog the server' – a mix of technological manners to ensure the MUD runs smoothly, and social manners governing the maintenance of LambdaMOO as 'a pleasant place for people to be'. On 'adventure' MUDs, these rules might extend towards practices such as 'pking' – the killing of characters in the game (Ito 1997). Protocols also exist to govern the treatment of 'newbies', the practice of 'lurking' (watching the game without participating), and the amount of power given to the 'wizard' overseeing the MUD. What we can see from this discussion, then, is a picture of MUDs as a complex cybercultural social experiment that has evolved (and is still evolving) its own 'subculture'. MUDs are entirely enabled by computer technology, making them one of the most prominent and popular manifestations of our category 'technological subculture' (some researchers suggest that MUDs are prototypical on-line communities; see Bromberg 1996). MUDs are, however, largely text-based subcultures, without the elements of stylization traditionally associated with subcultural work. By contrast, the next groups I want to look at – subcultures connected with cyberpunk – are engaged in embodied practices of resistance, and might be described as 'neo-tribal' collectivities.

## Cyberpunks

There are two important themes to cover in this section: the first is the depiction of subcultures in cyberpunk fiction and film, and the second is subcultures that borrow the aesthetic and philosophy of the cyberpunk genre to create group identities – such as the readers and writers collectively clustered around the cybermagazine *Mondo 2000*. Since these groups are indebted to the ideas and images of cyberpunk fiction, I'd like to begin by looking at the ways that subcultures are figured in that genre, and particularly in William Gibson's writing. Good general contextualizing overviews of cyberpunk are provided by Larry McCaffery (1991a, b) and Dani Cavallaro (2000). David Tomas (CR) provides a detailed and insightful discussion of what he names 'technicity' in Gibson's work – the production of tribal identifications through technological enhancements and interventions that produce 'technophilic bodies'. Tomas also explores the recycling of past subcultural forms in Gibson's 'technotribes'. This theme is echoed in George McKay's critical search for the 'punk' in cyberpunk. McKay suggests that cyberpunk is 'predicated on the past, touched by nostalgia' (McKay 1999: 51); Gibson himself refers to a 'kind of ghostly teenage DNA' which 'carried the coded precepts of various short-lived subcults and replicated them at odd intervals' across the landscapes of his work (quoted in Tomas CR: 177). In the rewirings of subcultural identity in Gibson's writing, then, a *bricolage* of technofuturism and recycled pasts is creolized to produce new hybrid subcultures. Tomas' discussion of Gibson's work is, therefore, a good place for us to start.

Tomas differentiates between *aesthetic* and *functional* modifications of the human body in cyberpunk: the former include forms of cosmetic surgery, grafting and transplant that restyle the body, the latter implant technology in order to enhance the body's capabilities. As discussed in Chapter 7, the ways in which technology intersects with the body have been a central concern in cybercultural theory; they have likewise been key concerns in cyberpunk (Cavallaro 2000). These enhancements and restylings are often adopted by the subcultural groups that populate the worlds Gibson describes:

> Various 'tribal' groups, the Panther Moderns in *Neuromancer* or the Low Teks in 'Johnny Mnemonic', equate stylistic effects of elective cosmetic surgery and the biotechnological manipulation of the body's surface with

technofetishistic baccanalian celebrations of the body as trans-species heterotopic site.

(Tomas CR: 177)

Technophilic cyborgian bodies, Tomas writes, rewire identification, producing subcultural and quasi-ethnic collectivities – such as the Panther Moderns and Lo Teks, as well as Big Scientists, Gothiks, Kasuals, Jack Draculas and so on – defined *technologically*; or, as he puts it, in terms of 'common technological kinship' (Tomas CR: 180). Dani Cavallero (2000: x) argues that this is part of what makes cyberpunk so interesting; that it 'amalgamates in often baffling ways the rational and the irrational, the new and the old, the mind and the body, by integrating the hyper-efficient structures of high technology with the anarchy of street subcultures' – as a genre, it juxtaposes multinational cybercapitalism with hi-tech gangs wandering ruined urban sprawls.

The functional enhancements Gibson's characters add to their bodies are attempts to improve aspects of their performance; these figures are depicted as having 'absorbed the hardware of information systems and bio-technology in cool fits of individualized, customized technophilia' (Tomas CR: 177) – the aim being to gain 'competitive edge' in the marketplace of the information economy. Johnny Mnemonic, for example, has his brain rewired to carry data, like a hi-tech smuggler. The theme of competitive edge (which Tomas also calls 'technological edge') is one that recurs in other technological subcultures, as we shall see.

A lot of the themes raised here have already been discussed in terms of cyberculture and the body; the key point to flag here concerns subcultural affinities that are formed around the body-technology interface. In particular, it is interesting to track manifestations of these imagined subcultures in contemporary culture. As Tiziana Terranova (CR: 269) writes: 'The extraordinary popularity of William Gibson's most imaginative icons . . . has turned fiction into an almost 'biblical' repertoire of images and cultural references whose contribution to the creation of the electronic culture as a whole cannot be underestimated'. One prominent contemporary cultural site to explore this is the US magazine *Mondo 2000*.

Both Terranova and Vivian Sobchack (CR) have written about *Mondo 2000* and its followers, and a compendium of the magazine's highlights was published in the early 1990s with the title *A User's Guide to the New Edge* (*Mondo 2000* 1993). Terranova (CR: 270) describes the magazine as 'the glossiest and hippest of the cybermagazines and possibly the most famous', with a large readership, styled as 'surfers on the New Edge' (mostly new professionals in the knowledge and information economy). The magazine offers a particular inflection of technophilia – the 'New Edge' – and is filled with ideas and images that resonate with cyberpunk. In order to explore the subcultural work around *Mondo 2000* and its New Edge, let's start with a quote from its editor, R. U. Sirius:

> The entire thrust of modern technology has been to move us away from solid objects and into informational space (or cyberspace). Man the farmer and man the industrial worker are quickly being replaced by man the information worker. . . . We are less and less creatures of flesh, bone, and blood pushing boulders uphill; we are more and more creatures of mind-zapping bits and bytes moving around at the speed of light.
>
> (quoted in Terranova CR: 271)

Vivian Sobchack (CR) critically summarizes the magazine's ethos, which she names 'utopian cynicism': '[i]ts *raison d'être* is the techno-erotic celebration of a reality to be found on the far side of the computer screen and in the "neural nets" of a "liberated", disembodied, computerized yet sensate consciousness' (Sobchack CR: 141). Sobchack gives special attention to the political implications of *Mondo 2000*'s project, characterizing its readers as 'New Age Mutant Ninja Hackers' engaged in what she calls 'interactive autism':

> Rather than finding the gravity (and vulnerability) of human flesh and the finitude of the earth providing the *material* grounds for ethical responsibility in a highly technologized world, New Age Mutant Ninja Hackers would look toward 'downloading' their consciousness into the computer, leaving their 'obsolete' bodies (now contemptuously called 'meat' and 'wetware') behind.
>
> (Sobchack CR: 142)

Sobchack reads 'interactive autism' as reflecting a withdrawal from RL, echoing our discussion of MUDders. Her analysis of *Mondo 2000* reveals a tension between the dream of existing as pure disembodied data and the continued presence of (often fetishized) bodies on its pages – most visibly manifest in the magazine's obsession with virtual sex. Remembering Tomas' distinction between types of technophilic body present in cyberpunk, we can, I think, read the *Mondo 2000* New Edge subculture as primarily one of *aesthetic* modification, of adopting a cyberpunk *style* (including, as Sobchack says, a cyberpunk writing style). While this style is accompanied by a distinct *attitude* – the New Edge – this is diluted by the admixing of a number of other subcultural counterdiscourses (New Ageism, 1960s hippiedom, excessive consumerism) into the magazine's philosophy. Other aesthetic variants of cyberpunk can be found associated with the 'fetish' and body-modification subcultures, where individuals construct their own versions of Gibsonian tribalism in similarly 'cool fits' of technophilic stylization (Polhemus and Randall 1996).

A subcultural take on the *functional* alteration of the technophilic body is realized more profoundly in other groupings; most notably, perhaps, in the Extropians. As Terranova (CR) explains, the subcultural cluster based around California's Extropy Institute is essentially an articulation of a professionalized countercultural technophilia. She quotes their FAQ file:

> Extropians have made career choices based on their extropian ideals; many are software engineers, neuroscientists, aerospace engineers, cryptologists, privacy consultants, designers of institutions, mathematicians, philosophers, and medical doctors researching life-extension techniques. Some extropians are very active in libertarian politics, and in legal challenges to abuse of government power.
>
> (quoted in Terranova CR: 272)

Extropianism, therefore, is a particular kind of subcultural project of the self, centring on becoming positioned at the forefront of post-human possibilities, ready to lead the way when the time is right. It represents a form of knowledge accumulation and personal transformation in many ways at odds with *Mondo 2000*'s New Edge, though both share what Terranova calls a 'rampant super-voluntarism' (275) which ignores RL social and political concerns. As two hi-tech subcultural formations, then, the 'Mondoid' New Edge and the Extropians articulate particular visions of the body's fate in cyberculture, which bear clear (but differently inflected) traces of cyberpunk. The last manifestation of a cyberpunk-like ethic – and sometimes aesthetic – is to be found in the most widely-known, and often most demonized technosubculture, described by Paul Taylor (1999: 169) as cyberpunk's 'real-world representatives': hackers.

## Hackers

Computer hacking has a particular kind of public image, associated with two acts: the breaching of high-profile computer security systems (The Pentagon, MI6, banks) and the writing and releasing of computer viruses (the most spectacular recent example being the 'Love Bug'; see Beynon and Dunkerley 2000). The hacker subculture similarly has a particular public image – of disaffected, geek-ish young men, whose technological expertise is matched by their social alienation. Hackers are, then, a prime example of contemporary 'folk devils', their activities resulting in a 'moral panic' – to use the terms from Cohen's (1972) work on mods and rockers. Hacking is accordingly criminalized and demonized as a 'fringe' activity that has the potential to wreak havoc in today's information society – exposing our 'trust/risk' relationship with computers.

However, a closer look at hackers and other members of the 'computer underground' complicates this picture. Paul Taylor (1999) provides an in-depth account of contemporary hacking, redefined from within the subculture as, at its broadest, 'an attempt to make use of any technology in an original, unorthodox and inventive way' (Taylor 1999: 15). There are hackers, to be sure, who practise their skills for personal gain (hacking banks, for example) or for illicit reasons (releasing a virus in an act of revenge), but this masks a whole spectrum of activities and a dense network of subcultural work.

Taylor reminds us that the term 'hacker' was originally used to describe the 'pioneering computer *aficionados* at MIT's laboratories in the 1950s and 1960s' (23). This 'first generation' of hackers was followed in the subculture's genealogy by the hobbyists and enthusiasts who worked to bring computing to 'the masses', and a 'third generation' who focused on computer games architecture. Only with the 'fourth generation' did hacking becomes synonymous with accessing *other people's* computers and data (and with virus writing). Taylor suggests the most recent iteration – the 'fifth generation' – is represented by 'microserfs' and by 'the co-optation of hacker skills by commercial computing' (23). The evolving subculture has thus gone through a number of important phases, ending – as is the case with so many subcultures – with absorption into the 'mainstream'. This lineage has left its trace in the 'hacker ethic' that expresses the common values of the computer underground. Taylor quotes the main points of this ethic from Levy's best-seller on hacking:

1. 'All information should be free.'
2. 'Mistrust Authority – Promote Decentralisation.'
3. 'Hackers should be judged by their hacking, not by bogus criteria such as degrees, age, race or position.'
4. 'You can create art and beauty on a computer.'
5. 'Computers can change your life for the better.'

(quoted in Taylor 1999: 25)

This neatly summarizes the technophilic, anarchic, egalitarian stance that governs the majority of hacking practice, at least until its co-option into corporate computer culture. Taylor fleshes this stance out by discussing with hackers their motivations, which he lists as:

1. Feelings of addiction.
2. The urge of curiosity.
3. Boredom with educational system.

4. Enjoyment of feelings of power.
5. Peer recognition.
6. Political acts.

(Taylor 1999: 46)

The way these different motivations play out in an individual hack obviously impacts on the perceptions of hacking outside of the subculture (and of that hack itself *within* the subculture – hackers follow each other's work). While those within the computer underground might like to emphasize hacking's benevolent aspects, the current climate of hacker panic means that the images circulating the mass media and popular culture tend to stress malevolence instead – see, for example, UK press coverage in the wake of the 'Love Bug', describing 'a fast-growing invisible menace to us all' (Burke and Walsh 2000: 19).

Andrew Ross (CR) also picks over the question of the kinds of work hacking does, and highlights a number of interesting ways in which hackers have defended their activities in the face of this demonization:

(a) hacking performs a benign industrial service of uncovering security deficiencies and design flaws; (b) hacking, as an experimental, free-form research activity, has been responsible for many of the most progressive developments in software development; (c) hacking, when not purely recreational, is an elite educational practice that reflects the ways in which the development of high-technology has outpaced orthodox forms of institutional education; (d) hacking is an important form of watchdog counter-response to the use of surveillance technology and data-gathering by the state, and to the increasingly monolithic communications power of giant corporations; (e) hacking, as guerilla know-how, is essential to the task of maintaining fronts of cultural resistance and stocks of oppositional knowledge as a hedge against a technofascist future.

(Ross CR: 255)

As we can see, these defences restate the hacker ethic and emphasize the social and cultural value of hacking. Set against this, of course, is the criminalization of hacking, and the recoding of hackers as at best juvenile pranksters and at worst as self-serving cybervillains equipped to use their stealth to bring down the world (or at least the world's info-systems), or to take our money and crash our computers. The contrast between benevolent hackers (who use their skills to shore up security systems and crack other hackers' codes) and malevolent hackers intent on world domination is vividly played out in the movie *The Net* – between the lone heroic figure of Angela Bennett and the shadowy, evil Praetorians (who invert benevolent hacking by hiding their virus inside computer security software).

Ross' essay focuses on one early and spectacular case of viral hacking in the US – the so-called Internet Worm – in order to plot the processes of demonization, and the resultant criminalization of hacking. As Taylor's work also shows, this criminalization is an ambivalent process, in that hackers continue to be seen as 'whizz-kids' with unrivalled expertise in programming; that's why they are simultaneously reviled and wooed by computing companies, who aim to domesticate their talents – to turn Praetorians into Angela Bennetts, whose talents can be used to hack the hackers.

Equally important, however, is Ross' discussion of other forms of computer resistance (hi-tech workplace sabotage, for example), and his call to expand our perception of hacking as a countercultural practice in order to accommodate the myriad ways that we might subvert the technologies around us. Crucially, he argues that cultural critics, too, should work more like hackers – that any technoscepticism or cybercritique must be founded on a 'hacker knowledge': we need to develop an insider's understanding of the things we are critical of, to be an 'enemy within'. This stance might be productively set against other forms of technosceptical subculture, especially those that seek the wholesale rejection of technology and a 'return' to pre-technological social and cultural worlds. The so-called Neo-Luddites are the most prominent manifestation of this kind of technophobia.

## Neo-Luddites

Anti-technological 'fringe' beliefs have gained recent notoriety following the case of the 'Unabomber', Theodore Kaczynski, who orchestrated a bombing campaign against key symbols of information society from his low-tech shack in Montana. His manifesto (published at his request in the *New York Times* and the *Washington Post* in 1995, and now, ironically, circulating on the Internet) rails against the negative impacts of advanced technologies and industrial society. He is thus aligned ideologically with other US Neo-Luddites such as Kirkpatrick Sale, who stages computer smash-ins to vent his frustrations, and Scott Savage, director of the Center for Plain Living, who refuses to recognize Daylight Saving Time (Katz 1996). Sale's 1995 book *Rebels Against the Future* blends technophobia and deep ecology, imagining a return to nature and to 'natural', traditional communities – it is itself a kind of Neo-Luddite manifesto. As a model of nostalgic, anti-technological neo-ruralism, Neo-Luddism enacts its own *bricolage* of 'fringe' beliefs, linking it to the conspiratorial subcultures already discussed. The romantic utopianism of Sale's vision also bears remarkable similarities, in its valuing of 'traditional' notions of family and community, to some versions of cybercommunity, especially those propagated by gurus like Howard Rheingold (Robins and Webster 1999) – except for their radically different imaginings of the place of technology in those communities.

In *Times of the Technoculture* (1999), Kevin Robins and Frank Webster attempt to salvage Luddism from its association with these Neo-Luddites, whose project they critique on a number of fronts. In its place, through a more careful reading of the history of the Luddites, Robins and Webster write a form of contemporary Luddism that has more parallels with hacking than with computer-breaking (which merely stages a literal up-dating of the Luddites' machine-wrecking). As a way of politicizing debates about technology – especially in its relation to capital – reclaiming Luddism might indeed be a powerful strategy. Combining the critical stances of the Luddite and the hacker in this way is the mythological subcultural figure of the 'Cyberpunk provo-geek techo-Luddite' conjured in Deena and Michael Weinstein's series of on-line countercultural caricatures:

> The Net is more technology to master in order to bring it down from the fuckin' insides! I'm the Unabomber hacking code. . . . Destroy the Net. Threaten security of private information, medical records and financial transactions in any way you can. . . . Perpetuate misinformation, disinformation, rumour and hate speech on the Net. . . . We infiltrate the Net as techno-geeks and then become the cyber-parasites that destroy it. . . . *We hate technology and we have mastered it – the ultimate cyber-punk horror story: the enemy within.*
>
> (Weinstein and Weinstein CR: 214–15; my emphasis)

Although written as a parody, Weinstein and Weinstein's 'cameo' shows how Luddism and hacking might coalesce in subcultural formations that resemble aspects of cyberpunk – and which offer a model for thinking critically about cybertechnology that resists the easy slide into unthinking technophobia. As Iain Boal (1995) notes, both technophobia and Luddism have become terms of abuse in contemporary culture, reserved for anyone who's 'off message' when it comes to new technology's promises; the kinds of perspectives brought in, for example, *Times of the Technoculture* or 'Hacking away at the counterculture' suggest ways to rework these terms productively.

## Summary

The aim of this chapter has been to explore a select number of subcultural or countercultural responses to cyberspace. These were divided into groups that make use of cyberspace to enlarge their project (as they do other media) and those whose very project embodies an engagement with cybertechnology. Although this separation isn't wholly satisfactory, it has enabled us to think through the kinds of subcultural activities that cyberspace supports and provokes. In the first category we looked at on-line fan cultures, conspiracy cultures and other 'fringe' groups (with a focus on the Far Right); the second category was illustrated by exploring MUDders, cyberpunks, hackers and Neo-Luddites. In each case, the aim has been to think through subcultural uses of cyberspace, in order to catch a glimpse of the range of activities that occur there. Moreover, as I said earlier in the chapter, I have tried to suggest that cyberspace *encourages* subcultural work. Because of the sheer amount and range of material accessible, on virtually every conceivable topic, we each have decisions to make about the kinds of things we are prepared to invest time and energy in while we are on-line. We have to prioritize our interests, or risk drowning in the datastream. The traces of our adventures in cyberspace build up a picture of aspects of our identities, and the sites we stay longest at manifest the priorities we have made. Moreover, our attitudes towards technology can be voiced collectively, whether we style ourselves as console cowboys or retreat into 'plain living'. Questions of identity and community are, in this way, reworked through the notion of cybersubculture.

## Hot links

### *Chapters from* The Cybercultures Reader

Susan Clerc, 'Estrogen brigades and "big tits" threads: media fandom on-line and off' (Chapter 13: 216–29).

Andrew Ross, 'Hacking away at the counterculture' (Chapter 16: 254–67).

Vivian Sobchack, 'New Age Mutant Ninja Hackers: reading *Mondo 2000*' (Chapter 8: 138–48).

Tiziana Terranova, 'Post-human unbounded: artificial evolution and high-tech subcultures' (Chapter 17: 268–79).

Richard Thieme, 'Stalking the UFO meme' (Chapter 14: 230–6).

David Tomas, 'The technophilic body: on technicity in William Gibson's cyborg culture' (Chapter 10: 175–89).

Deena Weinstein and Michael Weinstein, 'Net game cameo' (Chapter 12: 210–15).

Susan Zickmund, 'Approaching the radical other: the discursive culture of cyber-hate' (Chapter 15: 237–53).

### *Further reading*

Dani Cavallaro (2000) *Cyberpunk and Cyberculture: science fiction and the work of William Gibson*, London: Athlone.

Jodi Dean (2000) 'Webs of conspiracy', in Andrew Herman and Thomas Swiss (eds) *The World Wide Web and Contemporary Cultural Theory*, London: Routledge, 61–76.

Kirsten Pullen (2000) 'I-love-Xena.com: creating online fan communities', in David Gauntlett (ed.) *Web.Studies: rewiring media studies for the digital age*, London: Arnold, 52–61.

Kirkpatrick Sale (1995) *Rebels Against the Future: the Luddites and their war on the Industrial Revolution – lessons for the computer age*, Reading MA: Addison-Wesley.

Paul Taylor (1999) *Hackers: crime in the digital sublime*, London: Routledge.

Sherry Turkle (1997) *Life on the Screen: identity in the age of the Internet*, London: Phoenix.

Michael Whine (2000) 'Far right extremists on the Internet', in Douglas Thomas and Brian Loader (eds) *Cybercrime: law enforcement, security and surveillance in the information age*, London: Routledge, 234–50.

## Websites

http://www.hackers.com/index2.htm
'Commercial' hacking site, good archives and links, plus job opportunities!

http://www.geocities.com/Area51/Vault/3011/main.htm
'The Count's Page of Cyberpunk'. Billed as 'The Cyberpunk Authority', this has good info and links to sites covering cyberpunk writing, film, and subcultural practice.

http://www.ibiblio.org/usenet-i/hier-s/alt.tv.html
List of and links to Usenet alt.tv fan sites, from alt.tv.ab-fab to alt.tv.xuxa.

http://www.logicsouth.com/~lcoble/index.html
Frugal Squirrel's Homepage for Patriots, Survivalists, and Gun Owners: 'join in the fellowship of survivalism, share ideas, and make yourself at home' – extensive listing and links to US militia movement sites and articles.

http://www.oneworld.org/campaigns/wto/front.shtml
News and links on Anti-World Trade Organization protests.

http://www.ccs.neu.edu/home/eostrom/muds/lambdamoo.html
Basic (and a bit out-of-date) information on LambdaMOO and links to other MUD sites.

http://www.preservenet.com/theory/Sale.html
List of and links to Sale's key neo-Luddite tracts.

http://www.conspiracy-net.com/
Huge site – at the time of writing, it has 725 conspiracies logged!

# Chapter 9

# RESEARCHING CYBERCULTURES

Online fieldwork introduces new dimensions to our understanding of location and its relations to the production of knowledge and power. The virtual life worlds that we study foster new modes of interaction and representation, and with those, new realms of social, political, and ethical significance.

*Deborah Heath* et al.

THE PURPOSE OF THIS CHAPTER is to think through the possibilities and constraints of researching cybercultures, and to ask (and maybe even begin to answer) some questions about the practice of research on and in cyberspace. Debates about research on and in cyberspace have generated considerable heat, reflecting in part the on-going discussion of research in general, and in part the novel circumstances presented by new technologies. In particular, there has been a lot of interest in the suitability of applying accepted research techniques – such as ethnography or discourse analysis – to on-line settings. In addition, we need to think about the Internet's construction as a research resource as well as a research setting. What kinds of things exist in cyberspace that we can do research on and with?

It's become obvious to those of us who teach in higher education that the Internet is fulfilling a number of research roles for students, teachers and researchers. It is a huge resource, part library and part encyclopedia, which we all turn to with greater or lesser frequency for information. It is also an easily-accessible field site (as some people, such as Hine (2000) argue, in fact *too* accessible) for researching new social formations and new versions of existing social formations. It is a vast infrastructure and a material culture that impacts on everyday life in ways both spectacular and mundane (Star 1999). It has transformed the way we write, the way we work, the way we live, even the way we think. And, in universities like mine, it poses new challenges and offers new opportunities – as we dabble with virtual learning environments but also have to tackle issues of Internet-based plagiarism — and try to deal with the incredible variety of materials and uses offered.

We're still in the early stages of thinking about what cyberspace means for all of this, which is both positive and negative: positive in that there is lively debate and experimentation occurring all around us; negative because we still aren't close to developing a clear sense of all the issues at stake. Reading accounts of on-line research practice, I've been struck by the divergences of method and opinion about method, as well as by the different approaches to questions as fundamental as what cyberspace is. It unsettles a lot of previously-held views on information, knowledge and research, overturns (or at least questions) long-sedimented ways of working (for example, in publishing), and reopens debates in methodology, for instance around research ethics. We need to consider different strands of research, too — using online resources and methods to research offline things, using offline resources and methods to research online things, and using online resources and methods to research online things; or, to put it another way, we need to consider the issues that arise when (i) researching cyberspace, (ii) researching *in* cyberspace, and (iii) researching *cyberspace in cyberspace*. The ways we use what cyberspace has to offer in these different kinds of research practice each have their own impli-cations, many of which are still being thought through (Mann and Stewart 2000). And, of course, cyberspace never stands still, so neither can the ways we think about researching it and researching in it. These are the kinds of issues I want to explore in this chapter.

## Search engines and research engines

Let me start with something that has become a day-to-day issue in the knowledge economy that is contemporary university life: student use of the Internet. This is something that we, as teachers, have both promoted and cautioned about, and this mixture is, I think, revealing of a broader orientation towards the status of cyberspace in research terms. We have grown up with an established set of protocols about research and writing, some of which seem needlessly uptight, but which have been radically reshaped by the arrival on our desks and in our classrooms of networked computers. This arrival has manifest many of our hang-ups about the status of different kinds of informa-tion, knowledge and publication — telling stories about the practices of the academy, and the role of academics as self-appointed custodians of knowledge.

My colleagues who teach journalism, for example, get very cross when other academics dismiss this or that essay as *journalistic* — which is read as the opposite of scholarly. A similar uneasiness pervades our stance towards materials sourced in cyberspace: without the familiar infrastructure of peer review and so on, we are at sea when it comes to defining the *validity* or *reliability* of documents from the Internet. As John Butler (1998: 3) says, there is a 'high signal-to-noise ratio' on the Internet, which means that 'useful discussions [are] buried within a lot of idle chatter'. His response to this, in research terms, is to get a sense of what's useful – something that can only really be developed through experience. Moreover, he notes that 'while topics found across the Net are wide-ranging, most tend to be introductory. Many items, if converted to the printed page, would be considered flyers or brochures', adding that in cyberspace 'anyone can pose as an expert' (Butler 1998: 5). He frames this as a caution, rather than a welcome signal of the democratization of knowledge-production. Reading the same process from the opposite direction, Sadie Plant is more celebratory of the implications:

> The academy loses its control over intelligence once it is even possible to imagine a situation in which information can be accessed from nets which care for neither old boy status nor exam results. There is no selection on the Net.
>
> (Plant 1996: 37)

Now, this is a challenging way of seeing things; part of Plant's mission here is to disrupt the staid assumptions of academics. And it is very true that the current status of knowledge might be radically rewired by the Internet, shifting what we mean by labels such as 'expert'. Academics have established very rigid understandings of expertise, upon which institutions like universities rest (though these are increasingly challenged, and not just in cyberspace). In the face of incomparable types of information, we have to rethink who is an expert, and what it is they're an expert of – and this kind of rethink causes considerable unease among scholars (Fuller 1998). As Ananda Mitra and Elisia Cohen (1999: 197) suggest, the ways that we assess information gathered in cyberspace must be different, if we are to 'ensure that the authors who would be considered authentic and reliable by the traditional yardsticks are not privileged in cyberspace' – though, of course, there might be opposing arguments made, suggesting that those 'traditional yardsticks' *should* be transplanted to cyberspace, as debates over peer reviewing on-line show (Fuller 1998). While terms like 'reliable' and 'authentic' make me instantly queasy, Mitra and Cohen concur with Plant in as much as they would want to establish new ways of judging the usefulness of on-line materials. And I concur, too.

A lot of users, I think, fudge this to some extent by treating Internet documents as primary source materials (in the same way we often treat journalism) – as something to be 'decoded' or 'interrogated', to be contextualized as emerging from a very distinct site of knowledge-production that therefore needs handling in a particular way (something that we too infrequently apply to academic texts, however). Of course, this is true to some extent; to take one domain, we can see from thinking about web pages that these are produced in a whole range of different contexts, by a whole range of different authors, and for a whole range of different reasons. Mitra and Cohen (1999) suggest that the measurable popularity of a website might be one way of assessing its 'quality' – though this solution is unlikely to gain much endorsement from scholars who denigrate populism in all its forms. The question of 'quality' of information in cyberspace therefore vexes researchers, especially when the context isn't manifest – or, moreover, if the context isn't manifest in a way which researchers find legible. As Deborah Heath and her colleagues put it, 'information contained within the Internet domains of interest to us may be *materially available* without necessarily being *conceptually accessible*' (Heath *et al*. 1999: 457; my emphasis). We can find the sites, but don't know what to do with them once we're there.

For many users, in my experience, this leads to a general wariness, even dismissiveness, about websites – and a broader scepticism about what cyberspace has to offer. 'I went on the net, but couldn't find anything useful' goes the disappointed line – after all the hyped-up promise, it seems, the information superhighway isn't that super after all. In an empirical study of Internet usage, Debra Howcroft (1999) interviewed a range of users all working in the knowledge economy – academics, computer professionals and journalists. Among the key themes to emerge from the interviews were issues of information overload, feelings of boredom with the experience on being on-line, frustrations with the kind and quality of information accessible, and the perception that using the Internet was a waste of time and a distraction from other tasks. In short, going on-line was simultaneously overwhelming and disappointing, and failed to yield anything but basic information:

> Most of the interviewees agreed that the information available on the Internet did little to supplement their own area of expertise. It was primarily of value when they were trying to gain an overview of a topic area that was outside the boundaries of their own specialist domain.
>
> (Howcroft 1999: 295)

There are substantial queries, then, clustered around the Internet as a research resource. In part, this is a result of the hype, which has built up our expectations. We can temper this hype with our own experiences, and notice that, contrary to the predictions, the university isn't dead, and neither is the book; students still work with tutors, in classrooms, and the library still has stock on its shelves. In both cases, we've *augmented* what already exists, and transformed it in modest ways – so we might supply course materials on the university's website, or use email to contact students, and the library catalogue can be accessed from this machine in my office. And in terms of finding things out, we make attempts to navigate the complexities of cyberspace as a hybrid archive/library/shopping mall/field site, for example by making links on our home pages to sites we have judged to be useful or interesting. That move, of course, re-establishes the page writer as some kind of knowledge gatekeeper, as the one who assures the quality of the linked-up sites. (More on links in a moment.) What all this has to tell us, I think, is a tale about the problem of knowledge in the context of cyberspace. Perhaps one of the biggest myths to accrete to the Internet has been its projected role as a multi-tasking site of knowledge. As Howcroft puts it:

> It seems that there is an anonymous formula on the internet that assumes that more data will lead to more information, which will in turn generate more knowledge and wisdom. . . . The missing link in this mystical metaphorism, however, is the critical process that creates knowledge and wisdom from the mass of data.
>
> (Howcroft 1999: 283)

As is often reiterated in this context, information is not knowledge: knowledge comes from sorting, filtering and using information. It is as much about assessing as it is about accessing. It's also about understanding the *contexts* of production, distribution and consumption: who puts stuff on the net, from where and why – and how users find it, read it, make sense of it, and so on. One way into this is to consider how we find our way round in cyberspace: how we find sites, move from one to another – to look at the practices of surfing and browsing – and then to find ways of analysing or 'reading' the sites we discover.

## Hot links and cool sites

> The ontology of the World Wide Web is more than simply a question of space, sites, or pages; it is fundamentally concerned with links and motion.
>
> (Shields 2000: 145)

Computers have become valuable (if contested) tools in information-gathering, especially now they are networked and configured to be 'user-friendly'. We have been provided with the means to access huge amounts of information of all different kinds, and with help in finding what we want – up to a point. A frequent complaint voiced by student users (among others) is that searching the web for useful stuff is a time-consuming and sometimes overwhelming task. Moreover, the helpmates we have been given, such as search engines, aren't (yet) smart enough to really be of help. As my colleague Tracey Potts (1999: 82) says, the trouble with the search engine is that it 'discriminates only at the level of the signifier and does not distinguish between contextual use of words'. David Deacon and his colleagues (1999: 332) call search engines 'the catalogue of the Internet', adding that they have 'none of the librarian's informed discretion, or the sensitivity to users' needs found in a good library catalogue'. While intelligent search agents are promised in the futurology of artificial intelligence research, current search engines are anything but smart. Let me give you an example: some time ago, while researching a paper on lesbian and gay life in rural areas, I went looking on-line for a book called *Below the Belt: sexuality, religion and the American South* (Wilson 2000). I located the book on an Internet bookseller's site, and was offered the opportunity to 'click' for related sites. Thinking this would yield valuable extra research materials, I duly clicked, and was linked to a site selling authentic leather belts! Now, while these were very nice, and very reasonably priced, the ridiculousness of the link, connecting only at the level of the word 'belt', makes Potts' point very clearly.

Of course, this is a lazy commercial link, and not all links are like that. Looking at links is, in fact, one interesting way of thinking about websites, information and knowledge. Deborah Heath and her colleagues discuss the use of links to think about 'interactive knowledge production', arguing that hyperlinks are simultaneously 'vehicles for travel within and between Internet domains and online documents, and *part of the content* of such areas' (Heath *et al.* 1999: 456; my emphasis). Links are, therefore, much more than a technical, infrastructural device – they carry important information in their code. In their research on websites about medical genetics, Heath *et al.* show how links work as content and context, for example in joining 'official' medical database sites to support groups for people with particular genetic conditions. The networks mapped by hyperlinks gave them important 'clues' for understanding the intersections and the blockages between users of different kinds of sites, as well as revealing the kinds of 'tricks' that skilled users could utilize in order to 'decode' links.

Links are, in fact, a central component of the experience of the Web; we have got used to using them, clicking on them out of curiosity, moving around in cyberspace through these digital wormholes. Steven Johnson reminisces about the early experience of using hyperlinks:

> The eureka moment for most of us came when we first clicked on a link, and found ourselves jettisoned across the planet. The freedom and immediacy of that moment – shuttling from site to site across the infosphere, following trails of thought wherever they led us – was genuinely unlike anything before it.
>
> (Johnson 1997: 110)

Hypertext reconfigures the architecture of knowledge, and the practices of writing and reading; as Rob Shields (2000: 151) writes, 'links cannot be treated as merely thresholds or passages to other pages. The link is both part of the text and an index caught on the threshold of departure, signaling to another page or text' – links are 'arrows frozen in flight, but still imbued with an overall sense of being in flight, between here and there' (152).

In an effort to get a sense of this structure, some researchers have mapped hyperlinks between sites, tracing the dense and often serendipitous trails that those frozen arrows lead us through. Forms of software have now been devised to show us these tracings, such as Footprints and cookies, which can track a user through sites. As Dodge and Kitchin argue, such programs yield useful data on movement in cyberspace, as well as potentially reframing the activity of browsing or surfing the net:

> Web browsing is currently a solitary activity with users unaware of others who may also be looking at the same page, and unaware of the many previous users. This kind of knowledge, however, can be used to improve navigation, with current users benefiting from the efforts of those who have explored the space before. The integration of this information would transform solitary surfing into a more collaborative, social activity like walking around a busy city centre.
>
> (Dodge and Kitchin 2001: 120)

While many people will still want to walk the road less travelled, others will surely welcome seeing traces of other travellers, and maybe decide to follow in their footsteps. Think of your own experiences: you visit a site, and spot an intriguing link. One quick click and you're there, then you spot another link . . . Like travelling without a map, or doing the situationist *derive* (meandering the city streets as the mood takes you), clicking through links can take you into strange territories (Sadler 1998). It can bring dead-ends as well as treasure troves – fine if you're out for an amble, but less satisfactory if, like Howcroft's (1999) respondents, you need a quick answer to some burning question. Luckily, for those of us who don't want to surrender to the mysteries of cyberspace, it's also possible to retrace your steps, and get to home (page) again, thanks to the 'Back' button. As Wise (2000) reminds us, hypertext was developed to reflect the nonlinearity of human thought processes – and the complexity of maps that trace links clearly illustrates this. These maps are, therefore, fascinating documents, since they reveal the *higgledy-piggledy* business of thinking.

Moreover, as the study by Heath *et al.* of 'genetic knowledge production' shows, the links that we need to attend to extend beyond the hyperlinks between web pages and other online sites. As their work suggests, 'methodological strategies for mapping these emergent technosocial processes must be attentive to the nodes and interventions that link online and offline sites' (Heath *et al.* 1999: 451). Tracing these links is equally important if we are to understand how knowledge is produced, in acknowledgement that online resources are patched into offline worlds and lives in complex ways. For Heath and her co-researchers, this demands 'an itinerant methodological approach that traces connections between on- and off-line milieux' (452). We shall explore the implications of this in more detail later in this chapter. But before that, I want to think through one of the other prominent ways of examining the contents of cyberspace that I have already alluded to: the 'reading' of things like web pages as 'texts'.

## Textual approaches to cybercultures

One interesting attempt to outline strategies for analysing the web is that by Mitra and Cohen (1999), which focuses on textual analysis. While it is important to remember that the web is more than text, their essay is useful in picking through the key features of 'web textuality' and suggesting ways to think about them. Their proposal for a kind of 'critical text work' considers semiotic analyses of content (layout, style, etc.), a consideration of intertextuality (the relationships between texts) and the role of different reading positions in making the text (web page) meaningful. Borrowing from literary criticism and discourse analysis, Mitra and Cohen proceed to highlight six key features of web texts: intertextuality, nonlinearity, a blurring of the reader/writer distinction, 'multimedianess', 'globalness' and ephemerality. The intertextuality of web pages – the extent to which any text makes reference to other texts – is especially manifest through hyperlinks, and these determine most of the remaining characteristics, too. Pages are nonlinear since hyperlinks make nonsense of beginnings and ends – there is no origin-point (first page) and no final destination (last page). The text is, therefore, open, potentially infinite, and rhizomatic. The blurring of the reader/writer distinction arises since (i) anyone with the (increasingly available) technical knowledge can make their own site (Cheung 2000); and (ii) each reader 'constructs' the text through their use of links, customizing the connections between pages in a way the page's producer has little or no control over. The convergence of text, sound and image on the web gives pages their 'multimedianess', redefining the ways we interact with information in cyberspace, and giving websites a polysemous character in terms of content (Wise 2000). The potential for links to criss-cross the globe in disjunctive ways also brings polsemy, by opening the text up to different potential meanings. For example, both Mitra's (CR) work on 'India on the Internet' and Zickmund's (CR) on neo-nazi sites illustrates the heterogeneity of postings, responses and links between sites scattered geographically (and ideologically). Finally, web pages can appear and vanish without warning, rendering the web unstable – and thereby also destabilizing any 'text' we construct in it.

As we can see, the 'hypertextuality' of web texts is their key characteristic, from which all the others emanate. As Mitra and Cohen show, these characteristics all have implications for the ways in which we conduct research on web texts.

The first problem is: where to begin? As there is no beginning in the interlinked, nonlinear web, we either have to hope for the best and dive in, or devise some framework for deciding where a suitable starting-point might be. Web mapping tools and hit counters, Mitra and Cohen suggest, might indicate to us the popularity of some websites – and this might be a good place to start. But, as they say, to get over-bothered by the question of beginnings is to miss the point of the web – and in any case, given the ephemerality of pages and sites, the starting-point may vanish before you're done. Related to the question of where to start is the question of where (and when) to stop. There are always more links to follow – even if we hit a dead-end, we can back-track and choose a new route. But how many links do we need to follow in order to get a sense of an 'area' of the web? If we look at ten sites on a topic, does it matter that there might be a hundred more we haven't seen? Lastly, what are the implications of web texts' ephemerality? What if the site we've been focusing on suddenly one day disappears, replaced by the familiar '404' error message? Where the remains of past sites are archived, it might be possible to do some archaeological work (Wilbur CR) – but in many cases, sites simply disappear without a trace.

In answer to all these questions, Mitra and Cohen take a pragmatic approach, which is to emphasize the *provisional*, *located* and *contingent* nature of any findings: awareness of these issues means that research on the web is always a snapshot, from a particular time, of a limited number of sites, stitched together uniquely. Just as an anthropologist has to realize that her or his fieldwork is embedded in the locale and the period of their visit, so researchers exploring web texts must be mindful of the modesty of their knowledge-claims. As we shall see in the next section, similar issues and questions arise for those researchers attempting ethnographic work on or in cyberspace.

## Ethnographies in/of cybercultures

> While any ethnography is methodologically risky, cyberspace ethnography is vulnerable to unique disruptions.
>
> (Hakken 1999: 37)

Perhaps more than any other research strategy, ethnography has come to occupy a central yet controversial position in studies of cybercultures. There are serious methodological questions raised by the attempt to transplant ethnographic research into cyberspace that we need to explore here. These must also be set in the broader context of debate about ethnography as a research practice more broadly, notably in disciplines such as anthropology and sociology – and of the percolation of ethnography into popular domains such as docusoaps and other 'reality' programmes on television. This leads Ken Plummer (1999) to conclude that we now inhabit an 'ethnographic society', all of us 'people watching' (or at least docusoap watching). Debates about the status and practices of ethnography can't all be squeezed into this chapter comprehensively; instead, we shall address those that come up as and when we meet them in the specific context of ethnography in cyber-culture (and see also Hine 2000).

The very existence of the Internet and its easy accessibility make it a very attractive 'site' for fieldwork. As Steve Jones (1999b: 11) says, there has been something of an academic land-rush into cyberspace, matching those colonists who want to claim it as a community-space or an economic resource. Our senses of discovery and wonder, Jones writes, are 'titillated by the sheer scale and penetration of the Internet', as we marvel at the opportunities it offers us, from the comfort of our offices, to explore strange new worlds:

> the sheer availability of chat sessions, MUD/MOO sessions, e-mail, and the like provide us with a seductive data set, and it takes little effort to be of the belief that such data represent . . . well, *something*, some semblance of reality, perhaps, or some 'slice of life' on-line.
>
> (Jones 1999b: 12; emphasis in original)

Furthermore, in these days of tight finances in higher education, the Internet is a cheap-and-easy way to reach these worlds (a point reiterated a number of times by Paccagnella 1997). This can mean, of course, that researchers have less invested in their field sites, and can merely swoop in and out, grabbing data for their projects, or spend time 'lurking' – observing interaction without getting involved. Jones worries about the ethical impli-cations of what he names an '"easy come, easy go" opportunity for sociological work' (18), and I share those worries. We shall return to the ethics of online fieldwork in a moment. First, let me introduce one of the most hotly-debated aspects of online fieldwork (and something that has long troubled ethnog-raphy more broadly) – the question of verifiability. This becomes particularly controversial when it comes to the relationship between online and offline worlds: is it possible to do ethnography wholly in cyberspace?

Proponents of what is variously called virtual ethnography, cyberethnog-raphy and cyberspace ethnography argue that cyberspace is a distinct and dis-crete world, and should therefore be treated as such. Luciano Paccagnella (1997: 5), for example, writes that in 'ethnographic research on virtual communities the on-line world has its own dignity'. T. L. Taylor (1999: 443) makes the same argument in her work on virtual bodies and identities – that if we take seriously the phenomenology of on-line life, then we need not be too hung up on 'verifying' our findings IRL: 'the idea that verifiability can be achieved offline is often embedded in a larger epistemological claim I am less willing to accept'. This issue links us back to older methodological worries about 'truth', authenticity, validity, as already noted – arguments that have rumbled on for a very long time (Plummer 1999). In the end, Taylor argues that we should resist sliding back to a position that unproblematically repli-cates an offline/online boundary. Instead, she urges scholars to become as fully immersed in virtual worlds as the participants we are researching:

> being willing to fully inhabit the spaces we are researching, and adapting ourselves to the new methodological challenges they present, is likely the best (and possibly the only) way we will begin to make sense of life in these fluid landscapes.
>
> (Taylor 1999: 448)

This stance contrasts with that taken by Sherry Turkle (1995) in *Life on the Screen*, and by Danny Miller and Don Slater (2000) in *The Internet: an ethno-graphic approach*. Turkle only reported findings where she had met respondents face-to-face as well as on-line – or, in her terms, 'in person as well as in per-sona' (Turkle 1995: 324) – acknowledging that this may make her work seem conservative. Miller and Slater confess to a similar outlook on ethnography:

> An ethnographic approach is . . . one that is based on a long-term and multifaceted engagement with a social setting. In this regard we are both relatively conservative in our defence of traditional canons of ethnographic enquiry. This seems particularly important at the present time, when the term 'ethnography' has become somewhat fashionable in many disciplines. In some fields, such as cultural studies, it has come to signify simply a move away from purely textual analysis. In other cases, the idea of an Internet ethnography has come to mean almost entirely the study of online 'community' and relationships – the ethnog-raphy of cyberspace. . . . We assume that *ethnography means a long-term involvement amongst people, through a variety of methods, such that any one aspect of their lives can be properly contextualized in others. . . . An ethnography is much more than fieldwork.*
>
> (Miller and Slater 2000: 21–2; my emphasis)

David Hakken (1999: 45) echoes Miller and Slater too, chastizing those wayward academics guilty of 'donning the mantle of an anthropology of the contemporary but wearing it loosely', adding that 'misappropriation of ethnography is one reason why intellectuals find it hard to construct a convincing account of culture in cyberspace'. Like Miller and Slater, Hakken advocates multi-sited ethnography, with online and offline elements (see also Heath *et al.* 1999). Lyman and Wakeford (1999: 363) ask the pertinent question here: 'How much do we need to know about nonvirtual manifestations ("the real") to interpret the data that we collect online ("the virtual")?' We need, however, to broaden this question out, and think about (for example) the usefulness of seeing 'real' sites where people interact with the 'virtual' – as in Miller and Slater's time spent huddled round computers in Trinidad, or Wakeford's (1999) own work on cybercafés.

One way of reading this debate is as a predictable academic 'turf war' over the method of ethnography – as we see in Miller and Slater's dig at cultural studies, or Hakken's loose-fit anthropology. It's beyond the scope of my discussion here to join in with that spat. Instead, let's take the view that we're comfortable with different ways of doing ethnography, and focus instead on what seems to me to be the key issue here. To reiterate: *can we do ethnography solely online?* Christine Hine (2000) picks through this debate, siding with the more generous interpretation of ethnography, but (like Taylor) recommending active participation rather than passive observation. As she writes, this also means recognizing the distinctiveness of online life (and online research): 'how can you live in an online setting? Do you have to be logged on 24 hours a day, or can you visit the setting at periodic intervals?' (Hine 2000: 21). The researcher's depth of involvement should match participants' – indeed, in some respects, this distinction should disappear. Probably the most productive statement that Hine makes is to distinguish between different research contexts: 'the settings where we might observe Internet culture are different from the ones in which we would observe the Internet in use. One setting is virtual and the other a physical place' (40). While this maintains a distinction between real and virtual worlds that some scholars would want to contest (Taylor 1999), I feel that Hine's suggestion provides a useful practical solution to this particular problem. Moreover, to require face-to-face 'verification' of online ethnography may be unreflective of the context one is researching:

> Many inhabitants of cyberspace . . . have never met face-to-face and have no intention of doing so. To instigate face-to-face meetings in this situation would place the ethnographer in an asymmetric position, using more varied and different means of communication to understand informants than are used by informants themselves.
>
> (Hine 2000: 48)

This point reminds us of one key ethical issue in cyberspace ethnography – again echoing similar debates about power in the research process more broadly. Virtual ethnography restages some of these on-going debates, but also brings with it new ethical questions. It is important to sketch some of these here.

## Ethics in cybercultures research

> Every ethnography needs a warrant (what right do I have to tell this story?) and a credo (what are the damages I could do and how are they to be avoided?).
>
> (Plummer 1999: 645)

Qualitative methods like ethnography have a long history of wrestling with ethical questions of all sorts. There are serious issues to confront about the role and power that a researcher has, as someone who enters a social setting to conduct research in it – and this methodological baggage is carried into cyberspace, too. Let's start by considering the positioning of the researcher in cyberspace. As Hine (2000) says, the arrival on our desktops of computers through which to access cyberspace has made online research virtually irresistible. At the practical level, computers let scholars overcome time, money and other constraints that often prevent us from conducting the kind of in-depth ethnographies associated with anthropology. Here, through the wires, we have instant access to countless potential field sites and informants – and we don't even have to leave our offices! Moreover, we can be almost completely invisible, simply silently watching what's going on – something that's impossible in real life, unless we engage in the ethically problematic practice of so-called covert research (entering the field site in disguise, masquerading as a participant and not disclosing our real reasons for being there). The observer who only observes – who 'stays on the verandah' (Hine 2000) – has become an untenable role to occupy in 'real world' ethnography. When we enter cyberculture, however, the opportunities to stay on the *virtual verandah* can be seductive. There's even a ready-made role for us – that of the 'lurker'. Lurkers are people who watch things like chat rooms or MUDs without actively participating – a kind of virtual voyeurism. Before you set off to lurk, however, it's important to note that this is a discussion of ethics, and that lurking as a research technique is widely condemned by virtual ethnographers. At the very least, as Heath *et al.* (1999) suggest, lurking is not acceptable since it puts the researcher in a powerful and distant position – the academic is someone who gazes on others, appropriating their actions for the purposes of research. Lurking is a one-way process, and one of the strengths of ethnography is its emphasis on *dialogue* with respondents – recasting research as collaboration rather than appropriation. Moreover, the practice of lurking and then using material collected in research brings out questions of privacy in cyberspace: are chat rooms, discussion lists and so on 'public' or 'private'? There are different standpoints on this, and concepts of public and private vary across and between different kinds of online site (Mann and Stewart 2000). Given issues of database anxiety in this information age (Poster 1995), it seems sensible (and responsible) that researchers do not add to feelings of panic about unauthorised uses of information mined in cyberspace. Mann and Stewart (2000) survey arguments about ethics, confidentiality and lurking, and provide a broad ethical framework for online research, which highlights consent, confidentiality and the observance of netiquette, as well as offering practical advice on how to address these.

Set against research from the virtual verandah, then, is participation rather than observation. However, we should not simply see participation as the cure-all to ethical questions. For a start, we need to remember a distinction between overt and covert research – while many researchers have been disgruntled by the way that declaring their research aims means that no-one'll talk to them online (Ward 2000), there are immense ethical problems associated with covert participation. Again, this requires a mode of masquerade that amounts to deception, perhaps doubly so if we are attempting to pass as something we are not: if we are an 'outsider' rather than an 'insider' to the setting we're researching. That the act of masquerade is made easier in cyberspace does not mean that it is less ethically troublesome; neither does hiding behind the fact that everyone else could be lying about who they are. To rewire one of cyberspace's famous aphorisms, the fact that *in cyberspace no-one knows you're an ethnographer* does not answer the question of whether participants have a *right* to know that you are. Even if, as Daniel Tsang (CR: 432) says, it 'pays to have a sense of 'healthy paranoia' on-line', researchers shouldn't be aggravating that.

In addition, we have to remember that participation in any social setting transforms it – even if we do declare our intentions, our presence impacts on the behaviour of those around us. In some cases of overtly collaborative research, part of the agenda is to effect change – to intervene in the lives of respondents to enhance their well-being (Heath *et al.* 1999). Even when this is not the case, researchers have to recognize the effects that they have just by being there. While there are substantial practical gains in online research, such as comparative ease of access, there are also new limitations: the kind of sporadic involvement with a virtual field setting means we might miss some of the unintended impacts that our presence has. In common with offline participant observation, an awareness of these issues is paramount (Kendall 1999).

There are other serious ethical questions raised in cyberspace ethnography, but I do not have time to work through them all here. Ultimately, while David Hakken (1999: 210) argues that 'it may be more difficult for everyone to act ethically in cyberspace', it is important that scholars consider the ethical implications for different research strategies. Like the choice of methods, the exact shape of any ethical framework is context-specific; what's important is that it must be in tune with the field site, and must be accountable. Finally, we should remember what Howcroft (1999) wrote about information over-load, and Poster's (1995) comments on database anxiety. Firing off endless intrusive questions contributes to both these problems, and can be considered a form of spamming (Selwyn and Robson 1998). The machine on your desk-top might seem like a trouble-free gateway into limitless social phenomena, but all research online relies on the generosity of those we are researching (or, to put it more collaboratively, those we are *researching with*).

## A manifesto for cyberethnographers?

To round off our discussion of the pleasures and pitfalls of ethnography in cyberspace, I want to return to Hine's (2000) important work. *Virtual Ethnography* presents, I think, one of the best discussions and illustrations of the principles and practices of this kind of fieldwork. Hine picks her way through many of the methodological questions that arise, based on the expe-rience of researching online activities around the trial of British nanny Louise Woodward in the US in 1997. From the benefit of that experience she formu-lates a set of principles for virtual ethnography that I'd like to look at here. There are ten points (see Hine 2000: 64–5):

1. Virtual ethnography interrogates taken-for-granted assumptions about the Internet.
2. We need to see the Internet as both culture and cultural artefact.
3. The Internet transforms the notion of the field site, making the research mobile rather than spatially located.
4. Contesting the idea of the field site also means concentrating on flow and connectivity.
5. Virtual ethnography focuses attention on boundaries as well as connec-tions – especially between the 'virtual' and the 'real'.
6. Virtual ethnography is 'interstitial' temporally – it is not inhabited 24 hours a day, so immersion can only be intermittent.
7. Virtual ethnography can only ever be partial, and can never reflect the totality of the Internet.
8. The ethnographer is also a participant in using the media of cyberspace, and so reflexivity about online experiences should be foregrounded.
9. The ethnographer and informants are both present and absent to each other; virtual ethnography is 'ethnography *in*, *of* and *through* the virtual', so face-to-face interaction is unnecessary.

10. Virtual ethnography also means 'not quite' ethnography in purists' terms; it is adaptive, and 'adequate for the practical purpose of exploring the relations of mediated interaction'.

Hine concludes with pragmatics rather than principles, in response to the last point made – the one principle is that there are no once-and-for-all principles in an *adaptive* methodology:

> There are no set of rules to follow in order to conduct the perfect ethnography, and defining the fundamental components of the ethnographic approach is unhelpful. The focus of ethnography on dwelling within a culture demands adaptation and the possibility of overturning prior assumptions.
>
> (Hine 2000: 65–6)

In addition, and reinforcing points 4 (emphasis on connections) and 7 (about the partial nature of any virtual ethnography), Hine draws up a list of different sites 'in which the Internet is enacted and interpreted', to stress the need for mobile or multi-sited ethnography – or at least, the need to recognize the dense and complex sites that comprise the Internet. While she acknowledges that this list is incomplete, it's worth looking at here:

- Web pages
- Accounts of making web pages
- Instructions on how to make web pages
- Programs to help in making web pages
- Reviews of web pages
- Media reports on Internet events
- Magazines and newspaper supplements devoted to the Internet
- Fictionalized accounts of Internet-like technologies
- Computer equipment retailers
- Software developers
- Stock markets
- Newsgroups
- MUDs
- IRC
- Video conferences
- Accounts of the purpose of newsgroups
- Internet service providers' advertising and introductory materials
- Internet gateways and search engines
- Homes and workplaces where the Internet is used, and the practices we find there
- Training courses

- Conversations between friends, families and work colleagues
- Academic Internet studies like this one

(Hine 2000: 62–3)

In the case of her ethnography, Hine chose to focus on the Woodward case, and to incorporate from this list the dimensions relevant to exploring how the Internet shaped the discourses around the British nanny's trial. Depending on the specific focus of any research project, different aspects will become more or less significant. One dimension that Hine doesn't figure very prominently is the infrastructure of cyberspace – like Latour's (1992) missing masses, ethnography has tended to miss nonhuman elements. However, Susan Leigh Star (1999: 379) argues that we should 'attend ethnographically to the plugs, settings, sizes, and other profoundly mundane aspects of cyberspace', since in programs and protocols are embedded issues of power, culture and the potential for change.

That last component is, in fact, a key aspect of many discussions of online research: that it should embody a political commitment to change (Escobar CR). By showing how things are, issues of power, inequality and injustice are made visible, so that they can be addressed. Heath *et al.* (1999) refer to such acts as 'modest interventions', reflecting their contingency and partiality. Their modesty does not, however, diminish their importance. As Hakken concludes:

> The ultimate intent of an ethnographically led cyberspace studies . . . is to ground the process of imagining cyberspace on both a rich empirical understanding of what is actually taking place and to articulate ethically formulated intellectual rules of thumb to guide further imaginings. I believe it also to be a responsibility of cyberspace ethnography to explore diligently what the empirical study suggests regarding how best to imagine the future – *to help create cyberspace, not just be created by it.* . . . Because its imaginings can affect the future, cyberspace ethnography has a distinct moral charge. We study what is not because it will tell us what will be in any simple way, but *because in understanding what is (and what has been) we can learn ways of imagining that discourage practices that should be hindered, as ways that help us set goals we can attain.*
>
> (Hakken 1999: 228; my emphasis)

## Summary

To borrow Heath *et al.*'s phrase, this chapter has been my own modest intervention into discussions of research in, on and with cyberspace. It is not intended as a comprehensive review of techniques; nor is it a how-to guide. As Hine's work reminds us, it's neither possible nor desirable to attempt to write such guides – there are no once-and-for-all hard-and-fast rules here; methods must be adaptive. I have purposely limited the scope of this chapter, then, in order to get a focus on key issues. We have not, for example, discussed quantitative research such as the use of survey techniques to quantify the population of cyberspace (for a discussion of these, see Jordan 1999), nor the possibilities of integrating quantitative and qualitative methods in new ways in cyberspace studies (see Sudweeks and Simoff 1999). In addition, there are aspects of qualitative research that we have ignored, such as conversation analysis approaches (to email and discussion lists, for instance), or online interviewing and focus groups (see Mann and Stewart 2000). Neither have we explored other ways that networked computers can be used in research – such as their role in data analysis, storage and presentation (see Deacon et al. 1999). As tireless, obedient research assistants, computers have a variety of roles to play in the research process, and their presence has reconfigured many aspects of that process, from the initial selection of a topic right through to the writing-up and publication of research findings. Recognizing the multitasking that computers carry out for us in the research process also asks that we acknowledge our gratitude to them as participants. In the future, their place in research is likely to become even more central – which also makes even more pressing the debates around cyberspace methodologies.

What I have tried to do in this chapter, through a focus on particular methods and the debates they bring with them, has been to illustrate and explore some of the questions and issues that arise when conducting cyber-research – no matter what methods you use. As we have seen, some of these issues are familiar to offline methodologies, but new challenges and opportunities are also introduced in online research contexts. In this way, online research is reshaping the debates around method and methodology – and it is also reshaping online life. Indeed, as Hakken says, part of the purpose of researching cyberspace has to be to intervene, to 'discourage practices that should be hindered' and contribute to processes of knowledge-production and cyberspace-production in ways that contribute positively and politically to the on-going evolution of cybercultures.

## Hot links

### Chapters from The Cybercultures Reader

Arturo Escobar, 'Welcome to cyberia: notes on the anthropology of cyberculture' (Chapter 3: 56–76).

Ananda Mitra, 'Virtual commonality: looking for India on the Internet' (Chapter 44: 676–94).

Daniel Tsang, 'Notes on queer 'n' Asian virtual sex' (Chapter 27: 432–8).

Shawn Wilbur, 'An archaeology of cyberspaces: virtuality, community, identity' (Chapter 2: 45–55).

Susan Zickmund, 'Approaching the radical other: the discursive culture of cyber-hate' (Chapter 15: 237–53).

## Further reading

David Hakken (1999) *Cyborgs@Cyberspace? An ethnographer looks to the future*, London: Routledge.

Christine Hine (2000) *Virtual Ethnography*, London: Sage.

Steve Jones (ed.) (1999) *Doing Internet Research: critical issues and methods for examining the net*, London: Sage.

Peter Lyman and Nina Wakeford (eds) (1999) *Analyzing Virtual Societies: new directions in methodology*, special issue of *American Behavioral Scientist* 43: 355–490.

Chris Mann and Fiona Stewart (2000) *Internet Communication and Qualitative Research: a handbook for researching online*, London: Sage.

Daniel Miller and Don Slater (2000) *The Internet: an ethnographic approach*, Oxford: Berg.

## Websites

http://www.pitt.edu/~gajjala/cy.html

Cyberethnography webring hosted by Radhika Gajjala (aka Cyberdiva), outlining one approach to enthnography in cyberspace, and linking to other pages on virtual methods and methodologies.

http://ethnonet.gold.ac.uk

Website accompanying Miller and Slater's book, providing visuals and links to illustrate their Trinidad study.

http://www.MappingCyberspace.com

Great website of maps of cyberspace, showing the research techniques that aim to make visible to flows, nodes and spaces of cyberculture.

http://www.surrey.ac.uk/sru/SRU.html

The University of Surrey's quarterly update on social research, with a focus on methods and methodologies.

# Chapter 10

# LAST WORDS

I am not sure that I know what the Internet is; I am not sure that anyone does.

*James Costigan*

**W**HAT, FINALLY, CAN WE SAY about cybercultures? My aim in this book as been to explore some of the things that 'cyberculture' means, as a way of naming the relationships between the objects, images and experiences that together constitute cyberspace as culture and cultural artefact, to recycle Christine Hine's (2000) formulation. The book has been a modest introduction, partial and contingent – written as a way to think through with you some domains and dimensions of this inevitably multiplicitous thing. I am not sure, poaching from Costigan (1999), that I know what cyberculture is – but I would like to think that all the time spent buried in books, browsing the web and thinking with computers has at least contributed to the task of understanding and illustrating some components of cyberculture. To end with a summary-of-summaries, and to be brief (as I feel I've detained you long enough), here's what I consider to be the key points raised in and through the book:

- Cyberspace is created through the stories we tell about it. There are different kinds of stories, which I call material, symbolic and experiential stories. Material stories include looking at hardware and software – what we might think of as 'nerd stories' – as well as thinking about the material impacts of cyberspace, for example through considering issues of inequality in access. Symbolic stories are the tales told in popular culture – in fiction, films, songs, adverts – and everyday life; these stories give us a set of resources for thinking about cyberspace.

Experiential stories are tales of how we encounter cyberspace in the many places we interact with it. Importantly, the experience of cyberspace represents the mediation of material and symbolic stories, to give us what's sometimes referred to as Barlovian cyberspace.

- To get a handle on the culture in cyberculture, it is important to explore what conceptual and methodological tools are available to us. In terms of the former, there are theorists and theories that can help us interrogate cyberculture; we do not have to make a once-and-for-all commitment to one set of ideas, but we do have to make a once-and-for-all commitment to the practice of theorizing cyberspace as cyberculture. Theory is one kind of intelligent agent we need to take with us into cyberspace.

- Cyberspace is seen by many commentators as challenging accepted notions of community. From some perspectives, this is held as positive – RL communities are disappearing, and virtual communities can bring people back into meaningful social relations with one another. Other critics argue, however, that over-reliance on virtual communities leads to a withdrawal from RL, exacerbating the decline of real-world sociality. In between these two extremes comes the argument that cyberspace is augmenting traditional f2f social life, but neither replacing nor destroying it.

- Questions of cultural identity are seen as being reworked in cyberculture, as the medium offers new ways of understanding personal and collective identity. The possibility of reshaping who we are in virtual worlds is sometimes seen as liberating, but can also restage processes of domination. Moreover, the 'freedom' to play with identities online might be contributing to a loss of identity – a slide into individualism that has political consequences. Like the debate around online community, the arguments about virtual identity bring into relief the problematic negotiation of the cyberspace/meatspace boundary.

- Linked to issues of identity is the status of the body in cyberculture. Digital technologies are reconfiguring what we mean by the body and life, and what it means to be human. Work on prosthetic technologies, on cyborgs, on the posthuman and the Visible Human offers ways to explore the changing conditions and possibilities of embodiment in a world shared with robots, intelligent software agents, human–machine hybrids and artificial life-forms of all kinds. Thinking about cyborgs, and thinking as a cyborg, is one way to confront these issues head-on.

- Cyberspace also enabled particular kinds of subcultural work to take place – with part of its origins in 1960s counterculture, it is unsurprising to see non-mainstream uses proliferating in cyberspace. For some subcultures, such as fan cultures, media like the Internet offer another forum for the exchange of ideas, just as print media (fanzines) and audiovisual media (filk songs) have before. Other subcultures, however, have a more distinctly expressive relationship to new technologies, either as enthusiastic (if subversive) advocates – such as hackers – or as pessimistic doomsayers, as in the case of Neo-Luddites.

- To reiterate a point already made, in order to contemplate what cyber-culture means, we need the right tools to think it with. Some of these tools are theoretical, and others are practical: we need methods for conducting research into cybercultures that reflect the distinctiveness of new cybercultural formations. A multi-sited, mobile and adaptive set of methods offers the potential not only to describe cyberspace, but also to collaborate in the on-going process of meaning-making that will define what cyberspace becomes.

Now, if we add these points together, we still might not be able to say that we know what cyberculture is, but I hope we will have contributed to the on-going business of looking at some of the ways of talking and thinking about it. As Erik Davis (1998: 264) says, cyberspace is 'still under construc-tion, and therein lies its strength' – the possibility that we, as users and critics, can intervene in, in our own modest ways, helping to shape cyber-space as culture and cultural artefact – *cyberculture* – in all its emergent, rhizomatic complexity.

# Further reading

This guide should really be titled 'some books on cybercultures that David Bell likes'; it is a modest guide to further reading, shaped by the contents of my own bookshelves, and not claiming to be comprehensive or objective. There's so much published material out there, with more and more appearing all the time (this morning I wandered into our local bookshop, and saw Chris Gray's new book, *Cyborg Citizen*, on the 'New Titles' shelf – and made the decision that it was *too late* to include other than by nodding to it here). To look at this another way, earlier on in the work on this book, I went to amazon.com, the online bookseller, and did a quick search for books with 'cyberspace' in the title. The search produced 146 items, ranging from *The Parent's Guide to Protecting Children in Cyberspace* to *Career Opportunities in Computers and Cyberspace*, and from *The Domain Name Handbook* to *Hamlet on the Holodeck*. Clearly, I'm not in the business of surveying all the titles out there – all I can do is show you some books that I rate, and tell you why. The tv stations in the UK seem obsessed at the moment with programmes of lists – *The 100 Best TV Moments*, *The 100 Best Hit Singles* – and so, in recognition of this outbreak of 'list-eria' (as comedian Graham Norton calls it), here comes my own Top 20. The outbreak of list-eria has brought with it a secondary outbreak of heated debate about what's on and what's missed off – if you want to chat about my list, feel free to email me. There's nothing to be gained from citing books I don't like – and no point in pretending this is anything better than a list of books I do like. And because I'm also not in the business of ranking, they're listed alphabetically.

Janet Abbate (1999) *Inventing the Internet* (Cambridge MA: MIT Press)
A fantastic account of the prehistory and history of the net. Packed full of detail, this is a computer geek's dream book – in the best possible sense. I found it a real page-turner.

Michael Benedikt (ed.) (1991) *Cyberspace: first steps* (Cambridge MA: MIT Press)
Classic collection of cyberspace heavy-weights – very much of-its-time, but what a time it was! Captures the early 1990s buzz around cyberspace across a range of disciplines.

Dani Cavallaro (2000) *Cyberpunk and Cyberculture: science fiction and the work of William Gibson* (London: Athlone)
Good reading of the cyberpunk genre, set in the context of critical work in cyberculture. Establishes a 'mythology' of cyberpunk, and walks us through Gibson's work especially clearly.

Lynn Cherny and Elizabeth Reba Weise (eds) (1996) *Wired Women: gender and new realities in cyberspace* (Seattle: Seal Press)
Still one of my favourite collections of feminist and cyberfeminist interventions – great analyses of the implications for gender identities of new digital environments, and great use of personal experience to illuminate arguments.

Sean Cubitt (1998) *Digital Aesthetics* (London: Sage)
Hugely impressive exploration of the emerging aesthetics of computer culture, including discussions of digital art, virtual reality and the way computers and interfaces look.

Erik Davis (1998) *TechGnosis: myth, magic and mysticism in the age of information* (London: Serpent's Tail)
This is probably my very favourite book on cyberspace (and much more besides), tracking the 'secret history' of technology's irrational sides – its supernatural, mystic, paranormal dimensions. Fantastic.

Mark Dery (1996) *Escape Velocity: cyberculture at the end of the century* (London: Hodder & Stoughton)
A great account of the mid-1990s US cyber-scene, with interviews and critical commentary on cybersubcultures, the cyberarts, posthumanism and so on.

Mike Featherstone and Roger Burrows (eds) (1995) *Cyberspace/Cyberbodies/Cyberpunk* (London: Sage)
Definitive collection of essays from the *Body & Society* crowd – still remarkable for the strength and breadth of some of the readings on offer. My favourite: Robert Rawdon Wilson's 'Cyber(body)parts: prosthetic consciousness'.

David Gauntlett (ed.) (2000) *Web.Studies: rewiring media studies for the digital age* (London: Arnold)

A great student text, with techno-savvy chapters on topics from webcams to Xena fans. Manages to mimic the polysemy of the web in the covers of a book, by clicking through a huge range of perspectives and topics.

Chris Hables Gray (ed.) (1995) *The Cyborg Handbook* (London: Routledge)

Huge, smart and famous – the publisher's claim that it is a 'cult classic' under-sells it; this is a great big book, with essays ranging over all sorts of cyborgs and all sorts of ideas about cyborgs.

N. Katherine Hayles (1999) *How We Became Posthuman: virtual bodies in cybernetics, literature, and informatics* (Chicago: University of Chicago Press)

An astonishing read, in its ability to think about what it means to be posthuman from all kinds of angles, drawing on an amazing array of ideas, and written with a cool political commitment to its topic.

Tim Jordan (1999) *Cyberpower: the culture and politics of cyberspace and the internet* (London: Routledge)

A clear, critical overview of the current state of cyberspace; Jordan presents a series of 'myths' about the electronic frontier, which he then debunks or reworks to produce new, grounded ways of thinking about the net today.

Beth Kolko, Lisa Nakamura and Gilbert Rodman (eds) (2000) *Race in Cyberspace* (London: Routledge)

Fantastic collection of (mainly US) scholars interrogating the racial politics of the Internet and virtual reality. Some of the best work on the relationship between cyberspace and questions of identity, embodiment and politics.

Brian Loader (ed.) (1998) *Cyberspace Divide: equality, agency and policy in the information society* (London: Routledge)

Brilliant dose of hype-busting reality: reminds readers of the inequalities and injustices that cyberspace brings, keeping issues of social exclusion live in the on-going debates about the impacts of the Internet.

Larry McCaffery (ed.) (1991) *Storming the Reality Studio: a casebook of cyberpunk and postmodern fiction* (Durham NC: Duke University Press)

A decade old and still going strong, this is the classic compendium of pre-cyberpunk and cyberpunk writing, with an excellent show of critical essays mixed in.

Daniel Miller and Don Slater (2000) *The Internet: an ethnographic approach* (Oxford: Berg)

How good is this book? In providing a richly detailed ethnography of Internet use in Trinidad, it gives us a clear yet complex picture of the mutual shaping of technology and society. Contextualizes cyberspace's social locations brilliantly.

Marc Smith and Peter Kollock (eds) (1999) *Communities in Cyberspace* (London: Routledge)
Very useful collection of essays exploring different takes on one of the most vexed questions for cyberculture. The richness of the case studies grounds the broader theoretical agenda to think through what 'community' means (or could mean) in cyberspace.

Sherry Turkle (1995) *Life on the Screen: identity in the age of the internet* (London: Phoenix)
A book I keep going back to; as a model of one way of researching issues of identity on-line, it is unbeatable. Turkle's work on robots, interfaces and artificial intelligence provides valuable insights into our new posthuman relatives.

Catherine Waldby (2000) *The Visible Human Project: informatic bodies and posthuman medicine* (London: Routledge)
This is a fantastic reading of the intricacies and implications of the Visible Human Project, which moves out from those bodies to consider visual culture, biomedicine and artificial life.

Richard Wise (2000) *Multimedia: a critical introduction* (London: Routledge)
Slim but jam-packed, Wise's book does what it says: it guides us through the convergences and synergies that now comprise the multimedia landscape – with a critical edge that makes you stop and think.

# Glossary

I have limited this glossary to terms at the 'cyber' end of cybercultures, rather than the 'cultures' end. What I mean by this is that I have elected not to define terms like 'community' or 'subculture', but only those technical or neologistic terms associated with cyberspace. While I have some hesitations about doing this – since I wouldn't consider myself anything like an expert on these matters – I hope that the glossary might assist some readers to get to grips with the language of cyberculture. For a broader discussion, plus hints on correct usage, see Hale (1996). I've also included links in the form of references to texts that discuss in more detail some of the terms defined here. And if you still need to know more, RTFM (which I won't translate for you).

**ARPANET** The computer network developed by the US Department of Defense's Advanced Research Projects Agency, and forerunner of the Internet. See Abbate (1999).

**Artificial Intelligence** (AI) Simulation of human intelligence in machines – one of the most sci-fi like areas of computer research, and one that often provokes technophobic fears about smart machines taking over – like HAL in *2001*. See Turkle (1995).

**Artificial Life** (A-Life) Robotics and software programs that simulate biological systems or processes, such as evolution. Seen by some to herald a new, post-biological age. Computer viruses are sometimes considered as primitive forms of A-Life. See Hayles (1999).

**@** Symbol used to denote location in email addresses, as in d.bell@staffs.ac.uk, which points you to my email address at Staffordshire University. Now more widely used in everyday written language, especially in media such as advertising and brand names. See Hale (1996).

**Attachment** A file 'attached' to an email – things like documents and graphics can be carried by emails in this way, and opened by their recipients.

**Avatar** A cartoon-like virtual persona, used in MUDs and some other virtual environments to represent the user. See Taylor (1999).

**Barlovian cyberspace** Named after John Perry Barlow of the Electronic Frontier Foundation (EFF), the term is used to refer to cyberspace as it currently exists, in contrast to the purely imaginary Gibsonian cyberspace imagined in cyberpunk. See Jordan (1999).

**BBSs** Bulletin Board Services. One of the most talked-about forums for online interaction, BBSs are open computer systems accessed over the phone, into which subscribing users can input information for other users to read, download or respond to. Originally modelled on boards for pinning up notices, many bulletin boards are based around specific topics, and can be accessed through networked systems. A participant is called a BBSer. See Stone (CR).

**Bug** A software error or glitch that can cause malfunctions. The Y2K Bug was such a glitch, caused by programs failing to tell machines what to do when the year 2000 came, and their date-counters recorded '00'. It was predicted that this would confuse computers, who might think it was 1900, and that they therefore hadn't been invented yet. It arose since the program writers never imagined machines would still be running the same old programs by the millennium's end. In the UK, a huge government-sponsored 'compliance' programme was initiated, matched by an equally huge PR exercise, and the televised New Year's Eve celebrations included updates on Y2K bug disasters – which turned out to be few and far between. When we returned to work in January 2000, most of our machines were still working, and waiting for us.

**Chatroom** Virtual 'room' on a chat service such as IRC, in which multiple users can interact in real time, their messages appearing on all logged-on users' screens simultaneously.

**CGI** Computer-Generated Imagery. Cinematic special effects created using software programs, argued in this book to generate their own version of cyberspace.

**CMC** Computer-mediated communication. More than just a name for what people do in cyberspace, CMC has come to define a distinct approach to the study of things like email. CMC refers to text-based communications. See Jones and Kucker (2000).

**Conferencing** A term for forms of CMC which allow multiple users to communicate.

**Convergence** The ways in which different information, communication and entertainment technologies are both brought together (as in the web being accessible through your tv) or come to increasingly resemble one another, as with infotainment. See Bolter and Grusin (1999).

**Cookie** Tool for tracking movements through the web. Used to identify users and gather information about visits to websites.

**Cybercafé** A café offering Internet access for a fee. Often, at least in the UK, the emphasis is on the cyber at the expense of the café. For travellers and others without easy access to machines, cybercafés are useful places to send and receive email. See Wakeford (1999). Users, at least in San Francisco, are known as bitniks (Hale 1996).

**Cyberpunk** A subgenre of science fiction writing and cinema, associated with William Gibson, Pat Cadigan and others. Cyberpunk writing imagines a very particular kind of future, in which computer technology is ever-present and all-powerful. See Cavallaro (2000).

**Cyberspace** Notoriously difficult to define precisely or succinctly, scholars often point to William Gibson's famous definition, from his novel *Neuromancer* (1984) – since this is where the term was first coined. See also Gibson (1991). Think of it as the merging of the material, symbolic and experiential – as where we go to when we use the Internet, or email, or BBSs, or MUDs – and, as I suggest in Chapter 3, in the cinema, or the hospital.

**Cyborg** Literally a CYBernetic ORGanism, the term is now applied to numerous assemblages of the biological and the technological. See Gray (1995).

**Domain name** The suffix on webite URLs denoting the type of location: '.com' for commerical companies, '.ac' for academic institutions.

**Dot.com** Shorthand used especially by journalists to mean Internet-based businesses. The Nasdaq high-tech stock market, where shares in dot.com businesses float, has exhibited great volatility, leading economists and investors to conclude that we are not, in fact, witnessing a new economic miracle. See Martinson and Elliott (2000).

**Download** Getting a file, picture, document or whatever from the Internet (or any other network) and transferring it to your own computer. The opposite process, of transferring data from your computer to the net, is known as uploading (as is the imaginary process of transferring human consciousness to the net).

**EFF** Electronic Frontier Foundation. Founded in 1990 as self-appointed spokes-people for freedom in cyberspace, the EFF has its roots in the San Francisco counterculture of hippies and Deadheads (especially John Perry Barlow, ex-member of the Grateful Dead), and strong links with the WELL. Advocates of the 'frontierist' approach to cyberspace. See Jordan (1999).

**E-greetings cards** Also known as virtual postcards, these are images and animations that can be accessed on websites and then sent as email attachments. See Miller and Slater (2000).

**Email** Short for electronic mail. The basic form of asynchronous communication over the Internet, and the system for sending text messages (which can have other kinds of information added as attachments) to a specified address. See Kollock and Smith (1999).

**Emoticons** Use of keyboard characters to confer emotions in text-based communication, including smileys such as ;-) (winking) and abbreviated catchphrases (ROTFLOL – rolls on the floor laughing out loud).

**FAQs** Frequently Asked Questions. A document answering common questions about a site, product, newsgroup, often aimed at satisfying the curiosity of newbies – and now more widely used outside cyberspace.

**Flame** An abusive message posted to a newsgroup, BBS, or even via email; when people trade insults, things can escalate into a flame war. See Dery (1994).

**FTF/F2F** Face-to-face. When people meet IRL, rather than in cyberspace. Time spent f2f is sometimes known as facetime.

**FTP** File Transfer Protocol. Rules for transferring files between computers. FTP was one of the most important facilities written into the Internet, to allow users to share programs and data. See Abbate (1999).

**Geek** Originally a term of abuse for people overly-obsessed with computers – though now reappropriated as a badge of pride, as in groups such as Geekgirls. Other similar terms include anorak, spod, nerd, techie, gearhead and propeller-head. See Hale (1996).

**Gibsonian cyberspace** Term used to describe cyberspace as depicted in cyberpunk writing (hence Gibsonian, after William Gibson). See Jordan (1999).

**Hacking** Originally, any display of technical virtuosity or flashy geekism. Now more commonly used to mean gaining access to someone else's computer systems, for a variety of purposes. In popular culture, hacking tends to be conflated with breaching computer security systems for malicious reasons – a form of cybercrime – though this is more properly called cracking. Similar activities using the phone system are known as phreaking. See Taylor (1999).

**Hardware** The machinery – computers, wires, plugs, keyboards, monitors – that forms the material culture of cyberspace.

**Home page** A web page, usually the 'first' page of an organization's site, or a personal web page. Home pages often house links to other pages and sites. See Cheung (2000).

**HTML** Hypertext Markup Language. Formatting commands that convert files, documents, pictures and so on into web pages: 'The language that humans use to talk to web servers or browsers' (Hale 1996: 134).

**HTTP** Hypertext Transfer Protocol. Rules for linking files to each other on the web.

**Hyperlink** Connection between web pages in the form of clickable links, often embedded in the text. See Shields (2000).

**Hypertext** Document (such as a website) built up from hyperlinking other documents (such as web pages) together. More broadly, hypertext is the name for nonlinear connections between discrete bits of information. See Wise (2000). The linking of graphics, sounds and moving images in this way produced hypermedia.

**Interface** The so-called 'front end' of software applications – those things that appear on the screen (icons, tool bars, windows). The interface mediates between the computer and the human, for example by making software more 'user-friendly'. Interfaces that incorporate more than text-based commands are called GUI, or graphical user interfaces. See Johnston (1997).

**Internet** The worldwide network-of-networks, that together use the IP Protocol and can therefore be connected as a single network, though it endlessly branches and complexly connects, and supports a range of services, including email, the web, file transfer, IRC. Often shortened to the net.

**Intranet** An internal network within an organization, which may then connect to the Internet.

**IRC** Internet Relay Chat. System of real-time (synchronous) communication, or chat, through which users can talk to others who are logged on at the time. Lines of typed chat appear in a window on users' screens. IRC is divided by interests, known as channels. See Slater (1998). A system called ICQ (I seek you) permits chat users to see who else is logged on at any given time. Logged-on users congregate in a virtual space called a chatroom.

**IRL** In Real Life. Acronym for offline life used in text-based communication. RL is the same shorthand, for real life (as opposed to virtual or online life) – although some cyberspace advocates dislike the implication that the virtual world is any less 'real', and prefer terms such as meatspace.

**ISP** Internet Service Provider. An intermediary between Internet and user, available to subscribers, that provides ways of accessing Internet resources. An example is America Online (AOL).

**Jacking in** To enter cyberspace; to go online. Used in cyberpunk to describe the process whereby 'console cowboys' jack their minds direct into the matrix.

**Lurking** Passive, non-interactive reading of communication on a conference, newsgroup or BBS. Depending on your perspective, lurking is as harmless as 'people watching' or as intrusive as voyeurism.

**Mailing list** Discussion forum which participants subscribe to, to receive and send emails – often based around topics of shared interest.

**Modem** MOdulator/DEModulator. Device for connecting computers through telephone lines to the Internet. The modem translates between digital and analogue signals.

**MUDs** Multi-User Domains, Dimensions or Dungeons. Derived from role-playing games like Dungeons and Dragons, MUDs use computer databases to construct virtual worlds in which participants interact, often through text or avatars, building up an on-going collective 'story'. Social MUDs are less focused on game-playing, and instead provide a general social setting for interaction, often modelled on a house. MUD owners are known as Gods, and participants granted power to 'govern' MUDs are called Wizards. Participants are called MUDders, the practice is called MUDding, and when you've finished you've MUDded. LambdbaMOO is probably the best-known example of an object-oriented MUD, or MOO, where the program facilitates the building of rooms and objects. It was also the site of the infamous case of virtual rape documented by Dibbell (1999). See also Curtis (1999). Other variants include MUCKs, MUSEs and MUSHs.

**Netiquette** Generally accepted codes of conduct and behaviour on the Internet – for example around flaming or spamming and how to deal with it.

**Newbie** A newcomer to the Internet, or to a particular service on it (such as a chatroom). Newbies often irritate established users with their breaches of netiquette and their repetition of FAQs.

**Newsgroups** Public discussions online, divided into topics. Among the most prominent news forums in Usenet, which hosts thousands of groups on all imaginable topics. See Kollock and Smith (1999).

**Nick** Short for nickname. Pseudonym used in email, MUD, IRC, etc. Also known as 'handle', a term borrowed from CB radio culture.

**NITs** New Imaging Technologies. Medical devices for producing digital images of the body's insides, such as CAT scans and sonograms. NITs are argued by some critics to produce a distinct form of cyberspace. See Gromala (CR).

**NSF** National Science Foundation. ARPANET was split into two in the early 1980s, and the NSF took over the administration of non-military applications on NSFNet. See Slevin (2000).

**Packet** A unit of data. Files are split into standard-sized packets to be sent over the Internet, and each packet can take a different route to its destination. Once there, packets are reassembled. The process is called packet switching. See Abbate (1999).

**Posts/postings** Messages placed on newsgroups, discussion lists or BBSs.

**Prosthetics** Technological (or biomedical) devices augmenting the human body, such as artificial limbs and transgenic organs. Also applied to the externalizing of human facilities through technologies, as in Landsberg's (CR) work on 'prosthetic memories'.

**Protocol** The rules that govern how computers connect and communicate with each other; protocols allow different kinds of computers to access each other's files.

**Search engine** Database containing web information, compiled by 'robots' or 'spiders' that scour the web, adding in new finds. Search engines like Google and HotBot are a common way of entering cyberspace in the hunt for new information, though they are notoriously unselective in their search techniques.

**Server** A dedicated computer or program that hosts Internet sites, managing access to information by remote users.

**Software** Programs – instructions written by humans to tell computers what to do.

**Source code** HTML code specifying the content, layout and links of a web page.

**Spam** The equivalent of junk mail in cyberspace – unsolicited mail, or the sending of mail to multiple recipients indiscriminately. Chain letters on email and virus warnings are prominent forms of spam, contributing to the blizzard of emails.

**Surfing** Common term for travelling on the web, derived from channel surfing; synonym for (web) browsing.

**TCP/IP** Transfer Control Protocol/Internet Protocol. Protocols that facilitate the movement of programs and information between computers over the Internet – these let computers talk to each other across the Internet, regardless of their 'mother tongue'.

**Texting** Text-based communication using mobile phones, rapidly developing its own use of language, abbreviations and acronyms, although related to email. See Benson (2000).

**Thread** The trail of one particular discussion on a newsgroup or discussion list. See Stivale (1998).

**URL** Uniform Resource Locator. The address system used on the World Wide Web and other Internet locations, for example http://www/staffs.ac.uk/cultural/index. The URL indicates the method of access (http://www – the web), the server to be accessed (staffs.ac.uk – Staffordshire University's website) and the path of any file to be accessed (cultural/index – the cultural studies homepage).

**Virtual reality** Term coined by cyberguru Jaron Lanier to describe a computer-based system, combining software with forms of hardware (datagloves, goggles) that produce a simulated, 3-D environment into which the user is immersed. There has been a lot of hype about virtual reality, but it has yet to extend beyond a limited range of uses, including flight simulation and arcade games. See Rheingold (1991).

**Virus** A piece of software that is self-replicating, like a biological virus. More commonly refers to programs that spread from computer to computer, causing damage by infecting the hard drive, memory or programs. Viruses are the source of considerable anxiety among many computer users (Lupton 1994), although some virus hunters and breeders consider them to be primitive forms of A-Life (Ludwig 1996a, b).

**VRML** Virtual Reality Markup (or Modelling) Language. Code for linking 3-D objects and environments on the web; the VR version of HTML.

**Web browser** Software for 'travelling' on the web, looking out for enticing sites and then viewing them.

**Web page** An HTML document accessible on the web, often part of a larger website.

**Webcam** Digital camera linked to the web, offering either still or more frequently moving images. Reportedly invented by some boffins to keep an eye on the coffee machine at their workplace, webcam sites such as Jennycam offer the chance to watch other people's everyday lives, like a web-based docusoap. See Snyder (2000).

**Website** Collection of linked web pages, sometimes all from the same source (as in an organization's website), and sometimes linked across cyberspace.

**WELL** Whole Earth 'Lectronic Link. Bay Area (San Francisco) online community – probably the best-known and most talked-about virtual community out there, and the focus of Howard Rheingold's (1993) *The Virtual Community*. Grew from distinct Bay Area countercultural roots, and has strong links to EFF. See Davis (1998).

**Wetware** Cyberpunkish term for the human body; also referred to as 'meat'. When you're not in cyberspace, you're in meatspace.

**World Wide Web/WWW** A system or service for accessing information over the Internet, making use of hypertext links to provide text, still and moving images, graphics, sounds and files. Also often shortened to web or W3. Becoming increasingly popular and common, the web is most people's point of contact with cyberspace these days (Gauntlett 2000).

**Worm** Self-replicating program that moves independently through the Internet or other network – a form of virus. The most famous is Robert Morris' Internet Worm, which quickly visibilized the anxieties around hacking in cyberspace. See Ross (CR).

# Bibliography

Abbate, J. (1999) *Inventing the Internet*, Cambridge MA: MIT Press.

Anderson, B. (1983) *Imagined Communities: reflections on the origin and spread of nationalism*, London: Verso.

Anzaldua, G. (1987) *Borderlands/La Frontera: the new mestiza*, San Francisco: Aunt Lute Book Co.

Appadurai, A. (1996) *Modernity at Large: cultural dimensions of globalization*, Minneapolis: University of Minnesota Press.

Arizpe, L. (1999) 'Freedom to create: women's agenda for cyberspace' in W. Harcourt, (ed.) *Women@Internet: creating new cultures in cyberspace*, London: Zed Books.

Armitage, J. (1999a) 'Machinic modulations: new cultural theory and technopolitics', *Angelaki*, 4: 1–16.

Armitage, J. (1999b) 'Paul Virilio: an introduction', *Theory, Culture & Society* 16: 1–23.

Aurigi, A. and Graham, S. (1998) 'The "crisis" in the urban public realm', in B. Loader (ed.) *Cyberspace Divide: equality, agency and policy in the information society*, London: Routledge.

Aycock, A. (1995) '"Technologies of the self": Foucault and Internet discourse', *Journal of Computer-Mediated Communication* 1, available at: www.ascusc.org/jcmc/vol1/issue2/aycock.html (accessed January 2001).

Back, L. (1996) *New Ethnicities and Urban Culture: racisms and multiculture in young lives*, London: UCL Press.

Balsamo, A. (1996) *Technologies of the Gendered Body: reading cyborg women*, Durham NC: Duke.

Balsamo, A. (1998) 'Introduction', *Cultural Studies*, 12: 285–99.

Balsamo, A. (2000) 'Engineering Cultural Studies: the postdisciplinary adventures of mindplayers, fools, and others', in R. Reid and S. Traweek (eds) *Doing Science + Culture: how cultural and interdisciplinary studies are changing the way we look at science and medicine*, London: Routledge.

Bassett, C. (1997) 'Virtually gendered: life in an on-line world', in K. Gelder and S. Thornton (eds) *The Subcultures Reader*, London: Routledge.

Baudrillard, J. (1983) *Simulations*, New York: Semiotext(e).

Baym, N. (1998) 'The emergence of an on-line community', in S. Jones (ed.) *Cybersociety 2.0: revisiting computer-mediated communication and community*, London: Sage.

Beaulieu, A. (2000) 'The brain at the end of the rainbow: the promises of brain scans in the research field and in the media', in J. Marchessault and K. Sawchuk (eds) *Wild Science: reading feminism, medicine and the media*, London: Routledge.

Bech, H. (1997) *When Men Meet: homosexuality and modernity*, Cambridge: Polity Press.

Bell, D. (2001) 'Meat and metal', in R. Holliday and J. Hassard (eds) *Contested Bodies*, London: Routledge.

Bell, D. and Bennion-Nixon, L. (2001) 'The popular culture of consiracy/the conspiracy of popular culture', in M. Parker and J. Parrish (eds) *Age of Anxiety: the sociology of conspiracy*, Oxford: Blackwell.

Bell, D. and Binnie, J. (2000) *The Sexual Citizen: queer politics and beyond*, Cambridge: Polity Press.

Bell, D. and Kennedy, B. (2000) *The Cybercultures Reader*, London: Routledge.

Bell, D. and Valentine, G. (1997) *Consuming Geographies: we are where we eat*, London: Routledge.

Benson, R. (2000) 'The joy of text', *The Guardian Weekend* (UK), 3 June: 22–7.

Best, S. and Kellner, D. (1991) *Postmodern Theory: critical interrogations*, Basingstoke: Macmillan.

Beynon, J. and Dunkerley, D. (2000) 'A parable of our global times', in J. Beynon and D. Dunkerely (eds) *Globalization: the Reader*, London: Athlone.

Biagioli, M. (1999) 'Introduction: science studies and its disciplinary predicament', in M. Biagiolo (ed.) *The Science Studies Reader*, London: Routledge.

Bijker, W. and Law, J. (eds) (1992) *Shaping Technology/Building Society*, Cambridge MA: MIT Press.

Bloch, L. and Lemish, D. (1999) 'Disposable love: the rise and fall of a virtual pet', *New Media and Society*, 1: 283–303.

Boal, I. (1995) 'A flow of monsters: Luddism and virtual technologies', in J. Brook and I. Boal (eds) *Resisting the Virtual Life: the culture and politics of information*, San Francisco: City Lights Books.

Bolter, J. D. and Grusin, R. (1999) *Remediation: understanding new media*, Cambridge MA: MIT Press.

Bordo, S. (1993) *Unbearable Weight: feminism, western culture, and the body*, Berkeley CA: University of California Press.

Bourdieu, P. (1984) *Distinction: a social critique of the judgement of taste*, London: Routledge.

Branwyn, G. (1998) 'The desire to be wired', in J. Beckham (ed.) *The Virtual Dimension: architecture, representation, and crash culture*, New York: Princeton Architectural Press.

Bromberg, H. (1996) 'Are MUDs communities? Identity, belonging and consciousness in virtual worlds', in R. Shields (ed.) *Cultures of Internet*, London: Sage.

Brook, B. (1999) *Feminist Perspectives on the Body*, London: Longman.

Brook, J. and Boal, I. (eds) (1995) *Resisting the Virtual Life: the culture and politics of information*, San Francisco: City Lights Books.

Brooker, P. (1999) *A Concise Glossary of Cultural Theory*, London: Arnold.

Brunsden, C. (1997) *Screen Tastes: soap opera to satellite dishes*, London: Routledge.

Bukatman, S. (1994) 'Gibson's typewriter', in M. Dery (ed.) *Flame Wars: the discourse of cyberculture*, Durham NJ: Duke University Press.

Bukatman, S. (1995) 'The artificial infinite: on special effects and the sublime', in L. Cooke and P. Wollen (eds) *Visual Display: culture beyond appearances*, Seattle: Bay Press.

Burke, J. and Walsh, N. (2000) 'Coming to a screen near you', *The Observer* (UK), 7 May: 19.

Burrows, R. (1997a) 'Cyberpunk as social theory: William Gibson and the sociological imagination', in S. Westwood and J. Williams (eds) *Imagining Cities: scripts, signs, memory*, London: Routledge.

Burrows, R. (1997b) 'Virtual culture, urban social polarisation and social science fiction', in B. Loader (ed.) *The Governance of Cyberspace: politics, technology and global restructuring*, London: Routledge.

Butler, J. (1990) *Gender Trouble: feminism and the subversion of identity*, London: Routledge.

Butler, J. A. (1998) *Cybersearch: research techniques in the electronic age*, Harmondsworth: Penguin.

Byrne, E. and McQuillan, M. (1999) *Deconstructing Disney*, London: Pluto.

Cartwright, L. (1995) *Screening the Body: tracing medicine's visual culture*, Minneapolis: University of Minnesota Press.

Case, S. (1996) *The Domain-Matrix: performing lesbian at the end of print culture*, Bloomington: Indiana University Press.

Cashmore, E. and Rojek, C. (eds) (1999) *Dictionary of Cultural Theorists*, London: Arnold.

Castells, M. (1996) *The Rise of the Network Society*, Oxford: Blackwell.

Castells, M. (1997) *The Power of Identity*, Oxford: Blackwell.

Cavallaro, D. (2000) *Cyberpunk and Cyberculture: science fiction and the work of William Gibson*, London: Athlone.

Ceruzzi, P. (1998) *A History of Modern Computing*, Cambridge MA: MIT Press.

Cheung, C. (2000) 'A home on the web: presentations of self on personal homepages', in D. Gauntlett (ed.) *Web.Studies: rewiring media studies for the digital age*, London: Arnold.

Clark, N. (1995) 'Rear-view mirrorshades: the recursive generation of the cyber-body', *Body & Society*, 1: 113–33.

Clerc, S. (1996) 'DDEB, GATB, MPPB, and Ratboy: *The X-Files*' media fandom, online and off', in D. Lavery, A. Hague and M. Cartwright (eds) *Deny All Knowledge: reading* The X-Files, London: Faber & Faber.

Clynes, M. and Kline, N. (1995) 'Cyborgs and space', in C. Gray (ed.) *The Cyborg Handbook*, London: Routledge.

Cohen, S. (1972) *Folk Devils and Moral Panics: the creation of the mods and rockers*, London: MacGibbon & Kee.

Concannon, K. (1998) 'The contemporary space of the border: Gloria Anzaldua's *Borderlands* and William Gibson's *Neuromancer*', *Textual Practice*, 12: 429–42.

Costigan, J. (1999) 'Introduction: forests, trees, and Internet research', in S. Jones (ed.) *Doing Internet Research: critical issues and methods for examining the Net,* London: Sage.

Coupland, D. (1995) *Microserfs*, London: Flamingo.

Crane, D. (2000) 'In *medias* race: filmic representation, networked communication, and racial intermediation', in B. Kolko, L. Nakamura and G. Rodman (eds) *Race in Cyberspace*, London: Routledge.

Crawford, T. H. (1999) 'Conducting technologies: Virilio's and Latour's philosophies of the present state', *Angelaki*, 4: 171–81.

Cubitt, S. (1998) *Digital Aesthetics*, London: Sage.

Cubitt, S. (1999a) 'Introduction. Le reel, c'est l'impossible: the sublime time of special effects', *Screen*, 40: 123–30.

Cubitt, S. (1999b) 'Virilio and new media', *Theory, Culture & Society* 16: 127–42.

Cubitt, S. (2000) 'Shit happens: numerology, destiny, and control on the Web', in A. Herman and T. Swiss (eds) *The World Wide Web and Contemporary Cultural Theory*, London: Routledge.

Curtis, P. (1999) 'MUDding: social phenomena in text-based virtual realities', in P. Ludlow (ed.) *High Noon on the Electronic Frontier: conceptual issues in cyberspace*, Cambridge MA: MIT Press.

Danet, B. (1998) 'Text as mask: gender, play, and performance on the Internet', in S. Jones (ed.) *Cybersociety 2.0: revisiting computer-mediated communication and community,* London: Sage.

Davis, E. (1998) *TechGnosis: myth, magic and mysticism in the age of information*, London: Serpent's Tail.

Davis, K. (1995) *Reshaping the Female Body: the dilemma of cosmetic surgery*, London: Routledge.

Davis, M. (1990) *City of Quartz: excavating the future in Los Angeles*, London: Verso.

Deacon, D., Pickering, M., Golding, P. and Murdock, G. (1999) *Researching Communications: a practical guide to methods in media and cultural analysis*, London: Arnold.

Dean, J. (2000) 'Webs of conspiracy', in A. Herman and T. Swiss (eds) *The World Wide Web and Contemporary Cultural Theory*, London: Routledge.

Deleuze, G. (1995) *Negotiations: 1972–1990*, New York: Columbia University Press.

Deleuze, G. and Guattari, F. (1984) *Anti-Oedipus: capitalism and schizophrenia*, London: Athlone.

Deleuze, G. and Guattari, F. (1988) *A Thousand Plateaus: capitalism and schizophrenia*, London: Athlone.

Dery, M. (1994) 'Flame wars', in M. Dery (ed.) *Flame Wars: the discourse of cyberculture*, Durham, NC: Duke University Press.

Dery, M. (1996) *Escape Velocity: cyberculture at the end of the century*, London: Hodder & Stoughton.

Dery, M. (1997) 'An extremely complicated phenomenon of a very brief duration ending in destruction: the 20th century as a slow-motion car crash', in V2_Organisation (eds) *Technomorphica*, Rotterdam: V2_Organisation.

Dibbell, J. (1995) 'Viruses are good for you', available from http://www.levity.com/julian/viruses.html (originally published in Wired 3.02) (accessed January 2001).

Dibbell, J. (1999) 'A rape in cyberspace; or how an evil clown, a Haitian trickster spirit, two wizards, and a cast of dozens turned a database into a society', in P. Ludlow (ed.) *High Noon on the Electronic Frontier: conceptual issues in cyberspace*, Cambridge MA: MIT Press.

Dixon, B. (1997) 'Toting technology: taking it to the streets', in L. Gordon (ed.) *Existence in Black: an anthology of black existential philosophy*, London: Routledge.

Dodge, M. and Kitchin, R. (2001) *Mapping Cyberspace*, London: Routledge.

Donald, J. and Rattansi, A. (eds) (1992) *'Race', Culture and Difference*, London: Sage.

Driver, S. and Martell, L. (1997) 'New Labour's communitarianisms', *Critical Social Policy* 52: 27–46.

Druckrey, T. (ed.) (1999) *Ars Electronica: facing the future*, Cambridge MA: MIT Press.

Du Gay, P., Hall, S., Janes, L., Mackay, H. and Negus, K. (1997) *Doing Cultural Studies: the story of the Sony Walkman*, London: Sage.

Duncombe, S. (1997) *Notes From Underground: zines and the politics of alternative culture*, London: Verso.

Dyson, F. (1998) '"Space," "being," and other fictions in the domain of the virtual', in J. Beckham (ed.) *The Virtual Dimension: architecture, representation, and crash culture*, New York: Princeton Architectural Press.

Edensor, T. (2001) *National Identities and Popular Culture*, Oxford: Berg.

Edwards, P. (1996) *The Closed World: computers and the politics of discourse in Cold War America*, Cambridge MA: MIT Press.

Epstein, J. (ed.) (1998) *Youth Culture: identity in a postmodern world*, Oxford: Blackwell.

Farquhar, D. (1996) *The Other Machine: discourse and reproductive technologies*, London: Routledge.

Featherstone, M. (ed.) (2000) *Body Modification*, London: Sage.

Fenster, M. (1999) *Conspiracy Theories: secrecy and power in American culture*, Minneapolis: University of Minnesota Press.

Di Filippo, J. (2000) 'Pornography of the web', in D. Gauntlett (ed.) *Web.Studies: rewiring media studies for the digital age*, London: Arnold.

Fitzpatrick, T. (1999) 'Social policy for cyborgs', *Body & Society*, 5: 93–116.

Fleiger, J. A. (1997) 'Is Oedipus on-line?', *Pretexts*, 6: 81–94.

Foucault, M. (1979) *Discipline and Punish: the birth of the prison*, Harmondsworth: Penguin.

Foucault, M. (1981) *The History of Sexuality: volume one, an introduction*, Harmondsworth: Penguin.

Foucault, M. (1986) *The Care of the Self: the history of sexuality volume three*, Harmondsworth: Penguin.

Fox, A. (1997) '"Ain't it funny how time slips away?" Talk, trash, and technology in a Texas "Redneck" bar', in B. Ching and G. Creed (eds) *Knowing Your Place: rural identity and cultural hierarchy*, London: Routledge.

Freund, J. (1978) 'German sociology in the time of Max Weber', in T. Bottomore and R. Nisbet (eds) *History of Sociology Analysis*, London: Heinemann.

Fuller, S. (1998) 'Why even scholars don't get a free lunch in cyberspace: my adventures with a tunnelvisionary', in B. Loader (ed.) *Cyberspace Divide: equality, agency and policy in the information society*, London: Routledge.

Gandy, O. (1995) 'It's discrimination, stupid!', in J. Brook and I. Boal (eds) *Resisting the Virtual Life: the culture and politics of information*, San Franciso: City Lights Books.

Gauntlett, D. (2000) 'Web Studies: a user's guide', in D. Gauntlett (ed.) *Web.Studies: rewiring media studies for the digital age*, London: Arnold.

Gelder, K. and Thornton, S. (eds) (1997) *The Subcultures Reader*, London: Routledge.

Gibson, W. (1984) *Neuromancer*, London: Grafton.

Gibson, W. (1986) *Count Zero*, London: Grafton.

Gibson, W. (1988) *Mona Lisa Overdrive*, London: Grafton.

Gibson, W. (1991) 'Academy leader', in M. Benedikt (ed.) *Cyberspace: first steps*, Cambridge MA: MIT Press.

Giddens, A. (1991) *Modernity and Self-Identity: self and society in the late modern age*, Cambridge: Polity Press.

Goffman, E. (1959) *The Presentation of Self in Everyday Life*, Harmondsworth: Penguin.

Goldberg, D. T. (2000) 'The new segregation', in D. Bell and A. Haddour (eds) *City Visions*, Harlow: Prentice Hall.

Gonzalez, J. (2000) 'The appended subject: race and identity as digital assemblage', in B. Kolko, L. Nakamura and G. Rodman (eds) *Race in Cyberspace*, London: Routledge.

Gorman, A. (2000) 'Otherness and citizenship: towards a politics of the plural community', in D. Bell and A. Haddour (eds) *City Visions*, Harlow: Prentice Hall.

Graham, G. (1999) *The Internet: a philosophical inquiry*, London: Routledge.

Gray, C. (ed.) (1995) *The Cyborg Handbook*, London: Routledge.

Gray, C. (1997) *Postmodern War: the new politics of conflict*, London: Routledge.

Gray, C., Mentor, S. and Figueroa-Sarriera, H. (1995) 'Introduction: constructing the knowledge of cybernetic organisms', in C. Gray (ed.) *The Cyborg Handbook*, London: Routledge.

Guattari, F. (1995) *Chaosmosis*, Bloomington IN: Indiana University Press.

Haddon, L. (1993) 'Interactive games', in P. Hayward and T. Wollen (eds) *Future Visions: new technologies of the screen*, London: BFI.

Haddour, A. (2000) 'Citing difference: vagrancy, nomadism and the site of the colonial and post-colonial', in D. Bell and A. Haddour (eds) *City Visions*, Harlow: Prentice Hall.

Hafner, K. and Lyon, M. (1996) *Where Wizards Stay Up Late: the origins of the Internet*, New York: Simon & Schuster.

Hakken, D. (1999) *Cyborgs@Cyberspace? An ethnographer looks to the future*, London: Routledge.

Hale, C. (ed.) (1996) *Wired Style: principles of English usage in the digital age*, San Francisco: Hardwired.

Hall, S. (1973) 'Encoding and decoding in the media discourse', *Stencilled Paper No. 7*, Birmingham: CCCS.

Hall, S. (1995) 'The question of cultural identity', in S. Hall, D. Held, D. Hubert and K. Thompson (eds) *Modernity: an introduction to modern societies*, Cambridge: Polity Press.

Hall, S. (2000) 'Who needs "identity"?', in P. du Gay, J. Evans and P. Redman (eds) *Identity: a reader*, London: Sage.

Hannerz, U. (1996) *Transnational Connections: culture, people, places*, London: Routledge.

Haraway, D. (1992) 'The promises of monsters: a regenerative politics for inappropriate/d others', in L. Grossberg, C. Nelson and P. Treichler (eds) *Cultural Studies*, London: Routledge.

Haraway, D. (1995) 'Cyborgs and symbionts: living together in the New World Order', in C. Gray (ed.) *The Cyborg Handbook*, London: Routledge.

Haraway, D. (2000) *How Like a Leaf*, London: Routledge.

Harcourt, W. (ed.) (1999) *Women@Internet: creating new cultures in cyberspace*, London: Zed Books.

Harvey, D. (1989) *The Condition of Postmodernity: an enquiry into the origins of cultural change*, Oxford: Blackwell.

Hayles, N. K. (1999a) *How We Became Posthuman: virtual bodies in cybernetics, literature, and informatics*, Chicago: University of Chicago Press.

Hayles, N. K. (1999b) 'Simulating narratives: what virtual creatures can teach us', *Critical Inquiry*, 26: 1–26.

Hayward, P. (1993) 'Situating cyberspace: the popularisation of virtual reality', in P. Hayward and T. Wollen (eds) *Future Visions: new technologies of the screen*, London: BFI.

Haywood, T. (1998) 'Global networks and the myth of equality: trickle down or trickle away?', in B. Loader (ed.) *Cyberspace Divide: equality, agency and policy in the information society*, London: Routledge.

Heath, D., Koch, E., Ley, B. and Montoya, M. (1999) 'Nodes and queries: linking locations in networked fields of inquiry', *American Behavioral Scientist*, 43: 450–63.

Heath, S. (1980) 'Technology as historical and cultural form', in T. de Laurentis and S. Heath (eds) *The Cinematic Apparatus*, New York: St. Martin's Press.

Hebdige, D. (1979) *Subculture: the meaning of style*, London: Methuen.

Heelas, P., Lash, S. and Morris, P. (eds) (1996) *Detraditionalization: critical reflections on authority and identity*, Oxford: Blackwell.

Hess, D. (1995) 'On low-tech cyborgs', in C. Gray (ed.) *The Cyborg Handbook*, London: Routledge.

Hetherington, K. (1998) *Expressions of Identity: space, performance, politics*. London: Sage.

Hine, C. (2000) *Virtual Ethnography*, London: Sage.

Hine, T. (1991) *Facing Tomorrow: what the future has been, what the future can be*, New York: Knopf.

Hockley, L. (2000) 'Spectacle as commodity: special effects in feature films', in R. Wise, *Multimedia: a critical introduction*, London: Routledge.

Holderness, M. (1998) 'Who are the world's information-poor?', in B. Loader (ed.) *Cyberspace Divide: equality, agency and policy in the information society*, London: Routledge.

Holliday, R. and Hassard, J. (2001) 'Introduction', in R. Holliday and J. Hassard (eds) *Contested Bodies*, London: Routledge.

Howcroft, D. (1999) 'The hyperbolic age of information: an empirical study of internet usage', *Information, Communication and Society*, 2: 277–99.

Hoyle, F. and Wickramasinghe, C. (1983) *Evolution from Space*, London: Granada.

Ito, M. (1997) 'Virtually embodied: the reality of fantasy in a multi-user dungeon', in D. Porter (ed.) *Internet Culture*, London: Routledge.

Jameson, F. (1991) *Postmodernism, or, the Cultural Logic of Late Capitalism*, London: Verso.

Jary, D. and Jary, J. (eds) (1991) *Collins Dictionary of Sociology*, London: HarperCollins.

Jenkins, H. (1992) *Textual Poachers: television fans and participatory culture*, London: Routledge.

Johnson, S. (1997) *Interface Culture: how new technology transforms the way we create and communicate*, New York: HarperCollins.

Jones, S. (1995) 'Understanding community in the information age', in S. Jones (ed.) *Cybersociety: computer-mediated communication and community*, London: Sage.

Jones, S. (1999a) 'Preface', in S. Jones (ed.) *Doing Internet Research: critical issues and methods for examining the Net*, London: Sage.

Jones, S. (1999b) 'Studying the Net: intricacies and issues', in S. Jones (ed.) *Doing Internet Research: critical issues and methods for examining the Net*, London: Sage.

Jones, S. and Kucker, S. (2000) 'Computers, the Internet, and virtual cultures', in J. Lull (ed.) *Culture in the Communication Age*, London: Routledge.

Jones, S. G. (2000) 'Starring Lucy Lawless?', *Continuum: Journal of Media & Cultural Studies*, 14: 9–22.

Jordan, T. (1999) *Cyberpower: the culture and politics of cyberspace and the Internet*, London: Routledge.

Kaloski, A. (1999) 'Bisexuals making out with cyborgs: politics, pleasure, con/fusion', in M. Storr (ed.) *Bisexuality: a critical reader*, London: Routledge.

Katz, I. (1996) 'Pulling the plug on progress', *The Observer* (UK), 14 April: 20.

Kellner, D. (1995) *Media Culture: cultural studies, identity and politics between the modern and the postmodern*, London: Routledge.

Kellner, D. (1999) 'Virilio, war and technology: some critical reflections', *Theory, Culture & Society*, 16: 103–25.

Kember, S. (1999) 'NITs and NRTs: medical science and the Frankenstein factor', in Cutting Edge (eds) *Desire By Design: body, territories and new technologies*, London: I. B. Tauris.

Kendall, L. (1996) 'MUDder? I hardly know 'er! Adventures of a feminist MUDder', in L. Cherney and E. Reba Weise (eds) *Wired Women: gender and new realities in cyberspace*, Seattle: Seal Press.

Kendall, L. (1999) 'Recontextualizing "cyberspace": methodological considerations for on-line research', in S. Jones (ed.) *Doing Internet Research: critical issues and methods for examining the net*, London: Sage.

Kennedy, B. (2000) 'The "virtual machine" and new becomings in pre-millennial culture', in D. Bell and B. Kennedy (eds) *The Cybercultures Reader*, London: Routledge.

King, G. and Krywinska, T. (2000) *Science Fiction Cinema: from outerspace to cyberspace*, London: Wallflower.

Kirkup, G. (2000) 'Introduction to part one', in G. Kirkup, L. James, K. Woodward and F. Hovenden (eds) *The Gendered Cyborg: a reader*, London: Routledge.

Kneale, J. (1999) 'The virtual realities of technology and fiction: reading William Gibson's cyberspace', in M. Crang, P. Crange and J. May (eds) *Virtual Geographies: bodies, space and relations*, London: Routledge.

Kolko, B. (2000) 'Erasing @race: going white in the (inter)face', in B. Kolko, L. Nakamura and G. Rodman (eds) *Race in Cyberspace*, London: Routledge.

Kolko, B. and Reid, E. (1998) 'Dissolution and fragmentation: problems in on-line communities', in S. Jones (ed.) *Cybersociety 2.0: revisiting computer-mediated communication and community*, London: Sage.

Kolko, B., Nakamura, L. and Rodman, G. (eds) (2000) 'Race in cyberspace: an introduction', in B. Kolko, L. Nakamura and G. Rodman (eds) *Race in Cyberspace*, London: Routledge.

Kollock, P. and Smith, M. (1999) 'Communities in cyberspace', in M. Smith and P. Kollock (eds) *Communities in Cyberspace*, London: Routledge.

Kroker, A. (1992) *The Possessed Individual: technology and postmodernity*, Basingstoke: Macmillan.

Kroker, A. and Weinstein, M. (1994) *Data Trash: the theory of the virtual class*, Montreal: New World Perspectives.

Kuhn, A. (ed.) (1990) *Alien Zone: cultural theory and contemporary science fiction cinema*, London: Verso.

Land, N. (1998) 'Cybergothic', in J. Broadhurst Dixon and E. Cassidy (eds) *Virtual Futures: cyberotics, technology and post-human pragmatism*, London: Routledge.

Langton, C. (1999) 'Artifical life', in T. Druckrey (ed.) *Ars Electronica: facing the future*, Cambridge MA: MIT Press.

Latour, B. (1991) 'Technology is society made durable', in J. Law (ed.) *A Sociology of Monsters*, London: Routledge.

Latour, B. (1992) 'Where are the missing masses? A sociology of a few mundane artefacts', in W. Bijker and J. Law (eds) *Shaping Technology / Building Society*, Cambridge MA: MIT Press.

Latour, B. (1993) *We Have Never Been Modern*, Hemel Hempstead: Harvester Wheatsheaf.

Latour, B. (1999) 'On recalling ANT', in J. Law and J. Hassard (eds) *Actor Network Theory and After*, Oxford: Blackwell.

Lavery, D., Hague, A. and Cartwright, M. (eds) (1996) *Deny All Knowledge: reading* The X-Files, London: Faber & Faber.

Law, J. and Hassard, J. (eds) (1999) *Actor Network Theory and After*, Oxford: Blackwell.

Lee, J. Y. (1996) 'Charting the codes of cyberspace: a rhetoric of electronic mail', in L. Strate, R. Jacobson and S. Gibson (eds) *Communication and Cyberspace: social interaction in an electronic environment*, Cresskill NJ: Hampton Press.

Levinson, P. (1997) *The Soft Edge: a natural history of the information revolution*, London: Routledge.

Levinson, P. (1999) *Digital McLuhan: a guide to the information millennium*, London: Routledge.

Light, J. (1995) 'The digital landscape: new space for women?', *Gender, Place and Culture*, 2: 133–46.

Loader, B. (ed.) (1998) *Cyberspace Divide: equality, agency and policy in the information society*, London: Routledge.

Lourde, A. (1984) *Sister Outsider: essays and speeches*, California: Crossing Press.

Ludwig, M. (1996a) 'Introduction to *The Little Black Book of Computer Viruses*', in L. H. Leeson (ed.) *Clicking In: hot links to a digital culture*, Seattle: Bay Press.

Ludwig, M. (1996b) 'Virtual catastrophe: will self-reproducing software rule the world?' in L. H. Leeson (ed.) *Clicking In: hot links to a digital culture*, Seattle: Bay Press.

Luke, T. (1999) 'Simulated sovereignty, telematic territory: the political economy of cyberspace', in M. Featherstone and S. Lash (eds) *Spaces of Culture: city, nation, world*, London: Sage.

Luke, T. and O Tuathail, G. (2000) 'Thinking geopolitical space: the spatiality of war, speed and vision in the work of Paul Virilio', in M. Crang and N. Thrift (eds) *Thinking Space*, London: Routledge.

Lupton, D. (1994) 'Panic computing: the viral metaphor and computer technology', *Cultural Studies*, 8: 556–68.

Lupton, D. (1999) 'Monsters in metal cocoons: "road rage" and cyborg bodies', *Body & Society*, 5: 57–72.

Lupton, D. and Noble, G. (1997) 'Just a machine? Dehumanizing strategies in personal computer use', *Body & Society* 3: 83–101.

Lykke, N. (2000) 'Between monsters, goddesses and cyborgs: feminist confrontations with science', in G. Kirkup, L. James, K. Woodward and F. Hovenden (eds) *The Gendered Cyborg: a reader*, London: Routledge.

Lyman, P. and Wakeford, N. (1999) 'Introduction: going into the (virtual) field', *American Behavioral Scientist*, 43: 359–76.

Lyon, D. (2001) *Surveillance Society: monitoring everyday life*, Buckingham: Open University Press.

McBeath, G. and Webb, S. (1997) 'Cities, subjectivity and cyberspace', in S. Westwood and J. Williams (eds) *Imagining Cities: scripts, signs, memory*, London: Routledge.

McCaffery, L. (1991a) 'Introduction: the desert of the real', in L. McCaffery, (ed.) *Storming the Reality Studio: a casebook of cyberpunk and postmodern fiction*, Durham NJ: Duke University Press.

McCaffery, L. (ed.) (1991b) *Storming the Reality Studio: a casebook of cyberpunk and postmodern fiction*, Durham NJ: Duke University Press.

McIntyre, K. (1999) 'Me and my iBook', *Things*, 11: 99–102.

McKay, G. (ed.) (1998) *DiY Culture: party & protest in nineties Britain*, London: Verso.

McKay, G. (1999) '"I'm so bored with the USA": the punk in cyberpunk', in R. Sabin (ed.) *Punk Rock: So What? The cultural legacy of punk*, London: Routledge.

MacKenzie, D. and Wajcman, J. (1999) 'Introductory essay: the social shaping of technology', in D. MacKenzie and J. Wajcman (eds) *The Social Shaping of Technology* (second edition), Buckingham: Open University Press.

McLeod, J. (1997) *Narrative and Psychotherapy*, London: Sage.

McRae, S. (1996) 'Coming apart at the seams: sex, text and the virtual body', in L. Cherney and E. Reba Weise (eds) *Wired Women: gender and new realities in cyberspace*, Seattle: Seal Press.

Mann, C. and Stewart, F. (2000) *Internet Communication and Qualitative Research: a handbook for researching online*, London: Sage.

Marchessault, J. and Sawchuk, K. (eds) (2000) *Wild Science: reading feminism, medicine and the media*, London: Routledge.

Martinson, J. and Elliott, L. (2000) 'The year dot.com turned into dot.bomb', *The Guardian* (UK), 30 December: 23.

Menser, M. and Aronowitz, S. (1996) 'On cultural studies, science, and technology', in S. Aronowitz, B. Martinsons and M. Menser (eds) *Technoscience and Cyberculture*, London: Routledge.

Meek, J. (2000) 'Love Bug creates worldwide chaos', *The Guardian* (UK), 5 May: 1.

Meek, J. and Tran, M. (2000) 'Cost put at $1bn as love bug mutates', *The Guardian* (UK), 6 May: 10.

Mele, C. (1999) 'Cyberspace and disadvantaged communities: the Internet as a tool for collective action', in M. Smith and P. Kollock (eds) *Communities in Cyberspace*, London: Routledge.

Melucci, A. (1989) *Nomads of the Present: social movements and individual needs in contemporary society*, London: Hutchinson Radius.

Metz, C. (1977) 'Trucage and the film', *Critical Inquiry*, Summer: 657–75.

Michael, M. (1996) *Constructing Identities*, London: Sage.

Michael, M. (2000) *Reconnecting Culture, Technology and Nature: from society to heterogeneity*, London: Routledge.

Miller, D. (2000) 'The fame of Trinis: websites as traps', *Journal of Material Culture*, 5: 5–24.

Miller, D. and Slater, D. (2000) *The Internet: an ethnographic approach*, Oxford: Berg.

Mitchell, L. M. and Georges, E. (1998) 'Baby's first picture: the cyborg fetus of ultrasound imaging', in R. Davis-Floyd and J. Dumit (eds) *Cyborg Babies: from techno-sex to techno-tots*, London: Routledge.

Mitra, A. and Cohen, E. (1999) 'Analyzing the Web: directions and challenges', in S. Jones (ed.) *Doing Internet Research: critical issues and methods for examining the net*, London: Sage.

Mondo 2000 (eds) (1993) *A User's Guide to the New Edge*, London: Thames & Hudson.

Moore, D. (1994) *The Lads in Action: social process in an urban youth subculture*, Aldershot: Arena.

Moravec, H. (1988) *Mind Children: the future of robot and human intelligence*, Cambridge MA: Harvard University Press.

Moravec, H. (1998) 'The senses have no future', in J. Beckham (ed.) *The Virtual Dimension: architecture, representation, and crash culture*, New York: Princeton Architectural Press.

Moravec, H. (1999) 'The universal robot', in T. Druckrey (ed.) *Ars Electronica: facing the future*, Cambridge MA: MIT Press.

Morse, M. (1994) 'What do cyborgs eat? Oral logic in an information society', in G. Bender and T. Druckrey (eds) *Culture on the Brink: ideologies of technology*, Seattle: Bay Press.

Morse, M. (1997) 'Virtually female: body and code', in J. Terry and M. Calvert (eds) *Processed Lives: gender and technology in everyday life*, London: Routledge.

Morton, D. (1999) 'Birth of the cyberqueer', in J. Wolmark (ed.) *Cybersexualities: a reader on feminist theory, cyborgs and cyberspace*, Edinburgh: Edinburgh University Press.

Nakamura, L. (2000) '"Where do you want to go today?" Cybernetic tourism, the internet, and transnationality', in B. Kolko, L. Nakamura and G. Rodman (eds) *Race in Cyberspace*, London: Routledge.

Norris, C. (1992) *Uncritical Theory: Postmodernism, Intellectuals and the Gulf War*, London: Lawrence and Wishart.

Oudshoorn, N. (1994) *Beyond the Natural Body: an archaeology of sex hormones*, London: Routledge.

Ow, J. (2000) 'The revenge of the yellowfaced cyborg: the rape of digital geishas and the colonization of cyber-coolies in 3D Realms' *Shadow Warrior'*, in B. Kolko, L. Nakamura and G. Rodman (eds) *Race in Cyberspace*, London: Routledge.

Paccagnella, L. (1997) 'Getting the seats of your pants dirty: strategies for ethnographic research on virtual communities', *Journal of Computer-Mediated Communication*, 3, available at http://www.ascusc.org/jcmc/vol3/issue1/paccagnella.html (accessed January 2001).

Parker, M. and Cooper, R. (1998) 'Cyborgization: cinema as nervous system', in J. Hassard and R. Holliday (eds) *Organization/Representation: work and organizations in popular culture*, London: Sage.

Pearson, R. and Mitter, S. (1995) 'Offshore data processing', in J. Allen and C. Hamnett (eds) *A Shrinking World?* Oxford: Oxford University Press.

Penley, C. and Ross, A. (1991) 'Introduction', in C. Penley and A. Ross (eds) *Technoculture*, Minneapolis: University of Minnesota Press.

Pepperell, R. (1995) *The Post-Human Condition*, Oxford: Intellect.

Petchesky, R. P. (2000) 'Foetal images: the power of visual culture in the politics of reproduction', in G. Kirkup, L. James, K. Woodward and F. Hovenden (eds) *The Gendered Cyborg: a reader*, London: Routledge.

Pierson, M. (1999) 'CGI in Hollywood science-fiction cinema 1989–95: the wonder years', *Screen*, 40: 158–76.

Plant, S. (1996) 'Connectionism and the posthumanities', in W. Chernaik, M. Deegan and A. Gibson (eds) *Beyond the Book: theory, culture, and the politics of cyberspace*, London: London University Press.

Plant, S. (1997) *Zeros + Ones: digital women + the new technoculture*, London: Fourth Estate.

Plummer, K. (1999) 'The "ethnographic society" at century's end: clarifying the role of public ethnography', *Journal of Contemporary Ethnography*, 28: 641–9.

Polhemus, T. and Randall, H. (1996) *The Customized Body*, London: Serpent's Tail.

Porter, D. (ed.) (1997) *Internet Culture*, London: Routledge.

Porter, K. (2000) 'Terror and emancipation: the disciplinarity and mythology of computers', *Cultural Critique*, 44: 43–83.

Poster, M. (1995) *The Second Media Age*, Cambridge: Polity Press.

Poster, M. (1998) 'Virtual ethnicity: tribal identity in an age of global communications', in S. Jones (ed.) *Cybersociety 2.0: revisiting computer-mediated communication and community,* London: Sage.

Potts, T. (1999) 'Thrift-shop blues', *Things*, 11: 81–4.

Pullen, K. (2000) 'I-love-Xena.com: creating online fan communities', in D. Gauntlett (ed.) *Web.Studies: rewiring media studies for the digital age*, London: Arnold.

Reid, E. (1999) 'Hierarchy and power: social control in cyberspace', in M. Smith and P. Kollock (eds) *Communities in Cyberspace*, London: Routledge.

Reinel, B. (1999) 'Reflections on cultural studies of technoscience', *European Journal of Cultural Studies*, 2: 163–89.

Rheingold, H. (1991) *Virtual Reality*, London: Secker & Warburg.

Rheingold, H. (1993) *Virtual Community: homesteading on the electronic frontier*, Reading MA: Addison Wesley.

Rheingold, H. (1999) 'A slice of life in my virtual community', in P. Ludlow (ed.) *High Noon on the Electronic Frontier: conceptual issues in cyberspace*, Cambridge, MA: MIT Press.

Rieder, D. (2000) 'Bad web design: the Internet's *real* addiction problem', in D. Gauntlett (ed.) *Web.Studies: rewiring media studies for the digital age*, London: Arnold.

Roberts, L. and Parks, M. (1999) 'The social geography of gender-switching in virtual environments on the internet', *Information, Communication & Society*, 2: 521–40.

Robins, K. (1999) 'Against virtual community: for a politics of distance', *Angelaki: Journal of the Theoretical Humanities*, 4: 163–70.

Robins, K. and Webster, F. (1999) *Times of the Technoculture: from the information society to the virtual life*, London: Routledge.

Ross, A. (ed.) (1996) *Science Wars*, Durham NC: Duke University Press.

Ross, A. (1998) *Real Love: in pursuit of cultural justice*, London: Routledge.

Rushkoff, D. (1997) *Children of Chaos: surviving the end of the world as we know it*, London: HarperCollins.

Sadler, D. (1998) *The Situationist City*, Cambridge MA: MIT Press.

Sale, K. (1995) *Rebels Against the Future: the Luddites and their war on the Industrial Revolution – lessons for the computer age*, Reading MA: Addison-Wesley.

Sarup, M. (1993) *An Introductory Guide to Post-Structuralism and Postmodernism*, second edition, Hemel Hempstead: Harvester Wheatsheaf.

Sassen, S. (1999) 'Digital networks and power', in M. Featherstone and S. Lash (eds) *Spaces of Culture: city, nation, world*, London: Sage.

Sawchuk, K. (2000) 'Biotourism, Fantastic Voyage, and sublime inner space', in J. Marchessault and K. Sawchuk (eds) *Wild Science: reading feminism, medicine and the media*, London: Routledge.

Seabrook, J. (1994) 'Email from Bill', *New Yorker*, 69/45: 48–61.

Segerstrale, U. (ed.) (2000) *Beyond the Science Wars: the missing discourse about science and society*, New York: SUNY Press.

Selwyn, N. and Robson, K. (1998) 'Using e-mail as a research tool', *Social Research Update* 21, available at http://www.soc.surrey.ac.uk/sru/SRU21.html (accessed January 2001).

Shields, R. (2000) 'Hypertext links: the ethic of the index and its space-time effects', in A. Herman and T. Swiss (eds) *The World Wide Web and Contemporary Cultural Theory*, London: Routledge.

Shortis, T. (2001) *The Language of ICT*, London: Routledge.

Silver, D. (2000) 'Looking backwards, looking forwards: cyberculture studies 1990–2000', in D. Gauntlett (ed.) *Web.Studies: rewiring media studies for the digital age*, London: Arnold.

Simmel, G. (1995) 'The metropolis and mental life', in P. Kasinitz (ed.) *Metropolis: centre and symbol of our times*, Basingstoke: Macmillan.

Slater, D. (1998) 'Trading sexpics on IRC: embodiment and authenticity on the internet', *Body & Society*, 4: 91–117.

Slevin, J. (2000) *The Internet and Society*, Cambridge, Polity Press.

Smith, A. (1993) *Books to Bytes: knowledge and information in the postmodern era*, London: BFI.

Snyder, D. (2000) Webcam women: life on your screen', in D. Gauntlett (ed.) *Web.Studies: rewiring media studies for the digital age*, London: Arnold.

Sobchack, V. (1987) *Screening Space: the American science fiction film*, New York: Ungar.

Sokal, A. (1996) 'Transgressing the boundaries: towards a transformative hermeneutics of quantum gravity', *Social Text*, 46–7: 217–52.

Springer, C. (1996) *Electronic Eros: bodies and desire in the postindustrial age*, London: Athlone.

Springer, C. (1998) 'Virtual repression: Hollywood's cyberspace and models of the mind', in J. Beckham (ed.) *The Virtual Dimension: architecture, representation, and crash culture*, New York: Princeton Architectural Press.

Springer, C. (1999) 'Psycho-cybernetics in the films of the 1990s', in A. Kuhn (ed,) *Alien Zone II: the spaces of science fiction cinema*, London: Verso.

Stallabrass, J. (1999) 'The ideal city and the virtual hive: modernism and emergent order in computer culture', in J. Downey and J. McGuigan (eds) *Technocities: the culture and political economy of the digital revolution*, London: Sage.

Star, S. L. (1995) 'Introduction', in S. L. Star (ed.) *The Cultures of Computing*, Oxford: Blackwell.

Star, S. L. (1999) 'An ethnography of infrastructure', *American Behaviorial Scientist*, 43: 377–91.

Starlin, J. and Graziunas, D. (1992) *Lady El*, New York: ROC Books.

Sterling, B. (1986) 'Preface', in B. Sterling (ed.) *Mirrorshades: the cyberpunk anthology*, New York: Arbor House.

Sterne, J. (1999) 'Thinking the Internet: cultural studies versus the millennium', in S. Jones (ed.) *Doing Internet Research: critical issues and methods for examining the Net*, London: Sage.

Stivale, C. (1998) *The Two-Fold Thought of Deleuze and Guattari: intersections and animations*, London: Guilford.

Stone, A. R. (1995) *The War of Desire and Technology at the Close of the Mechanical Age*, Cambridge MA: MIT Press.

Sudweeks, F. and Simoff, S. (1999) 'Complementary explorative data analysis: the reconciliation of quantitative and qualitative principles', in S. Jones (ed.) *Doing Internet Research: critical issues and methods for examining the Net*, London: Sage.

Synnott, A. (1993) *The Body Social: symbolism, self and society*, London: Routledge.

Tasker, Y. (1993) *Spectacular Bodies: gender, genre and action cinema*, London: Routledge.

Taylor, M. and Saarinen, E. (1994) *Imagologies: media philosophy*, London: Routledge.

Taylor, P. (1999) *Hackers: crime in the digital sublime*, London: Routledge.

Taylor, T. L. (1999) 'Life in virtual worlds: plural existence, multimodalities, and other online research challenges', *American Behavioral Scientist*, 43: 436–49.

Tenner, E. (1996) *Why Things Bite Back: predicting the problems of progress*, London: Fourth Estate.

Terranova, T. (2000) 'Free labor: producing culture for the digital economy', *Social Text*, 63: 33–58.

Thornton, S. (1995) *Club Cultures: music, media and subcultural capital*, Cambridge: Polity Press.

Thornton, S. (1997) 'General introduction', in K. Gelder and S. Thornton (eds) *The Subcultures Reader*, London: Routledge.

Thrift, N. (1995) 'A hyperactive world', in R. Johnston, P. Taylor and M. Watts (eds) *Geographies of Global Change: remapping the world in the late twentieth century*, Oxford: Blackwell.

Tirado, F. J. (1999) 'Against social constructionist cyborgian territorializations', in A. J. Gordo-Lopez and I. Parker (eds) *Cyberpsychology*, Basingstoke: Macmillan.

Tönnies, F. (1955) *Community and Association*, London: Routledge and Kegan Paul.

Tulloch, J. and Jenkins, H. (1995) *Science Fiction Audiences: watching* Doctor Who and Star Trek, London: Routledge.

Turkle, S. (1997) *Life on the Screen: identity in the age of the Internet*, London: Phoenix.

Turkle, S. (1998) 'Cyborg babies and cy-dough-plasm: ideas about self and life in the culture of simulation', in R. Davis-Floyd and J. Dumit (eds) *Cyborg Babies: from techno-sex to techno-tots*, London: Routledge.

Turkle, S. (1999) 'What are we thinking about when we are thinking about computers?', in M. Biagioli (ed.) *The Science Studies Reader*, London: Routledge.

Virilio, P. (1989) *The Museum of Accidents*, Toronto: Public Access Collective.

Virilio, P. (1995) 'Red alert in cyberspace!', *Radical Philosophy*, 74: 2–4.

Virilio, P. (1997) *Open Sky*, London: Verso.

Wajcman, J. (1991) *Feminism Confronts Technology*, Cambridge: Polity Press.

Wakeford, N. (1996) 'Sexualized bodies in cyberspace', in W. Chernaik, M. Deegan and A. Gibson (eds) *Beyond the Book: theory, culture, and the politics of cyberspace*, London: London University Press.

Wakeford, N. (1999) 'Gender and the landscapes of computing in an Internet café', in M. Crang, P. Crang and J. May (eds) *Virtual Geographies: bodies, space and relations*, London: Routledge.

Waldby, C (2000a) 'The Visible Human Project: data into flesh, flesh into data', in J. Marchessault and K. Sawchuk (eds) *Wild Science: reading feminism, medicine and the media*, London: Routledge.

Waldby, C. (2000b) *The Visible Human Project: informatic bodies and posthuman science*, London: Routledge.

Ward, K. (2000) 'A cyber-ethnographic analysis of the impact of the internet on community, feminism and gendered relations', unpublished PhD thesis, Staffordshire University.

Waters, M. (1995) *Globalization*, London: Routledge.

Watson, N. (1997) 'Why we argue about virtual community: a case study of the Phish.net fan community', in S. Jones (ed.) *Virtual Culture: identity and community in cybersociety*, London: Sage.

Webster, A. (1991) *Science, Technology and Society*, Basingstoke: Macmillan.

Webster, F. and Robins, K. (1998) 'The iron cage of the information society', *Information, Communication & Society*, 1: 23–45.

Weeks, J. (1995) *Invented Moralities: sexual values in an age of uncertainty*, Cambridge: Polity Press.

Weibel, P. (1999) 'Virtual worlds: the emperor's new bodies', in T. Druckrey (ed.) *Ars Electronica: facing the future*, Cambridge MA: MIT Press.

Wellman, B. and Gulia, M. (1999) 'Virtual communities as communities: net surfers don't ride alone', in M. Smith and P. Kollock (eds) *Communities in Cyberspace*, London: Routledge.

Wendall, S. (1996) *The Rejected Body: feminist philosophical reflections on disability*, London: Routledge.

Wertheim, M. (1998) 'The medieval return of cyberspace', in J. Beckham (ed.) *The Virtual Dimension: architecture, representation, and crash culture*, New York: Princeton Architectural Press.

Whine, M. (1997) 'The Far Right on the Internet', in B. Loader (ed.) *The Governance of Cyberspace: politics, technology and global restructuring*, London: Routledge.

Whine, M. (2000) 'Far right extremists on the Internet', in D. Thomas and B. Loader (eds) *Cybercrime: law enforcement, security and surveillance in the information age*, London: Routledge.

Whittaker, J. (2000) *Producing for the Web*, London: Routledge.

Whittle, S. (2001) 'The trans-cyberian mail way', in R. Holliday and J. Hassard (eds) *Contested Bodies*, London: Routledge.

Williams, R. (1974) *Television: technology and cultural form*, London: Fontana.

Williams, S. and Bendelow, G. (1998) *The Lived Body: sociological themes, embodied issues*, London: Routledge.

Wilson, A. (2000) *Below the Belt: sexuality, religion and the American South*, London: Cassell.

Wilson, R. R. (1995) 'Cyber(body)parts: prosthetic consciousness', *Body & Society*, 1: 239–59.

Wise, J. M. (1997) *Exploring Technology and Social Space*, London: Sage.

Wise, R. (2000) *Multimedia: a critical introduction*, London: Routledge.

Wollen, T. (1993) 'The bigger the better: from CinemaScope to IMAX', in P. Hayward and T. Wollen (eds) *Future Visions: new technologies of the screen*, London: BFI.

Wolmark, J. (1999) 'Introduction and overview', in J. Wolmark (ed.) *Cybersexualities: a reader on feminist theory, cyborgs and cyberspace*, Edinburgh: Edinburgh University Press.

Woolgar, S. (1996) 'Science and Technology Studies and the renewal of social theory', in S. Turner (ed.) *Social Theory and Sociology: the classics and beyond*, Oxford: Blackwell.

Young, I. M. (2000) 'A critique of integration as the remedy for segregation', in D. Bell and A. Haddour (eds) *City Visions*, Harlow: Prentice Hall.

Zack, N. (1998) 'Introduction', in N. Zack, L. Shrage and C. Sartwell (eds) *Race, Class, Gender, and Sexuality: the big questions*, Oxford: Blackwell.

Zurbrugg, N. (1999) 'Virilio, Stelarc and "terminal" technoculture', *Theory, Culture & Society*, 16: 177–99.